A Life

On

The Toilet

A Life On The Toilet

This book is all about something none of us even want to contemplate, never mind actually suffer ... bowel cancer. Actually, it's officially known as colorectal cancer. In my case, the 10cm tumour was mainly in my rectum.

Lovely! Some vile thing growing in my arse – just what I've always wanted ... NOT! And, I'm sure, just what you always wanted to read about too. Pardon? Was that a 'Not really' comment somewhere there?

DEDICATION

For all those who got me through it and in some cases are *still* getting me through it. You all know who you are.

Idiot's Note

Consider FEAR. It is an intangible 'something', an emotion which nearly all human beings experience. Some suffer it only rarely; others seem to carry it around with them most of the time. I am one of the latter. In fact, I have become so used to Fear as an almost constant companion, it has now taken on an actual life of its own. Or should I say 'his' own (because I'm sure it's male).

I spoke to a psychologist about this. She laughed when I described the entity I had imagined and told me that, when dealing with psychological problems in children, externalising whatever the problem is can often make it easier to deal with. She added that, in creating this entity, externalising is exactly what I have done. Ah. I should be able to cope easily with everything from now on, then.

Meet Psyche-Imp: He is a fetching deep blue colour. He has a very long nose, much more like a pointy stick than a nose, but it must be a nose because it sticks out of his face over a wide, thin-lipped mouth often grinning to show hundreds of tiny, dirty, little spiky teeth. Of course, being an imp, he also has long, pointy ears to match his nose. His eyes are large, slanting, bright yellow, with vertical pupils like a hunting cat. He doesn't have hair as such, just a few damp strands of something resembling wet seaweed sticking out of the top of his head. He has a raspy, menacing voice too; it's a bit like the sound made when raking gravel.

Although he is probably only about a foot tall under most circumstances, he does have a tendency to grow and now and again, he shrinks a bit. His, spindly limbs are incredibly strong for all their frail-looking appearance. Most importantly, he follows me everywhere. In fact, I have to carry the little bastard a lot of the time and he is spiteful; very, very spiteful.

A Bit Of Background

I've never lived a particularly healthy lifestyle. I mean, for a start, I've smoked since I was about thirteen years old.

I started off, coughing, choking and spluttering on the foul things (as most teenagers do) to be one of the crowd; to be grown up and all that. Women who smoked looked sophisticated (or so we all thought).

In fact, I had to work really, really hard to start smoking; it wasn't easy. At first, I just took the occasional puff (thinking how foul it tasted) and trying to look as if I was an old hand at the habit. Pretty soon, someone noticed I didn't inhale and pointed it out and so the peer pressure really began.

I tried to inhale and choked my lungs up. I can even remember the actual event. I've suffered all my life from a phobia of vomiting, so if I get to actually retch on something or for any reason, I have a major panic attack. Thus all my efforts are then concentrated on *not* throwing up. That first time should have been enough to put me off for life. Sadly, the peer pressure was stronger than the fear and I persisted and insisted and just bloody kept at it until I could inhale without my eyes watering and my lungs going off for a walk somewhere cleaner.

Add to that that I've always hated red meat – yes, I know they say eating red meat gives you bowel cancer. What they actually say is eating TOO MUCH red meat and/or processed meat (like bacon) gives you cancer. I've not really eaten meat at all since I was about thirteen or fourteen – about the same time as I started smoking. I occasionally eat chicken and white fish, but never the good, oily fish one should eat to be healthy. So in a way, I suppose I'm a vegetarian. The problem there of course is that I've always hated vegetables too!

In fact, apart from really bland and boring stuff, I am fairly suspicious of food in general. I'm so scared it might be bad or 'off' and so I never want to 'chance' good food in case it makes me sick! So, again since I was about thirteen or fourteen, at that age when adults have a really, really hard time in actually making teenagers do anything they should do and stopping them from doing stuff they shouldn't do, I was living an unhealthy lifestyle.

That I am inherently lazy as well does not help matters. Not for me the regular sports or jogging, although back then, when I was young, I could run if I wanted to. It just wasn't 'cool' to run. It wasn't 'cool' to be fit either. Well, not if you were a girl. I seem to recall that the most important things in life back then were being stick thin, wearing fashionable (if awful) clothes and shoes with massive heels and platforms ... oh yeah, and LOTS of make-up.

Already I can hear those readers who have got this far thinking to themselves something along the lines of "Oh, well. You really brought it upon yourself then, didn't you?" I guess I did. But try telling a fifteen year old rebel that some strange woman thirty eight years from now is going to be having a terrible time with her arse and what's up it and she'll sneer, look everywhere but at you and probably make some nasty, spiteful comment as soon as you stop to draw breath.

Anyway, as I got older my diet did improve somewhat. I was healthy enough. I walked everywhere and I walked fast (remember, it wasn't 'cool' to run). I was stick thin, but I was strong and could carry more loaded shopping bags than any other girl I knew. I could also lift quite heavy things with minimum effort too.

Apart from the odd cold here and there, I was extremely fortunate in that I was rarely unwell in any way. I took my health entirely for granted. I also assumed that I was as immortal as every other teenager (despite the few friends I lost along the way to motorcycle accidents, car smashes and drugs). At least I never did drugs. I was actually too scared to try them in case they made me vomit. So that's probably the only positive thing about the phobia.

I had a few fainting fits when I was in my late teens. These were probably due more to not having eaten anything for a few days than to anything more serious. Back then I was the same as I am now. If I feel nauseous, nothing on this earth can persuade me to eat anything at all, and barely drink anything either.

Drink. In the days of my early teens, I did drink alcohol – because it was 'cool' and also because it was against the law and I wasn't having anyone telling me what I could and couldn't do. By the time I was eighteen and it was actually legal for me to drink, I had really gone off the stuff. I'd drunk so much one Christmas that I managed to give myself a kidney infection. That was painful. I'd never got absolutely bladdered before. Certainly, I never drank enough to make me stagger about, forget where I'd been or what I'd done and absolutely never enough to make me sick. I just drank nearly all the time. When other people were pouring cola down their necks, I was pouring whisky and dry ginger down mine.

Anyway, I hit the age of about eighteen and a half, had a kidney infection and the doc at the time said it was probably due to my 'excessive' intake of alcohol. The kidney infection was painful, I remember that. I also felt nauseous, I vividly remember that too and that I didn't want anything to eat on Christmas day. So I quit the evil drink, increased the cigarettes to make up for the loss and carried on regardless.

Well, there's the basic background to me. Over the years between the ages of eighteen and thirty nine, I managed to get pregnant seven times – despite the plan never to have any children at all and certainly not that many. It didn't seem to matter what kind of contraception I used, none of it ever worked; not even if I used two or three together. My friends told me I was 'cock-eyed'. In other words, I only had to look at a bloke and think, "Oh, he's cool/pretty/beefy/strong" (any of those or similar) and I was 'up the duff' as they used to say.

Needless to say, I continued in my very unhealthy lifestyle (with a very brief break to do some strength type gym work when I was in my mid twenties, when my muscles became huge) blissfully unaware that I was setting myself up for the Big 'C' later in life.

Having said all that, anyone can get cancer. There are probably thousands of people all over the country who have never lived such an unhealthy lifestyle as I have. They've never smoked or drunk more than was good for them. They've eaten a sensible diet, everything in moderation, kept themselves strong and healthy and fit – and still got this bloody horrible disease. I feel really, really sorry for those people. That's truly an awful thing, to have to suffer this without ever having done anything at all to bring it upon yourself.

So now I'm thinking to myself as I write, "Do I actually *deserve* to have cancer?" There isn't actually a sensible answer to that. Some people will say straight away, "Of course you do, look at the way you've behaved and the things you've done which you shouldn't have done and the things you haven't done which you should have done." Others would say something like "No-one *deserves* to get cancer, no matter what they've done."

Since I've found out that I've got this damnable disease, I swing from one extreme to the other in my opinions. On some days, I feel like crap and think I fully deserve everything I've got. On other days I think the other way, that nobody deserves any disease. It's all relative in the end. The fact is, I *have* got it and you, dear reader, are going to learn an awful lot more about my arse and toilet habits than you really want to.

Maybe it's a good time to put the book down now and think to yourself that it might be a better idea to go and find something by Tom Sharpe or Sir Terry Pratchett. At least those two can make you laugh. I might make you laugh in places, but it's not intentional. Sometimes I do have to laugh at myself, but for the most part, I whine. I moan too. I complain a lot and oh – did I mention this? I'm scared shitless.

Actually, if I really *was* scared shitless, I probably wouldn't spend half so much time on the toilet or eat Imodium (Loperamide) like sweeties. Perhaps I should rephrase that last remark to something more appropriate like I AM SCARED TO DEATH. Because actually, if I'm one of the very unlucky ones (and there are plenty of them) that's just exactly where I'll end up, and long before my time too. I'm only fifty three. There is a possibility that I might not actually make it to be fifty four. And that really is a scary thing because that day is only seven months away.

Now I'm being over-dramatic. I do that rather a lot too. It's in my nature. The slightest little thing will send me into hysterics – crying, shouting or generally moaning. A silly little thing will happen and all of a sudden, my whole life is completely buggered.

Strangely, I didn't react like that to the news that I had a growth the size of a grapefruit growing up my arse. I took it all very calmly and quietly and walked away thinking something along the lines of "Well. That's that, then." I think I thought I was dead already.

Actually, I really rather hoped I was asleep and just having a particularly creative nightmare. I'm very creative. However, I couldn't have created this nightmare in my very wildest nights of horrible dreaming. It's far worse than that. This is REAL.

Chapter One: Looking Back

Now I'm looking back over my wild and mis-spent youth, I think there was something wrong in my guts probably all my life. Although I was largely healthy, I did often get bouts of diarrhoea. I didn't feel ill or unwell in any way, I would just have diarrhoea for a few days then it would go away. My parents were not the sympathetic kind (but that is a whole other story) so nothing much was ever made of it and I guess I just learned to live with it.

In every pregnancy except one of the seven it happened again. Sometimes, there was blood in the diarrhoea and that scared me. I scare quite easily. I think I may have mentioned that before. It's bloody Psyche-Imp; he creeps up and whispers all kinds of frightening rubbish in my ear and I believe it all. I don't get scared over the things that ordinarily scare people either; I cope well with those. I get scared over stupid, silly little things like vomiting, spiders, being all on my own. Unfortunately, there being blood in my doings, although quite scary, never frightened me enough to go running to the doctor about it. Anyway, I was kind of scared of doctors – well maybe I was suspicious of doctors rather than scared. I didn't like hospitals, avoided sick people like the plague and felt that a doctor's waiting room was probably the best place to catch some foul disease. There or a trip into Woolworth's. Sadly, I didn't think I'd ever catch the foulest of diseases.

Anyhow, this isn't all about my youth, or my pregnancies, or in fact about anything other than the fact that I have bowel cancer and I fully intend to tell you, dear reader, and in fact, anyone else who'll listen, what it's been like up until now. My biggest problem is deciding where to start because, as I said, I think there may well have been problems in my guts from quite a young age.

I think I will start in nineteen ninety three. That's what, eighteen years ago. Of course, I haven't had cancer for eighteen years. Well, I shouldn't think I have, but who knows? Maybe it has taken eighteen years or so to grow. After all, this is a really BIG tumour.

Chapter Two: Still Looking Backwards

I was just going through a really messy and very unpleasant divorce. I was doing pretty well under the circumstances (which I don't want to go in to here). There was a sudden lull in the unpleasantness and I got a bout of very bad, explosive diarrhoea. How bloody inconvenient is that? Apart from the fact that I worked full-time as well as being a mother and a shortly-to-be-single-parent, I was busy; very busy indeed. In fact, I was far too busy to keep running to the toilet. But that is exactly what I had to do; about fifteen times a day for well over a week. Back then, if there was such a drug as Loperamide, nobody had heard of it (unless it was prescribed for them). I just had to keep drinking plenty and I ate – almost constantly as a matter of fact because I felt so very hungry.

Down the hatch went multiple bowls of cornflakes, loaves and loaves of bread, pounds of butter, lots and lots of cheese, eggs and chicken. And very shortly afterwards, out it came again! Of course, it was changed somewhat by the time it came out. Into liquid form, for a start!

After about four days, I realised that the diarrhoea occurred mainly in the mornings into the early afternoon. Being a resourceful type (when it suits me and Psyche-Imp is asleep or causing trouble elsewhere), I rearranged most of my day so that I could actually get things done. One of the things I got done was to make an appointment to see the local doctor, whom I only knew from having had to consult him over back problems; slipped discs to be exact.

I haltingly told the doctor my symptoms. It was a bit embarrassing to have to tell a man the contents of my 'doings' after all. He was very kind. He asked about my life in general and it soon came out that I was having a rough time, what with the messy divorce, custody of the kids and all that. Plus my job was quite high pressured too. He examined my tummy, pressing and tapping on my abdomen here and there. He didn't ask to do any kind of rectal examination and I was very pleased about that as I would probably have run, screaming, from the room if he had suggested it anyway.

He sat down whilst I straightened my clothing and got off the examination couch, then announced to the room in general that, in his professional opinion, I was suffering from Irritable Bowel Syndrome brought on by Anxiety. I had no reason to disbelieve him since I was feeling pretty anxious by then, not least by the fact that I needed the toilet! He gave me a prescription for something called 'Colofac' which is, apparently, an antispasmodic drug and would help. He advised me to cut down on dairy products, eat a lot more 'fibre' (that is fruit and vegetables and brown bread rather than the cheap and nasty white bread I was using) and then he said 'good evening' and that was the end of that.

I went to the chemist and collected the prescription. When I got home, I opened the bag and contemplated the enormous brown/red pills in the blister pack. I've never been any good at taking pills. I can't swallow a contraceptive pill without chewing it first. I didn't read the enclosed leaflet of patient information (they weren't that good back then anyway). I popped out a pill, stuffed it in my mouth and began to (try) to chew it as I chewed up all other pills. Whilst doing so, I put the kettle on to make a cup of tea to wash it down with. I never got that far. When my teeth finally cracked the hard shell of the pill, it tasted so utterly vile that I retched. The pill fell out onto the kitchen floor in three pieces and Psyche-Imp came running and helped to exacerbate a major panic attack so that I had to concentrate all my efforts on not throwing up.

After about fifteen minutes, I recovered myself, kicked Psyche-Imp out of my way, shooed the dog (who was sniffing the bits of pill on the floor) away, cleaned the bit of pill up and put the pack in the cupboard – never to be touched again.

I went through a further three days of dreadful debilitating diarrhoea, during which time I drank tea, ate nothing at all and sucked Extra Strong Mints as if my life depended upon it. Psyche-Imp came along frequently and tried to make me panic so much that I vomited; there was no getting rid of him. His little scratchy voice whispered in my ear and every time I tried to lie down, he danced about on my stomach, making me feel sick again.

Then, quite as suddenly as it had started, the diarrhoea stopped. Of course, I didn't know for sure it had stopped, so I was still staying very close to a toilet in case I needed to sprint – that was about the only exercise I got in those days, apart from rushing round like a blue-arsed fly after my children, the shopping, work and things in general. The sprint to the toilet so as not to disgrace myself (especially at work) was the only real running I ever did.

Within another day or two I began to eat again, very cautiously, avoiding dairy foods as the doctor had suggested, but definitely not eating brown bread – which I and my children considered to be the equivalent of poison – and not eating very much in the way of fruit and vegetables either.

By the end of the second week after the bout of diarrhoea, I was back to my old bad eating habits and had forgotten all about the episode. Anyway, I was far more concerned with other things and just grateful that I did not have to try to conduct my life from the seat of the toilet. Since there were no cordless landline phones or mobile phones back then – well, not unless you were a millionaire – this made life considerably better all round.

The divorce was over and done with and I had to move house with the children. Moving is always very stressful and this particular move was even worse than usual. You would have thought, with the amount of anxiety and stress I was going through, I should have had terrible diarrhoea, but I didn't. I just got on with everything and went back to my normal habit of 'going' about once every third day. Basically, I could concentrate on doing what needed to be done, which was great.

So, we arrived at our new home, three hundred miles away, where I knew no-one and had no job to go to either. It seemed I would have to depend upon welfare benefits, not something I had needed to do before. I took it all in my stride, although I was somewhat dismayed at the amount of money the welfare benefits involved, or did not involve should I say. Even so, I managed to move my children, my pets, my furniture and about a thousand houseplants into a new house in a completely new area without even one bout of diarrhoea! How strange. When I look back, I think to myself that moving is always one of the most stressful things one can do, particularly after such a horrible divorce, and moving into a completely new area with no friends or support makes it even more stressful and yet I was completely well.

After about a week, since the doctor surgery was right opposite my home, I took myself and my children there to register as patients. Everyone seemed very nice. We all had a very brief medical to check we were healthy – and we *were* declared healthy. Our medical records would be sent from the old doctor surgery soon we were told. In the meantime, any problems, we were to give them a ring and make an appointment.

There weren't any problems. Not for any of us. The kids started at their new schools, I went looking for work (and found none at all) and we started our new lives. We still live in the same place, which is a great surprise as we were certainly not welcomed with open arms.

In fact, I've lived here for nearly seventeen years and I still only have two friends! How's that? I am a gregarious person by nature and certainly I would regard myself as friendly and outgoing, but making friends in this place is just impossible if you weren't born and bred here.

The kids had the same problems. They came home in various states of distress, often with cuts and bruises. In short, they were bullied horribly. I was stressed and upset (of course). I took myself off to the two schools, one a secondary and one a primary, and spoke with the head teachers and many other staff members. I complained bitterly. No-one really took much notice. This is an ex-mining village and we were 'outsiders'. It was to be expected and would eventually get a lot better. I was very, very stressed indeed, not to mention lonely and unsupported. Yet I didn't get diarrhoea. Not even a little bit.

Life carried on like this for weeks, which stretched into months and then into more than a year and I still had no diarrhoea. It never occurred to me to question the previous doctor's diagnosis. After all, the absence of illness doesn't usually cause one to go see a doctor, does it?

Through the Lonely Hearts column of the local newspaper, I met a couple of people, mostly men; people don't tend to advertise for simply same-sex friends or company, do they? Mostly the men were totally unsuitable, (of course; otherwise why on earth would they need to advertise themselves?). In any event, answering these ads meant I sporadically had someone to talk to aged over thirteen and sometimes even someone with whom to go out (with the children too).

Well into my second year here, I had met two men through the lonely hearts. One was rather nice. He was ex air-force and worked for the forestry commission. He liked me, liked my kids and didn't push things too far. He didn't drink alcohol, only smoked cigarettes occasionally and was just a little shy, but very pleasant.

The other one was quite charismatic, although I did recognise him straight away as a kind of rogue wild-boy. He smoked and drank and wasn't averse to 'funny fags' either. In fact, he smoked rather a lot of that particular illegal weed, which I hated.

So why on earth did I end up between the sheets with the latter of the two? Don't ask me. I have no idea. I was very careful with contraception too. No way did I want to get pregnant; I already felt totally useless as a single parent. The other (nice) fellow gracefully withdrew. I gave him a dog which needed re-homing and never saw nor heard from him again.

The other chap got me pregnant. Of course, I helped with that too. In fact, I'd already decided I didn't like him at all or the way he drank alcohol and still drove his car or the fact that he smoked that nasty weed in my house and it made me feel sick. I sent him packing; I didn't know I was pregnant. I shouldn't have been pregnant at all. I'd been very careful indeed and there had only been a few occasions.

The first symptom of being pregnant was that I got diarrhoea. Again. I was gutted. Fortunately, this house has two lavatories, one upstairs and one downstairs. For well over a week, I spent most of the day in one or other of them and got very little done at all. Psyche-Imp turned up again and howled with laughter as the world, metaphorically speaking, fell out of my bottom.

Then I missed my period and totally panicked. I made an appointment for the doctor, spent most of the waiting time in the toilet and then told him I thought I might be pregnant. My medical records still had not been transferred from the previous surgery. I didn't even mention that I'd got awful diarrhoea. I was far more concerned with the fact that I couldn't bear to have another baby. And I had started to feel very sick. Not just in the mornings, but all day, every day. The doctor obligingly gave me some very good anti-emetic pills. (Just as well really. If he hadn't done so, I would have gone to the chemist and bought some for myself). I scuttled home to spend another miserable day in and out of the toilet. Psyche-Imp had a field-day!

I think I mentioned the diarrhoea to the midwife at the first ante natal appointment. I told her I always got awful diarrhoea whenever I was pregnant. She didn't seem concerned. She told me the same as every other midwife had told me; basically the same general advice on diet and so on. I also mentioned the fact that my previous doctor had diagnosed Irritable Bowel Syndrome. She said it was the stress of living in a place where I had no friends, where my children were bullied constantly and I could find no work. This would be enough to give anyone an attack, pregnant or not. Apparently, she also told me, there were some pills people could take for diarrhoea but not when pregnant. I would have to make sure I ate well and drank plenty of fluids and just put up with it.

Somehow, I did put up with it. It sounds so stupid now, but I got used to running to the toilet up to twenty times a day. I was actually quite unwell in general in that pregnancy. I had chest pains, I had back pains, I had swollen feet and ankles and in fact, I spent most of my time in bed, on the toilet or lying down on the settee. At one point, when my back was really bad, I started sleeping on the living room floor! The midwife suggested I try that as it would help my back. It didn't.

So the diarrhoea continued. I couldn't go anywhere where there wasn't a toilet close by. This meant that shopping was a particularly difficult task. Also, I didn't drive in those days and had to rely upon either a taxi or a bus. It was usually a taxi because they could drop me right outside the public toilets in town, not to mention stop and wait sometimes whilst I charged through a thorny hedge into the nearest field!

In every other pregnancy except the first one, the diarrhoea stopped within a week or so of the birth. Even after the first baby, it had stopped after three weeks. On this occasion, the diarrhoea did not stop at all. It continued and life became a monotony of putting the baby down mid-feed to rush to the toilet. I was extremely lucky in that I had a very good and patient baby.

Eventually, after two months, I went back to the doctor to complain about the continuing diarrhoea and the fact that I still felt sick all the time.

My medical records never had arrived as promised from the previous surgery, but the doctors here had seen enough of me through the pregnancy and various consultations with the children with their injuries from the bullying they suffered, to give an immediate diagnosis: Anxiety. They refused to give me anything for the anxiety they insisted I was suffering and which was causing the diarrhoea because I had (in that very first consultation) told them that I used to be given Valium years ago for stress and panic attacks. They thought I was an ex-addict of Valium trying to get hold of more of the drug!

Very dissatisfied indeed, I hurried home across the road and continued with my life of living in the toilet with brief trips to the kitchen or lounge. I am certain for many months after Damon was born, I never saw a complete television programme or film. I never ate an uninterrupted meal and I certainly never did anything else uninterrupted by the need for the toilet either. It became almost impossible to attend to the things I needed to attend to, like meetings with teachers about the various bullying events; parent's evening and so on.

Due to the fact that my bowel simply could not behave normally, my whole life changed. I became a recluse. I rarely went out anywhere at all. Whenever I did in fact go out, I was limited to where I could go as to whether or not there was a toilet either on the premises or within sprinting distance. Please bear in mind that when one has an urgent need for the toilet, it is not possible to sprint very far without having a (very embarrassing) accident.

I took to wearing sanitary pads even when I wasn't on my period and to carrying spare knickers in my handbag. I am afraid to say, I often had to use them. I went out less and less and in the end, I could barely bring myself to even trot across the road to see the doctor – which I had done several times during the previous few months.

Every consultation, every time, they sent me away with the diagnosis 'Anxiety' and assured me it would get better. "Do relaxation exercises;" "sleep more;" "meditate;" "master the relaxation breathing exercises." One of the doctors also made a referral to a Cognitive Behavioural Therapist – who had to come to my home because I couldn't stay away from the toilet! Of course, I never mentioned Psyche-Imp, but I did say I suffered terrible panic-attacks if I felt sick – which was almost daily – and so I often felt terrified.

During the same period, despite eating ever so much more than I ever had in my life before (once the anti-emetic pills had worked, I was always hungry), I began to lose weight. I also began to experience other rather strange symptoms which included dizzy turns – sometimes to the point where I would fall over – a lot of sudden waves of nausea; back pain; leg pain; sudden weaknesses in my legs, twitching of my limbs and a few other weird sensations too.

Finding these to be rather frightening, especially the dizziness, I returned to the doctor to complain about them. Imagine my surprise when the doctor dismissed every single symptom with the phrase, "I told you before, you're suffering from anxiety."

The thing is it wasn't simply one doctor who said this. There were about seven doctors in the actual practice and I believe I had seen six of them. They all said the same thing.

I didn't *feel* anxious – at least, only about being caught out without a toilet nearby if I had to go out anywhere – but they all said it; and they all said it *every* time I visited the doctor for any symptom at all. In fact, over a period of two years I visited those doctors more times than I had previously visited doctors in my whole life put together.

My poor little baby boy; he had so far spent his life being cared for by a mother who constantly put him down and rushed off to the toilet when he may or may not then be picked up by his sister. He must have thought it was normal I suppose.

Unfortunately, there was then a huge catastrophe in our home. I mean a REAL catastrophe. We were all minding our own businesses when a car came careening off the road straight through the front wall of the house. My daughter was standing in front of that window at the time. She was run over. Had it not been for the fact that the radiator under the window had come away and actually covered her body before the car ran over it, she would probably have died. In fact, all the children living at home had a 'very near death experience' that evening. My son, Zakh, eight years old at the time, who was seated sitting in an armchair on the other side of the room to the window, had a spear of glass from the shattered double-glazing whistle past his shoulder and embed itself into the wall. Damon, only just two years old, had a house brick skim the top of his head before landing at the far end of a very long lounge.

Total carnage ensued; wrecked house; terrified and traumatised children; some pets missing, some pets shaking with terror and hiding in the ruins – and me.

Funnily enough, rather than making me run to the toilet, this particular stress caused the diarrhoea to abruptly stop.

To be quite honest, I really wasn't thinking about diarrhoea. I farmed my children out between the two friends I had made in the village, tried to find my pets, dealt with firemen who came to pull the wrecked vehicle out of the house, workmen who came to place 'house-jacks' between the remains of floor and ceiling to hold the house upright, and who then fenced the area off – oh yeah, and with a reporter from the local newspaper.

Once it had been established that no-one had died, the children were safe, most of the pets were accounted for, I took myself off to bed in the ruins and read for hours by torch light. The electricity had been switched off by a quick thinking workman; at least I could make a cup of tea by boiling water in a pan on the gas cooker.

Fortunately for me, the workmen had managed to isolate the heating from the rest of the house water supply so I had water and working toilets. However, it turned out I didn't, apparently, need the toilets so urgently any more.

By six the following morning a missing dog had returned, one of my daughter's friends had taken the other dog to her house and two cats (who I suspect had hidden somewhere) had reappeared and were clinging to me and purring the nervous purr.

There then followed a period of about three days during which time I kind of existed in a cloud of builders, workmen, insurance assessors and an awful lot of rubberneckers. However, knowing the children were all safe meant I could simply stay put, care for the pets and salvage what few precious items I could. And I didn't need to go to the toilet any more than any other person would. How very strange. My dizzy turns had stopped too and mostly, the pains and stiffness in my limbs had also ceased. During the long nights alone (which was peculiar too, because I have never liked to be totally alone – even Psyche-Imp was absent), I had plenty of time to think about it. I decided I would visit the doctor and challenge the diagnosis.

I did just that. The doctor looked at me; he appeared to be pitying me. However, he had no explanation as to why it could be that my 'anxiety' symptoms had miraculously disappeared during a time of utter chaos and stress. I think he gave me sleeping pills, although he might not have done. I cannot really recall now. In any event, I came away from the consultation thinking that the particular doctor I had seen was clearly some sort of idiot. I certainly did not trust him anymore. Not that I really had very much faith in any of them in the first place.

Gradually, over the next week or two, the children returned home – to a building site. Our landlord had no other property to offer us so we were required to live in the remains of our house as it was being repaired and rebuilt. This was neither comfortable nor pleasant. However, the diarrhoea had stopped as had most of the other symptoms, so we all just got on with it.

Not very long after the house-wrecking disaster, and whilst I was exploring the possibility of suing the car driver's insurance company for damages (as was my landlord), another catastrophe occurred quite out of the blue.

Damon had always been a particularly healthy baby. He had eaten and grown well and was big and advanced for his age. He was two and a bit and had a vast vocabulary – although he did forget how to speak after the car through the house incident and so needed speech therapy, but the medics said that was 'shock'. Apart from that he was a fine, strapping, healthy little boy.

One morning he was sick. It was only then that I realised this child had never, ever vomited before, not even as a tiny baby along with a burp. He was very traumatised by the event, as was I, of course. Vomiting was the most terrifying thing I could imagine. I coped all right with my house falling around my ears but I didn't cope nearly so well with a puking child!

After the initial vomiting and distress, Damon quickly recovered and indicated he was really hungry. I left it an hour or two then decided he must know if he was hungry, so I gave him food. He seemed fine. A little later, he vomited again. This time, he was not so fine. He appeared sleepy and he cried because his tummy hurt.

My reaction to this (apart from suppressed panic – when diarrhoea should have set in again, but didn't) was to do what I would always do for a child with a tummy bug: withdraw food for a while, certainly until they cease vomiting and give them plenty of either electrolyte solution or flat lemonade to drink. After all, this was child number seven and I was hardly a novice at these things.

Some sixth sense niggled away in my brain though. That night I kept my little son downstairs in a small bed I made up on the settee. My daughter, Kae and I took turns to sit up beside him. Several times in the night he roused and grizzled because his tummy hurt, was very thirsty and drank a lot of flat lemonade before going back to sleep. Kae and I took two hour shifts each.

My last 'shift' was between six and eight in the morning. The other children got up at eight, so I would be awake from then anyway. Sadly, I dozed off to sleep with my book over my face. The children duly got up at eight – and to all intents and purposes Damon was dead.

Diarrhoea should have set in immediately. It didn't. I did all the things one should do, which included calling an ambulance. I had established that he was breathing (just) but he was deeply unconscious and even pain stimuli administered by paramedics could not rouse him. I left the other children in the care of my daughter and went off to hospital with Damon in an ambulance.

After loads and loads of questions, even almost accusations that I had somehow caused his condition by withholding food, it was established that he had no blood sugar. His reading (on the British scale) was zero point eight – almost nothing – hence the hypoglycaemic coma. Once they'd found a vein and got some dextrose going in, actually two lots of dextrose, he returned to consciousness and was mightily distressed and pissed off to find himself surrounded by strangers and in an unfamiliar place.

I shook a lot; I did feel nervous and anxious, of course I did. When blood sugar was mentioned I thought to myself, "Ah. It must be diabetes." Wrong. It definitely wasn't diabetes but they didn't know what it was. Damon was admitted to hospital and I stayed with him. Significantly, I had no diarrhoea! This convinced me that the doctors at my surgery were all complete idiots. If this was not enough anxiety and stress to cause diarrhoea and all the other 'anxiety' symptoms, nothing was.

After a few days, Damon was discharged and we went home. However, we had to keep returning to the hospital for test after test after test for many months.

Every time we went, the hospital suggested some other terrifying disease and tested for it. These included leukaemia, some rare disease of the adrenal glands, brain tumour and others. I became more and more anxious and stressed but I had no more diarrhoea.

In fact, at one point, taking pity on me, the lady doctor at the practice saw me and gave me a small prescription of Valium to help me cope. I didn't take them very often, but they were certainly useful in keeping me going when I felt a complete nervous wreck. However, I still didn't have diarrhoea. I shook – from head to toe; I had difficulty sleeping; I was terrified to let my child out of my sight for a second, but I did not have diarrhoea or dizzy turns – even though I wasn't eating much at all.

Finally, we got a diagnosis: Medium-Chain Acyl CoA Dehydrogenase Deficiency. You've never heard of it? Neither had I. In fact, neither had any of the doctors at the surgery, or indeed at the hospital! They'd brought in a specialist from another hospital and he found it.

It's a metabolic condition and it is quite rare. It is also genetic. With two people carrying the affected gene, whether they are merely carriers or sufferers themselves, they have a one in four chance of producing a child with MCADD.

I was instructed that Damon, although he looked very strong and healthy, was in fact very fragile and could go from perfectly fine to comatose or dead in a matter of hours. He had to be fed regularly. He had to keep his blood sugar levels up quite high as he could not manufacture his own blood sugar from body reserves.

Most of all (and the physician had no idea of course that he was talking to a confirmed emetophobe) should my child vomit or become ill in any way, I must bring him straight to the hospital children's ward as it was not possible to safely nurse him at home. He told me I would be given a letter as a 'quick pass' so as to avoid the Accident and Emergency Department altogether and go straight to the children's ward. I was given telephone numbers, told my doctors would be informed and taught about the disease and sent off on my way.

I should have been straight in the toilet. In fact, I should have – if my doctor's diagnosis of 'anxiety' was correct – have rushed to the toilet and sat there forever with the world falling out of my arse. It didn't happen. Not at all. My errant bowels had returned to their pre-diarrhoea state of once every third day (whether I ate anything or not).

I spent the next week researching everything I could about this strange disease MCADD. I had recently acquired a computer and the internet and I was actually quite terrified by what I found out. It was far more common in the United States and a support group there showed that kids died of this thing on a regular basis. I should have been rushing to the toilet, but I wasn't.

Zakh, who was by that time nine years old, came home from school with a tummy bug. He vomited. He had the diarrhoea. Psyche-Imp appeared as if by magic and danced a little jig round and round the upstairs bathroom shouting "Your baby's gonna die and then you're gonna puke and die too!" I had a total panic attack. Not for myself (for a change). I had read enough and been told enough to know that it was vital that Damon did not catch this bug. I did my best to isolate Zakh, whilst still caring for him – oh yes, and I scrubbed and scrubbed everything ... with neat bleach.

My hands were raw as I never used gloves. The house reeked of bleach (which is better, I suppose, than reeking of vomit) and I was exhausted and very, very anxious. But I did not have diarrhoea. After three days, thinking I had actually beaten the bug (the other two kids caught it but recovered very quickly), I relaxed a little. I forgot to mention that, during this time, I had not eaten anything myself. I had survived through it all on simply cups of tea and Extra Strong Mints.

Then, quite suddenly, on the third morning, Damon began to vomit. Not just a little like the other kids had done, but an awful lot. Every twenty minutes in fact. I rushed to the phone and called the children's ward of the hospital to tell them I would be bringing him in. The nursing sister on the other end of the phone had never heard of me or my little boy – or indeed MCADD. She told me I was talking absolute rubbish and that my child had a simple tummy bug – and she didn't want a vomiting child on her ward. I should pull myself together and get on with it. She hung up.

Damon was only semi conscious at the time. *Why* didn't I call an ambulance? I think I didn't because the nurse had so thoroughly convinced me that I was stupid. I should have had immediate diarrhoea; I didn't.

Uther, who was thirteen back then, had the bright idea of obtaining glucose powder and feeding it, via water, in small doses, to Damon. He reasoned that, even if Damon vomited, because glucose is so quickly absorbed, it would be taken up in part by his body no matter how short a time it remained in his stomach. We did this. For twelve days. And for those twelve days, my little one continued to be semi conscious and vomit all the time. By the time he began to recover a little and his diarrhoea started, I was a nervous wreck. But I still didn't have diarrhoea myself.

Cutting short a long-winded description of the following events, as my little boy recovered ... I had a complete nervous breakdown. I could not eat at all (except Extra Strong Mints). I could not get a cup of tea to my mouth to drink it because I shook so violently. My whole body shook. I could not sleep. I felt ten thousand per cent terror at all times and Psyche-Imp sat on my shoulder with his legs crossed picking his nose and flicking bogies at everyone he could see. Kae called the doctor.

By sheer luck, the best doctor in the practice visited me at home. He was very kind, very patient and he said mine was the worst case of breakdown or anxiety he had seen in his more than thirty year career. He put me on Valium for a start. I would not take pills I didn't know, for fear they would make me vomit. He also referred me to the Mental Health Team and specifically, a Psychologist.

I cried after the doctor went. Then, when Kae pointed it out, I realised I had not wept at all through any of the disasters we had endured as a family. I had not cried, in fact, for several years, never mind months. Of course, once the tears began, they wouldn't stop! However, I still did not have diarrhoea.

My appointments began with the Psychologist. She was a pleasant woman and extremely good at her job. She began picking apart the reasons for my state of mind. There was a great deal to unpick. Over a period of about seven weeks, I began to get understand the depth of my troubles.

However, the diarrhoea began again. It was quite sudden. I woke up one morning, stretched and got out of bed and opened the curtains. I saw a beautiful, sunny day outside. The sky was such a glorious blue; the birds were singing. I opened the window and felt the warm fresh air on my face and thought, "What a beautiful day!" Then the world fell out of my arse! There was no warning. I hadn't even felt the need to 'go'. It simply happened and was very, very smelly and messy and completely ruined an otherwise wonderful day. I think my first word as it happened was probably my favourite swear-word, "Bugger!"

Cleaning up was difficult. I had to keep running to the toilet. Fortunately for me, the bedroom was exactly opposite the bathroom. I used a lot of bleach. I had to scrub the carpet in my bedroom, soak my underwear and nightclothes in a solution of bleach and cold water, and of course, take a bath. This was equally difficult as I had to keep getting out of the water to use the toilet! At no point did I feel ill. At no point did I actually feel anxious in any way at all. In fact, I was just irritated as hell.

By lunch-time, the diarrhoea had stopped. I then began to eat. I was starving. I ate loads and loads, including, I have to add, plenty of vegetables and by that time in my life, I had got used to brown bread too. So, plenty of fibre went in.

For the next several days, all that came out of me was virtually water. And it smelled awful! I couldn't do anything or go anywhere because, once the urge came upon me I had merely seconds to get to a lavatory and I quite often didn't make it in time. I had to telephone the Psychologist that week and cancel my appointment. Did I say already that I was seeing the Psychologist once a week?

When I still had the diarrhoea the following week, the Psychologist very kindly changed the appointment time to the afternoon. This was very accommodating of her as she was a very busy woman. Even so, during the consultation, I had to 'run' several times.

After two months of continual diarrhoea and the return of my 'dizzy turns', back and kidney pain and various other symptoms, I went to visit the doctor one evening. The Psychologist had encouraged me to go. She felt that it needed investigating. I saw one of the doctors I had seen previously. He dismissed the symptoms as 'anxiety' once again and wrote a prescription for some more Valium (which I hadn't taken for over a month). I insisted that it was not anxiety. That was being treated (very successfully) by the Psychologist. Anyway, how could it be anxiety when there were no aggravating factors in my life and I had only just got out of bed and was thinking nothing more than, "What a beautiful day!" when it began? The doctor was clearly ruffled at being challenged. He informed me, quite coldly, that he knew his job and I was suffering from anxiety and nothing more than that. He didn't even examine me!

I lived in the toilet for most of the following year. Every single day was the same. I would wake up, rush to the toilet, explode for the first time of the day, and then, if I was lucky, manage to get myself downstairs before exploding again. Between the next two explosions, also if I was lucky, I could make myself a cup of tea. And during the following explosions, again relying on nothing more than luck and timing, I could drink the tea – and any more cups of tea I managed to make. Or, if someone else (Kae, for example) were here in the house, she could make the tea and I would drink it between, and sometimes during, explosions from my nether regions.

I also developed an extremely unhealthy habit in that year. Feeling so incredibly hungry all the time, I often put bread in the toaster, rushed to the toilet, washed my hands, buttered the toast and took it with me to eat on the toilet during the next explosion.

I could, quite literally, go nowhere at all – except to the Psychologist once a week. The explosive and unpredictable diarrhoea no longer ended by lunch-time. It could last all day. Sometimes it lasted well into the evening too. I lost count of the number of bowel 'accidents' I suffered during that year.

Mostly -- although not always – at night I seemed to be all right. Once I had emptied myself and settled into bed, so long as I lay very still indeed, I could go to sleep. Sometimes I woke up at some ungodly early hour to go to the toilet, but mostly, I was able to sleep around six to seven hours.

I was so very hungry all the time too. I ate and ate and ate. I should have been the size of a house. I did not limit myself to meals. I had constant snacks too: potato crisps, sweets, biscuits, at least five meals a day and still I was starving – all the time.

The Psychologist became more and more concerned as the year wore on. I was losing a great deal of weight. I also had an awful lot of pain in my back, legs and shoulders. I suffered pins and needles in weird places, altered sensation in my body and limbs at odd times – and of course, the ever present diarrhoea. She told me to go to the doctor again. I refused. I explained to her, very patiently that, in my opinion, if I went to the doctor with my head tucked under my arm and said something like, "Excuse me, my head seems to have fallen off. Do you think you could arrange to have it stitched back on, please?" that the doctor would dismiss me by telling me I was only suffering from anxiety!

By the end of the year, the Psychologist was concerned enough to make the doctor appointment on my behalf and to come along with me. My weight had dropped from nine stones and two pounds (my normal weight, albeit low for such a tall woman) to a little under eight stones, despite the fact that I never stopped eating.

Now, the general practitioner I actually saw, in company with the Psychologist was, in fact, the senior partner. This doctor had not seen me since my pregnancy, during which time, it turned out, he had been extremely alarmed and had actually thought they might 'lose' me because I was so very ill whilst pregnant.

When I walked into the doctor's office along with the Psychologist that evening, the good doctor greeted me warmly and then said, "Good God, woman! What have you done to yourself? You look terrible!" I barely said a thing. I sat there listening to the Psychologist as she soundly told the doctor off for his colleagues' behaviour. Clearly, she said, they should have investigated my symptoms, instead of insisting that I was suffering from anxiety and sending me to see her. She assured him that my mind was absolutely fine, especially in view of all she had learned I'd coped with in my life and that these physical symptoms were very real indeed and were physical in nature not related to mental ill health.

The doctor agreed wholeheartedly. He wrote referrals there and then for both gastroenterology and neurology to have all my symptoms thoroughly investigated. I felt a huge wave of relief, although, to be absolutely honest, I couldn't wait to get out of there because I was starving and had in mind a very large chicken curry for my supper.

The diarrhoea continued as I waited for the referral appointments. My huge appetite also continued. The doctor had taken some blood tests at the consultation. I was barely surprised to have a telephone call from the surgery which informed me that I was very anaemic and that I should come to the surgery for some iron tablets. I declined. I explained to the woman who called that she should tell the doctor I am unable to take oral iron – because it gives me diarrhoea. Since I already had dreadful diarrhoea, I didn't want any more. Years ago, before I had come to live in this area, whenever I became anaemic, which happened frequently, the doctors down there sent me to hospital for blood transfusions. The woman assured me she would pass this on to the doctor.

The hospital appointments arrived. Gastroenterology was only a short wait, but neurology was months. I telephoned the hospital to see if the neurologist had a private clinic (for which I would have to pay) where he could see me sooner. He did. I immediately asked his secretary to send me a private appointment with all speed. I was determined to get to the bottom (ha-ha) of these symptoms as soon as possible in order that I could recover and get back to living a life again.

I went off to the gastroenterology appointment. I was naive and stupid and knew nothing at all about gastroenterology or its investigations. The consultant was a woman named Doctor Ross. She was brusque almost to the point of rudeness and looked very tired and very bored. She barely seemed to listen to me and then told me she intended to shove a snake with a camera on it down my throat, give me a barium enema and a snake with a camera on it up my arse, but not all at once.

I freaked. I tried to explain my phobia of vomiting. She'd never heard of emetophobia (very odd for a gastroenterologist, I thought) and told me not to be so pathetic. When I insisted they could not send a camera 'down' at all, she suggested a general anaesthetic to do the investigation. I refused that too – on the grounds that the only two general anaesthetics I had ever had in my life had made me very, very sick.

The consultant got extremely irritated with me. In the end, I agreed to a colonoscopy and nothing else. I fled from the hospital in a state of panicked relief. Panic because of the 'near-miss' of having a camera forced down my throat and relief that I had escaped the dreadful consultant. I hurried home, stopping only to get something to eat on the way.

Two days later, and three days before the private neurology appointment, the diarrhoea suddenly stopped. Of course, having spent so long with diarrhoea, I was deeply suspicious. How could I be certain, I mused, that it actually had, really stopped? I still felt I couldn't go out anywhere, just in case it began again.

Despite my fears, after a 'normal bowel motion' earlier in the day, I took myself off to the neurologists' private clinic in the evening. He examined me thoroughly, seemed a pleasant enough man, and asked me a great many questions. He told me he would refer me to Liverpool Fazakerly hospital to have a number of investigations done. These would include a lumbar puncture (no problem, I thought to myself. It cannot be worse than an epidural anaesthetic and I'd had a few of those). I would also have electrical tests on all my muscles, which he assured me, although uncomfortable, would not be painful. I would also have a brain scan and a full body MRI scan.

Entirely satisfied, I went home, certainly feeling lighter in the mind than I had for several weeks but feeling the ever present hunger as well. I stuffed my face that night and really enjoyed my food as well, even though I more than half expected the diarrhoea to begin again the next morning.

The diarrhoea did not begin again at all. I felt healthy and well – at least, apart from being starving hungry all the time and my weird pins and needles, aches and pains continued, but they didn't make me feel unwell. I began (very cautiously) to go out and do normal things again, which included shopping, gardening, going to the kids' schools for appointments and other mundane things.

After about six weeks of this, an appointment letter arrived for my planned colonoscopy. It was not on the 'urgent' list and would be in three months' time. Enclosed in the appointment letter were two sachets of a medication called Picolax – which is a powerful laxative.

I read through all the information enclosed within the letter, rang up to confirm the appointment date and time – and forgot all about it; after all, it was three months away. I then got on with the business of being a mother, housewife and gardener.

An appointment arrived for the Fazakerly hospital. I had a few problems in arranging transport and the children's care for the day. After all, the hospital was in Liverpool some forty miles from my home and I would be there all day and not get back until the evening. Still, arrangements were made and I felt confident that everything would be all right.

On the day of the appointment, I felt extremely anxious indeed. I had no idea why; it seemed silly to be anxious about a few tests, but anxious I was. Off I went, with my then partner (Peter) driving; he'd taken a day off work in order to take me to the hospital. It was not a pleasant journey. I felt nauseous with anxiety. I took a Valium pill to counteract that and an anti-emetic pill as well. I felt fine by the time I got to the hospital.

The nurses who greeted us were pleasant and friendly. They showed me to the bed prepared for me. I didn't need to get undressed. I was permitted to eat and drink normally. All I had to do was wait.

After about an hour or so, a very friendly nurse came to see me. She looked a little embarrassed. She asked if I knew what tests I was supposed to be having. I told her. She wrote them all down, along with the name of the Consultant Neurologist who had referred me, offered me a cup of tea and went away.

A little later, another nurse came and told me and Peter that there had been a mix up. For some reason, although the bed had been reserved for me, the tests had not been booked. They would need to 'shuffle things around a bit' in order to get them done. This would mean I had a much longer wait than previously thought to look forward to. However, I was not to worry, they would sort it all out and everything would be fine.

Rather miffed, but not in the least alarmed, I settled down with a puzzle book to wait. Another nurse altogether came to speak to me about the lumbar puncture I was to have. I would need to lie flat afterwards for a minimum of two hours in order to avoid getting a 'lumbar puncture headache'. I suddenly remembered an epidural I'd had which had left me with just such a headache. It had lasted two weeks and no painkiller would touch it. I began to get nervous. The nurse told me they hadn't yet found 'a slot' for my procedure and that also they would try to get the other tests done first in order that I could rest properly after the lumbar puncture and before going home. I would be leaving the hospital at about eight in the evening, she thought.

Well, I waited and waited and waited. No tests happened. No slots to fit me in appeared. By four thirty in the afternoon, having been at the hospital lying on that bed since eight in the morning, absolutely nothing had happened! At that point, I decided to go home. I got up, made my way to the nurse station with Peter and told them that I really could not wait any longer, not least because I had children and responsibilities at home. They should contact me with another appointment when they had everything booked, planned and sorted out.

The senior nurse asked me to return to the same hospital at eight the next morning, by which time, she assured me, everything would be fixed and in place. I nodded my agreement and left, stopping only to buy a sandwich from the hospital shop before it closed.

On the way home, we stopped at MacDonalds and I ate a huge meal. When I got home, I prepared a family meal and ate that too. During the evening, I had several snacks as well. I still felt hungry.

It was only really at bed time that night that I realised I had not had any symptoms; no pain, pins and needles or anything else for over two weeks. It seemed pointless to go back for investigations when everything had resolved. However, Peter insisted that I should do so.

My best friend of some twenty odd years, Rosemary, arrived from the South that evening and she said she would come to the hospital too. We sat up late, chatting and laughing. During the chat and laughter, my anxiety levels began to build. I had trouble sleeping. In fact, I didn't really sleep at all.

When we got up at ridiculously early o'clock to make the second journey in two days, I was a nervous wreck. We made the journey, pulled up outside the hospital and I suddenly said, "I can't do this. I want to go home."

Rosemary completely understood; she very obligingly turned the car around and home we went. I telephoned the hospital when I got home, apologised for wasting their time and settled down to a large and relaxed breakfast. The hospital staff member who took the call advised me to come back. She assured me all the tests were booked and that I had time to make the journey again and get started straight away. I refused. What was the point, I argued. All my symptoms had vanished anyway. It must have been anxiety after all.

I really enjoyed having Rosemary to stay. We went all over the place. Although my diarrhoea had never returned, Rose suffers herself from Irritable Bowel Syndrome. (I truly think that woman knows the location of every public lavatory in England, Scotland and Wales). She always needed the toilet wherever we went. I didn't. Apart from always being hungry, I was healthier than I had ever been, although I was extremely pale, despite the fact that I had a bit of a tan from my constantly being outside gardening.

We took the kids to the zoo and had a wonderful day, laughing like loons. We went into Wales and saw some wonderful places. We went to the park and we went shopping in Wrexham (spending far too much money, I might add). It was great. All too soon, Rose had to go home. This in itself was enough to cause me anxiety, although we spoke on the phone for at least two hours every Friday – sometimes more often.

One evening, when Rose rang me, we were discussing the planned colonoscopy. She had herself undergone the procedure. She recommended that, once I'd taken the Picolax, I stay very close to a toilet because it acted almost immediately and continued for several hours, although she said she had been able to sleep, despite knowing she would have to take the second dose in the morning and start all over again.

I began to think about the planned procedure. I had at that time, gone nearly four months with entirely normal bowel motions and I really couldn't bear the thought of deliberately inducing diarrhoea. When Rosemary went home later that day, I sat down at the computer and wrote a letter to the consultant of the gastroenterology department.

I explained that my symptoms had resolved and that I was healthier than I had ever been and furthermore that I really could not bring myself to deliberately induce diarrhoea, having been free of it for so many months and able to live a normal life. I enclosed the sachets of Picolax and went happily off to post the letter.

I never gave gastroenterology another thought. For the next several years, everything was fine as far as diarrhoea went. My bowel behaved itself and I was able to live a normal life in that regard. From time to time, the pains returned in my back or legs. The strange pins and needles and altered sensations came and went as well, but until I actually suffered a frozen shoulder, which was incredibly painful, I was very healthy indeed.

I have to tell you, dear reader, that during those years, there were times of extreme stress and anxiety inducing events, but the anxiety would manifest itself with a *feeling* of being anxious or worried or frightened. Sometimes I got so scared I shook; sometimes I felt sick with fear (and the disgusting little Psyche-Imp put in another appearance). I still took the doctor prescribed anti-emetics three times a day every day (in case I felt sick). But the diarrhoea never returned. I concluded from this that my doctors were all idiots and that no way were any of my previous or current symptoms linked to anxiety.

Chapter Three: Possibly Where Cancer Started

I went to see the doctor one evening with my frozen shoulder and some other thing (which I cannot now recall) which was bugging me. This time, I saw a lady I had never seen before. She listened to what I had to say, consulted my records and remarked, "You know, I think I know what may be wrong with you. Have you ever heard of Fibromyalgia?" I said I had never heard of it. The doctor told me she would make a hospital referral and that the lady consultant I was going to see was very patient and kind and the appointment would not be stressful in any way. She gave me some painkillers for my shoulder too.

I went off to that hospital appointment, which arrived very quickly. The lady was indeed very pleasant and she asked me all manner of questions (a lot of which seemed irrelevant at the time). She concluded I did have Fibromyalgia. She further told me that many doctors do not believe the condition exists, but that every single symptom I had – along with several other things – PMS for a start – would indicate that I had suffered from it for years. She examined me thoroughly and then she gave me a prescription for a drug called Amytriptilene, which she said would relieve all the symptoms in time, including the frozen shoulder, which had by then moved to the other side of my body.

Feeling delighted that I was not in fact a mental case and really did have something wrong with me after all – which is bizarre because who actually *wants* to have something wrong with them – I left the hospital and went straight to a pharmacy to collect my new drugs.

I took the pills for just about two weeks. I can't say they made any difference at all to any of my weird pains and pins and needles. I kept taking them, but I did notice I was getting pain in the centre of my chest now and then, which I'd never experienced before. It wasn't severe, more annoying than anything. However, when I started getting a bit breathless whilst taking my dogs for a walk, I decided a trip across the road to the doctor was in order.

The doctor (one of the ones who always used to tell me things were anxiety) listened to what I told him. He also listened quite carefully to my chest. He couldn't hear anything in there (apart from what he should hear, I assume). After a little questioning, he learned I was taking Amytriptilene; at that point he told me that particular drug was actually known to sometimes cause heart problems and advised me to stop taking it – especially as I hadn't noticed any difference in symptoms. He didn't offer me anything else instead, and to be honest, I didn't ask for anything. I simply came home and stopped taking them.

I still hadn't had any diarrhoea. I was fairly active – at least, I got about, did the shopping and the housework and took my two dogs for a walk every day. I actually felt quite good. What felt even better was not rushing across to the doctor surgery twice or three times a week. Once again, I took my health for granted, even though now and again, I began to get the odd chest pains and breathlessness. I simply tried to cut down the cigarettes a bit – which of course immediately resulted in smoking more than ever. In the end, I just got on with being alive, took no notice of any of the symptoms and took painkillers if they got too bad.

That situation continued for several years. Looking back now, I think I was actually gradually slowing down more and more but, because it was such a gradual decline, I didn't really notice it. Certainly, I no longer had the energy for gardening and my precious garden began to resemble a jungle, which dismayed me, although the dismay itself did nothing to spur me onward. Once or twice I went out to try and tackle it but it had got too bad and I couldn't fix it. As always, I took the same way out: "Bugger it!"

My appetite had lessened a great deal since the diarrhoea stopped and in fact, for the first time in my life, I had a bit of a tummy and some breasts. At first, I was pleased about it. Then, as they got bigger and bigger, I did the normal female thing and decided I disliked them! I should say this was after having spent the whole of my life wishing for a more womanly figure. Now it was arriving (along with a very early menopause), I was as dissatisfied as any woman would be who has been able to eat whatever she likes all her life and remain stick thin.

When my appetite disappeared almost completely about two years ago, I decided it was a psychological way of making me stop gaining weight. I lived on brown bread toasted, with lashings of butter and jam or marmalade, ready salted potato crisps – around four packs a day – and very little else. Every now and then I would fancy something like egg or chicken, or even more bizarrely, bacon or ham. When I fancied these things, I ate them, otherwise I hardly ate anything.

For many, many years I had drunk nothing at all except strong tea with a little milk and no sugar. I actively dislike cold drinks and had found that drinking coffee, delightful though it is, tends to make my bowel motions more watery – which I really wanted to avoid. So, day after day after day, I drank around twelve cups of tea, one cup of weak coffee – and nothing else.

At about the same time as the appetite disappeared again, I began to have a lot more of the pains, pins and needles and odd sensations I'd had before. I took myself across the road to the doctor surgery and saw yet another doctor who had previously dismissed everything as anxiety.

I asked him if there was anything else I could take for the Fibromyalgia symptoms because the Amytriptilene disagreed with me. His response was amazing. He leaned forward and patted the back of my hand. He actually said: "Ah. Been looking on the internet have we and think we have Fibromyalgia?"

Coldly and with great venom I replied: "No. Doctor Lim, the Rheumatology Consultant at the Wrexham Maelor Hospital diagnosed me with Fibromyalgia four years ago. The Amytriptilene she prescribed gave me chest pains so your colleague told me to stop taking it. But I need something else as the symptoms are bothersome again."

Apparently unrepentant and in no way embarrassed at his own disgusting behaviour, the doctor simply explained to me in a tone of voice one usually reserves for recalcitrant children or the mentally retarded that Amytriptilene is very well tolerated by everyone, has no known side effects and then handed me a prescription for them. He advised me that if I was 'anxious' or 'frightened' of taking them, I should reduce the dose by half!

I collected the tablets at the desk, came home and dropped them in the bin unopened. I silently fumed to myself at the way the doctor had treated me and the tone of voice he had used to speak to me. I then decided that, unless I was very nearly dead, I would not consult the doctors at all. Clearly, they were entirely and absolutely useless and had already made up their minds about me. They must think me a terrible hypochondriac.

Unfortunately, over the next year and a half, the breathlessness and the chest pains began to increase significantly. In the end, I had no choice but to return to the doctors – albeit with no feelings of confidence that they'd be any help.

It actually seemed to depend which doctor I managed to see. Both the lady doctors listened to me and took me seriously. All the men (the senior partner had retired as had the doctor I originally signed up with) treated me as a fool and a hypochondriac.

Both female doctors advised me to stop smoking. One of them referred me to the chest pain clinic at the hospital, although not as an 'urgent case' as I said I didn't have the pain all the time, only when I really overdid things and alongside other pain. What I didn't tell her at the time was that 'really overdoing things' meant walking with the dogs, carrying a bag of shopping from the car or walking up or down the stairs.

I woke in the middle of the night not long after that consultation. I had dreadful pain in my left chest, side, shoulder and arm. I felt like I couldn't breathe. In fact, I actually thought I was having a heart attack. Since I couldn't move to reach the telephone – which was on the left-hand side of the bed, I couldn't ring an ambulance either. I knew shouting out would not wake my sons and without them awake, an ambulance crew would not be able to get in anyway.

I lay there, thinking I would probably die and that it would be horrible for my sons to discover my corpse in the morning. Gradually, over the period of an hour or so, the pain subsided and I felt better. I read for a while and then fell back to sleep.

The next day, we were in the process of clearing out the garage, which involved quite a lot of heavy lifting and hauling stuff about. I used to pride myself on my strength, wiry and unfit though I was, but I found the process difficult and I soon got breathless. I decided to pay a friend's son to help Damon and his friend Zeke to do it instead. I then retreated to the safety of the lounge and sat on my backside. I was writing a book back then and so I could at least keep my hands busy.

All of this is completely irrelevant, you understand, but I'm putting it in any way as this book is about ill health in general and how easy it becomes to ignore the serious things (particularly when doctors have you pegged as a raving hypochondriac or a mental case).

Two days later, when I was at the charity shop on a hot day unloading several large heavy boxes from my car (because the charity shop was manned by little old ladies who couldn't possibly lift such heavy stuff), I experienced the chest pain again. I sat in the car afterwards with this awful pain in my chest, unable to breathe and wondered if I would die before I got home. I knew I shouldn't really drive, but on the other hand, all I could think of was the burning need to get home. So I drove, sweating profusely and puffing like a steam train.

When I arrived, I immediately went to the computer and checked my symptoms on NHS Direct. The advice was to call an ambulance. Not happy with that, I checked another site and another. Every one of them said the same thing.

So I called my car insurance company and added Zakh to my car policy. Once that had been arranged and feeling more breathless and suffering more pain by the minute, I called the ambulance. When I'd done that, I called Damon and Zakh (who were busy arguing) downstairs and told them what was wrong and that Zakh was now insured to drive the car. I also handed Zakh my bank card in case I had to stay in hospital. I didn't want them to starve.

When the paramedics came, they did an ECG test, which was normal. They took my blood pressure and blood sugar, which were also both normal. However, they didn't like my 'colour' or the fact that I was sweating, so they decided to take me to hospital. On the way there, they sprayed something under my tongue and gave me an aspirin to suck.

By the time we reached the hospital, I felt absolutely fine and more than fine. I also felt a total fraud for wasting their time. They hauled me inside anyway and I was wired up to various monitors and questioned closely by several doctors and a couple of nurses. My sons arrived a little while later and sat beside me while the machines went beep and ping. I continued to feel fine.

After a few hours, a doctor came to speak to me. He told me I had angina and I should go home and see my general practitioner as soon as possible and get myself some GTN spray and some drug or other.

Pleased to be released and relieved that I wasn't going to die (well, not that day, anyway) I went out and allowed Zakh to drive us all home.

Sure enough, when I attended across the road at the doctor surgery a few days later, they prescribed the GTN spray and some pills or other and told me to take it easy and not to keep rushing around. I didn't bother to tell them I haven't rushed around anywhere for years. There didn't seem to be any point. They also sent me in to the nurse for some blood tests because the tests done at the hospital seemed to imply I was suffering from very acute anaemia again.

A few days later, I received a phone call from the doctor surgery. The lady told me I needed to visit the doctor as my blood tests had come back and showed me to be anaemic. I needed to come along and get some iron tablets. I thanked her for taking the trouble to call me but explained I am unable to take iron (again) as it causes chronic diarrhoea. They did not call again.

I usually experienced chest pain on exertion – and not always. Sometimes, I could walk all the way up the hill with the dogs. Other days I could only get half-way. I did not always use the GTN spray because it caused a harsh headache when I did. Gradually, and I do mean gradually, I stopped taking the dogs out every single day. They didn't seem to mind and I really didn't feel able to do it.

When the appointment arrived for the chest pain clinic, I went off to the hospital with few expectations. I saw a pleasant enough doctor, who explained that I would need some tests done on my heart in order to establish what was causing the angina. I listened carefully to the explanation of a special scan done in the Nuclear

Medicine department, which would involve a radioactive dye being put into my veins so that it would show up on the scanner. The appointment was brief and I was allowed to go home, after being told the appointment would arrive by post.

Over the few weeks during the wait for that appointment, I had a few short-lived attacks of diarrhoea. They lasted two or three days, drained me and made me feel quite sick as well. Psyche-Imp reappeared from wherever he hides when I am mentally strong and tried to make me panic uncontrollably but I kicked him in the groin turned my back on him. I continued to take my anti-emetic pills and hoped the diarrhoea would not escalate into anything like it had done in the past. Fortunately, it did not.

One of my complaints to the doctor some months before had been depression – caused mainly, I thought, by the pains, pins and needles and other symptoms. That doctor had referred me straight away to the mental health team and I was allocated a CPN (Community Psychiatric Nurse). This very friendly fellow, Arne, visited me at home every now and then and we seemed to talk mainly about general things. He was interested that I'd had a book published. In fact, he even bought a copy! He very kindly offered to drive me to the heart scan appointment. I accepted.

One of the things which rather irritated me with the heart scan was the restriction on what I could not have to eat and drink for some forty-eight hours prior to the procedure. This included tea (even caffeine-free tea), coffee, chocolate, and a number of other things I took for granted. I knew this would be difficult as I really dislike any cold drinks and the prospect of either milk or water for two days and nights did not fill me with joy I can tell you.

It was very difficult and to be totally truthful, I nearly died of dehydration over that period. I just couldn't seem to swallow water and I simply detest milk. I managed a few sips here and there and it had to be bottled water. By the time the Arne arrived to take me to the hospital, I was half asleep (lack of caffeine, no doubt) and very much aware that I was not only a nicotine addict but a caffeine addict too! All I could think about was a cup of tea and how soon it would be before I could drink one.

When we arrived, the nurse questioned me closely as to whether or not I had taken anything containing caffeine or chocolate. I assured her I had not. She rigged me up to an automatic blood pressure machine and went off to do something. I glanced at the reading. It was really very high indeed. In fact, it was so high, Arne remarked upon it when the nurse came back. She was very brusque and told him sharply, "I expect she's just anxious about the procedure, that's all."

I interrupted her. "I'm not in the least anxious about the procedure. I just want a cup of tea. Let's get on with it please."

The nurse took me into a small room, sat me on a chair next to an examination couch and a small steel trolley full of packs and syringes. I proffered my right arm; I have an excellent vein in my inside elbow ideal for needles, injections and drawing blood.

Rather than draw blood or give me an injection, the nurse tossed a small grey paper-pulp bowl into my lap. "I'll give you this now," she said casually, as she rummaged on the trolley, "this stuff sometimes makes people sick and I don't want vomit all over the floor in here."

Psyche-Imp leaped out from behind the nurse, putting his fingers in his large ears and blowing a raspberry. He grinned widely, showing his rows of sharp teeth. "Hah hah ha ha!" he crowed. You're gonna be sick! Ha ha ha!" Panic overwhelmed me in the blink of an eye. I leapt up from the chair and dashed to the door, throwing the bowl away in my haste. Unfortunately, the door was locked and I began to wail and beg to be allowed out. The nurse stared at me in open astonishment. She made a remark about never having seen anyone react to a little needle like that in the whole of her career.

I tried to explain that it was not the needle which had upset me but the possibility I may vomit. I was unable to make myself clear. In truth, I was totally hysterical and this is no surprise. Psyche-Imp jumped onto the nurse's shoulder and mimed sticking his fingers down his throat. I shrank further into the corner and shook from head to toe.

The nurse went out to the waiting area, leaving me pressed into the corner and brought Arne into the room. She explained I had completely freaked out but she had no idea why. I gabbled out my panic and he translated. The nurse stared. She tried to persuade me to sit down again and allow her to inject the stuff, but I was having none of it. She further tried to explain that very few people actually vomit, she had just been taking precautions in case I was one of the five per cent who do. I still flatly refused to comply. I could feel my heart pounding in my chest; I found breathing difficult.

All I wanted to do was to get out of there as quickly as possible.

Thinking I was clearly mentally retarded, the nurse then went to fetch the doctor who would be performing the test – should I permit it – clearly believing I would be somewhat frightened into submission by his presence. I was not in the least intimidated. I did calm down a little and explained my phobia to the doctor, who had never heard of emetophobia and thus had no idea of the terror the nurse's remark would cause. Nothing would persuade me to go ahead with the test and in the end, with a sigh of resignation, Arne escorted me from the department. He drove me home and chatted about normal things. He did not reproach me in the least for the way I reacted.

Things continued much as before. I stayed away from the doctors and hoped things would get better on their own. However, when the GTN spray ran out, I knew I would have to see a doctor in order to get another one. I made the appointment, mightily miffed because I would have to see the doctor who taunted me about the Fibromyalgia he thought I'd 'found' on the internet.

As it happened, that doctor was very kind to me. He understood, so he said, why I had been unable to have the heart scan. He also told me that it was his belief that I was bleeding 'somewhere inside', hence the anaemia. He had me fill in a questionnaire about my bowels and said he was making a referral to gastroenterology. I did tell him I needed no such intervention and that I was fine. Nothing on the form suggested (to me) that there was anything wrong in there. The doctor gave me some more GTN spray and explained that severe anaemia like mine can cause angina and it was his firm belief there would be something to be found. I accepted the prescription and fled. I did not trust the man in the least and was convinced in my own head he was simply trying to frighten me.

A few weeks later, an appointment arrived to see a heart specialist at the hospital. There would be nothing invasive about this appointment, simply talking and perhaps an examination. I happily accepted this.

Two days before that appointment, I received a letter from the gastroenterology department, asking me to attend; I ignored it. After all, I hadn't got diarrhoea anymore and I certainly wasn't ill.

I went off to the heart appointment. The doctor, a consultant, was charming, witty and kind. He listened to my description of the chest pain and remarked that it did not sound like true angina, but he was very interested that the GTN spray relieved not only the chest pain but also any other aches and pains I had. He ordered a chest X-ray and some blood tests and bade me farewell.

I allowed blood to be drawn – again. In fact, so much blood was drawn from me that day I felt like I should have been given a cup of tea and biscuit and allowed to lie down for a while to recover!

The chest X-ray took only a couple of minutes and off I went home again. The doctor had assured me that he would send the results of both tests to me personally as well as to my doctor, which made me a lot happier. It had been my mention of an attack of pleurisy a few months previously which had prompted the X-ray in the first place, but I could breathe well again (except when my chest hurt) and I had no cough, despite the cigarettes I smoked regularly. In any event, the pleurisy had been on the right and the pain was on the left, so I was not worried that anything would be found.

Over the next week or two as I waited for the results, I suffered once or twice with diarrhoea. It wasn't serious, in my opinion and it didn't last long. My friends remarked that if I wasn't careful, I would end up confined to the house again as I had been before. I knew it wasn't that bad and laughed it off. In fact, when the gastroenterology department telephoned me and asked me why I had ignored their letter and tried to make an appointment for me, I declined. I told them I didn't need an appointment with them and was just fine. The nurse on the phone sounded doubtful and reminded me that my doctor had asked me to attend. I told her my low opinion of my doctor and said I would not be coming at all, thank you all the same.

A letter arrived from the heart specialist. It was in regard to my blood tests. The results showed I was deficient in vitamin B12, most other vitamins and minerals and in particular, was extremely anaemic. It went on to say that I should attend at the doctor surgery for this to be corrected.

If I am honest, I had no idea what vitamin B12 was, so I looked it up on the internet. Cobalt – of all things. What a strange thing to be deficient in! I went out immediately and bought myself some multi-vitamins – the chewable kind. When I came back, I made an appointment at the surgery to see the nurse for the B12 injection.

Those injections hurt! I'm not scared of needles at all but knowing I had to have one a week for goodness alone knew how long was not pleasant after having had the first one. I still refused any iron tablets. I'd had them many times before I moved to this area and every time taking them resulted in extreme diarrhoea and feeling so insanely generally ill I'd prefer to curl up and die. I asked the nurse if I could have a blood transfusion like I used to have before I moved to the area. She told me I would need to see the doctor to ask about that. So I had to wait to see the doctor.

It was one of the female doctors. She did listen to me and she said that blood transfusions are almost never given for anaemia any more. The only other option was an iron infusion. I felt so desperate; I even asked if I could have one – despite having suffered anaphylactic shock to one many years previously. The doctor felt, at that stage, an infusion was not necessary but encouraged me to take the multi vitamins, try to improve my poor diet and also to remember to come weekly for the B12 injections. She assured me I would soon feel much better. I remember I actually believed her too!

I did try to eat better, really I did, but I had no appetite. I felt permanently tired, weary to the bones and often far too nauseated, despite my regular anti-emetic pills to want to eat anything very much at all.

The results of the X-ray arrived. I was surprised to see that there was something to be seen – on my right lung. The letter suggested it could be scarring from the pleurisy I'd suffered a few months before. It went on to say I should arrange for my doctor to make me an appointment to have a chest CT scan.

Off to the doctor again. For someone who really dislikes and distrusts doctors, I seemed to be virtually living at the surgery across the road from my house!

Fortunately, the doctor had also received the same letter as me so there was no argument about booking a CT scan. She reassured me that it was indeed probably simply scarring from the pleurisy and told me the scan would be quick and painless and would not take long.

I did have to wait a few days for the scan and the letter stated that I must eat and drink nothing at all for four hours before it. Imagine my surprise when, two or three days before the appointment date, I received a telephone call from the hospital at around two in the afternoon, asking if I could come that day at seven in the evening. I agreed that I could. The nurse reminded me to eat and drink nothing at all from three in the afternoon. I put the phone down, checked the time and rushed to the kitchen to make myself a cup of tea and a sandwich before the deadline!

When I arrived at the hospital, I was ushered into a waiting area. It was all very cosy and pleasant. A nurse came along and told me I would need to strip to my knickers and put on a hospital gown – which she gave me. They then intended to put a needle in my hand in order to inject a 'dye' to make the scan show things more clearly. I smiled and nodded, accepted the two page form to fill in and sat down.

There were so many questions on the form. I hadn't taken my spectacles with me, so I had trouble and it took time to complete with Peter's help. Although we'd split as a couple, we were still friends and Peter had since qualified as a nurse.

When I got to the part where I had to list any allergies, I gasped. There were only two, short line spaces for these – and I have a lot of allergies! So I completed as many as I possibly could in the space provided and added a few on the margin of the page.

I left the form, on its clipboard, on the small table and scuttled into the cubicle to change. As hospital gowns go, this one was a fetching royal blue and actually covered everything it should without leaving my boobs or my arse hanging out. When I came out of the cubicle, there was another lady sitting on one of the chairs, filling in a form just like the one I had just done.

The nurse came back to collect me and lead me to the scanner. She had my clipboard in her hand. Her expression was one of deep concern. Waving the clipboard under my nose, she queried the allergies section. Amongst my allergies is Iodine. She wanted to know what happened with Iodine. I told her I had once been prescribed an Iodine lotion for a gynaecological problem and that it had caused my 'bits' to go bright red and swell up enormously. The nurse shuddered and said, "No-one is swelling up on my watch. I'll have to go and see the doctor. Sit down please. I'll be right back."

I did sit down and I wondered, vaguely, what the nurse could have meant. Whatever were they planning on using Iodine for? I got my answer quite quickly. Apparently, the needle they had planned to put into my hand was so that they could inject Iodine into my blood-stream. Iodine was the 'dye' they had intended to use! I did actually ask what would happen if they injected something into me which made me swell up and go red on the outside. The nurse replied, "I don't know, but none of us want to find out, thank you very much! Least of all you!"

So I had the scan, which turned out to be of my chest and abdomen. It didn't take long and did not hurt in the least, although the CT scanner makes some very loud and alarming noises. I think the worst part of the whole thing is being required to lay flat on one's back for the duration (never good for anyone with back pain).

A few weeks later, I suffered, for the very first time in my life, a bout of constipation. I had the urge to 'go' and it was an urgent urge too. I rushed to the toilet, fully expecting the world to fall out of my bottom, but nothing happened. Not even a fart! I sat there for a while; I confess, I strained a little too, but still nothing happened. In the end, I gave up.

As it happened, I had a friend visiting me that day. She suffers constipation most terribly. I described my futile effort at going to the toilet and Caroline actually laughed. We sat and talked for a while about how terrible constipation is for those who suffer it. To be honest, at that point, I wasn't that sympathetic. After all, it was only one time. I felt sure I would 'go' later on. Caroline, however, had been hospitalised and undergone all manner of very undignified examinations, treatments and enemas not just once, but many, many times. She had to take laxative medicine to allow her to 'go' at all. It sounded pretty awful.

Several times that day, the same happened. I had a pressing urge to 'go'. I felt 'full' and that if I went, I might be there for some time. Every time, nothing happened at all. I began to get a very uncomfortable feeling in my lower abdomen. As the day progressed into evening, the uncomfortable feeling turned to pain. By ten o'clock that night, I was desperate! I really needed to 'go', but no matter how I tried, nothing happened.

Surprisingly, I slept well that night, despite my feeling of being very full and the griping pains on and off in my stomach. At no point was I particularly worried, more intrigued than anything else. This was an entirely new experience for me. I felt sure that I would be able to 'go' in the morning.

Now, dear reader, if I told you that the bulk of the next day was spent toilet related, you would probably assume, in view of my 'history', that the constipation had turned overnight, into diarrhoea. Well, you'd be wrong. I still had constipation, but I kept running to the toilet with great urgency, only to have nothing happen at all.

By the evening of the second day, I'd managed to pass a tiny bit of wind and nothing else. I felt faintly alarmed. How on earth could I have become so blocked up? I telephoned Caroline. She promised to call and visit the next day. That night, I didn't sleep at all well. In fact, I kept dozing off, only to wake up less than an hour later with griping pains and the urgent need for the toilet, only to get there and either pass nothing at all or simply a small and weak fart. I began to get irritated. I was tired and I need my beauty sleep.

The next morning I actually managed to have a cup of tea before the urge to rush to the toilet overtook me. I felt cross and weary, but I dashed to the toilet anyway and plonked myself down. My fat, ginger cat, Loki came sauntering in and decided to sit on my lap.

This turned out to be rather comforting; a fat, ginger tabby sitting on my bare legs against my bare, sore tummy and purring like a traction engine, really did feel nice. He looked up into my face and said, "Meowl?" It sounded so like a question that, even as the griping pains began, I had to laugh. "I can't poo, Loki," I replied. For answer, Loki stuck his claws into my bare knees and purred louder.

With quite a lot of straining, I eventually produced some wind and a little of what I assumed was watery poo. How strange I thought, as I remained seated, contemplating the walls, the basin, the cat. It was only when I stood up that I realised what I had actually passed was simply blood-streaked mucus. At that point, I think I was quite alarmed. Loki remained, winding around my feet, just as if he were concerned as well.

I rang Caroline – after all, she is an expert on all things 'poo' related. She reassured me and told me not to worry; apparently, this quite often happens when one gets a little blocked up. She in fact told me that one can go up to about ten days, sometimes more, without 'going' at all before really nasty things begin to happen – like faecal vomiting. I was shaking as I put the phone down. NO WAY was faecal vomiting going to happen to ME! I made a mental note to go out and get myself a laxative of some kind later in the day.

As it happened, I was going nowhere that day – except to the toilet. I must have spent almost all day either going to, coming from or sitting on that toilet. And, on every single occasion, Loki came too. Bless him. I'm not sure if he knew there was something wrong, or whether he was just being a cat and was nosey. Whichever it was, he was a great comfort to me, especially as the griping pains got worse and worse.

I did have the occasional pang of hunger, but to be honest, I felt so full and blocked I hardly dared to eat anything at all for fear of making things worse. When

Caroline came round during the afternoon, she brought with her a punnet of raspberries and a punnet of plums and told me to share them with her.

I don't actually like plums but I do enjoy raspberries. We ate them together whilst chatting and laughing about the fact that I had to keep getting up and running and the cat went running too.

With encouragement from Caroline, we went outside into the garden and began a little weeding. She told me to ignore the urge and wait. Instead of running to the toilet, she said, wait until you can actually feel something coming. She also advised me to wear a pad. That way, if I waited until something was actually coming and then ran for the toilet, if I didn't quite make it, the pad would catch the damage and my undergarments would not be soiled.

This advice worked reasonably well during the afternoon, except that I did make the run indoors to the toilet on about five occasions because I was absolutely certain something was coming. The something turned out to be just more mucus containing streaks of blood again. I began to wonder what on earth I'd done or eaten which could have caused such a strong blockage.

Caroline told me to stop stressing, get on with the weeding and reminded me it was my turn to make the coffee. I did make the coffee and I did do quite a lot more weeding too. I said to Caroline that, if I had not 'been' by the following afternoon, I intended to make an emergency appointment at the doctor surgery – not the one opposite my house, that's only open in the morning – the one up the road in Chirk, which is the main surgery.

That evening, despite not feeling hungry, I took Caroline's advice and ate a great deal of vegetables, including those which I knew usually upset my stomach. Things like onions and cauliflower. I had also been drinking coffee all day, which I knew for a fact made me go if I had more than one cup in a day.

In general, I felt all right, I just kept getting the griping pains and the urge for the toilet. It seemed, the more I rushed to the toilet and strained, the more blood and mucus I lost, but nothing else. I looked down at my stomach, which didn't look hugely bloated, even though it felt as if it was.

I slept through most of the night, only waking once and in that period of wakefulness, I managed a very long, loud and satisfying fart. Feeling a little better, I went back to sleep.

In the morning, I rushed straight to the toilet, certain that I really would 'go' as I felt a very pressing need indeed. I didn't need to strain. I passed quite a lot of blood-streaked mucus and a great deal of wind. Loki sat on my lap. He didn't seem to mind, even though my own eyes were watering because the wind smelled just terrible.

I subjected myself to a bowl of cereal for breakfast, with milk. I dislike milk, apart from a little in my tea or coffee, and it is guaranteed to make me 'go'. I also had strong coffee rather than tea. This was now day four of not 'going' and I was determined that if there was any way I could 'eat my way to relief' I would do so. The previous evening, I had sent Damon to the shop to get a wholemeal loaf with seeds in it. I followed the cereal with two slices of this bread. I didn't even bother to toast it. I made what I call a 'Paddington sandwich' –

that is a marmalade sandwich. Anyone who has read Michael Bond's stories of the little bear, Paddington, will recognise this term.

I spent the day doing very little other than run to and from the toilet. On these occasions, I passed nothing at all. I called Caroline mid afternoon and asked her if she would kindly accompany me to the doctor surgery in the evening. She said she would. I put the phone down and ran back to the toilet.

It seemed sensible to put a book in the toilet and a bottle of spring water (Caroline advised that water is good for making one 'go'). Loki sat on my lap and I sat on the toilet, reading a book and occasionally drinking water – certainly not something I would ordinarily do. Oddly, the water was refreshing and I had no trouble in getting through a whole half litre bottle.

Caroline arrived and we sat together drinking coffee and talking about everything else other than the toilet for a couple of hours. Just before we had to leave, I visited the toilet to see if anything happened. It didn't. Resigned, I put Loki back on the floor, put my shoes on my feet and went out to the car with Caroline.

Although I had an appointment, I had to wait at the surgery for nearly forty minutes before I was seen. I knew where the toilet was situated and was surprised that I didn't need to make a dash for it. I asked Caroline to come in to the consultation with me. She was used to such consultations and I wanted to be sure (since I didn't trust my doctors) that things went as they should.

I explained to the doctor that I hadn't been for four days, that I had a constant urge to go and was very full and uncomfortable indeed. I also added that I'd drunk water and coffee and that I'd eaten everything I could think of which would normally make me 'go'.

To be fair to the doctor, he didn't dismiss me as suffering from anxiety. He listened carefully, asked a few questions, such as what my 'normal' bowel habit was and how long it had been that way. I told him I generally went once a day, every day, in the morning after my first cup of tea. He asked about my diet, which I admitted was relatively poor and included no meat, only a few vegetables, a very little fruit and usually, only tea to drink. I also added that I'd been taking multi-vitamins to make up any shortfall on vitamins and minerals and that I was still having the B12 injections weekly.

The doctor had me lie down on the examination couch. He pressed all around my abdomen – quite hard. Nothing particularly hurt. He said he could find no obvious lumps or bumps which would imply a blockage. Then came the shock. He wanted to do a rectal examination.

I was appalled. I have a history of sex-abuse and as I've got older, I have become more and more averse to any kind of intimate examination. I am not sexually active and have not been so for well over ten years – something which makes me very happy and content. Having 'done' the menopause as well, I am blissfully free of everything related to sexual activity (except the hot flushes which continue with menopause for years). I refused. In fact, I flatly refused and had to fight the panic urge to run out of the door.

The doctor was very kind indeed. He did not insist. He merely asked if I would permit one of the female doctors to do the examination at another time. Relieved, I agreed I would allow this. He wrote me a prescription for something he called 'a kind of laxative, more a stool-softener' and told me to use it daily and if I still hadn't 'been' by the following Wednesday, to contact the surgery and make an urgent appointment with one of the lady doctors. He also told me not to worry unduly and that I would be fine even if I did not 'go' for about ten to twelve days – exactly what Caroline had said.

Unfortunately, due to the forty minute delay in being seen, the local chemist was closed when Caroline and I left the doctor surgery. She took the prescription and said she would pick it up for me in the morning. I drove us back to my house and we watched television together and laughed at Damon and Zeke acting the fool. Then she went home.

About an hour after she'd left, I had the 'urge' and I dashed to the toilet, Loki running along behind me, his tail straight up in the air in expectation of a nice cuddle. I plonked myself down, picked up the cat and with no straining or effort at all, I passed something about the size and shape of a golf ball. I made a great fuss of Loki and told him it was his furry body and purring which had 'done the trick'.

Relieved, I then sent Caroline a text, telling her I had 'been' just a little. She sent a text back saying she would still pick up the prescription as I may need it in the future. I settled down to watch one of my favourite television shows, feeling very relieved indeed.

Later that evening, I had cause to 'go' again. Off I went to the toilet, with Loki following as had become usual. This time, I passed what I can only describe as a 'normal bowel motion'. I was simply delighted. This was great and what a shame I had wasted the doctor's time earlier.

Just as I was getting ready for bed, I needed to go again. I was not surprised. After all, I mused to myself as I plonked myself on the toilet seat with the cat on my lap, it had been four days. I clearly had a lot to get rid of, not least all the vegetables and coffee. Loki seemed delighted too. He sat on my lap and purred like a traction engine.

During the night, I woke up and thought, "Oh dear! I'd better hurry!" I rushed to the toilet again. Once more, I passed another normal bowel motion. By the time Loki appeared at the door, I had finished. I made a big fuss of the cat anyway. After all, he'd probably been fast asleep somewhere and had taken the trouble to come to me even in the middle of the night. In fact, I believe I went to the kitchen and gave him a handful of kitty treats. I went back to bed and drifted off to sleep without a care in the world.

I had only just got up when Caroline arrived in the morning. She had a big bag from the chemist. I opened it and saw several packs of the medication the doctor had prescribed. I told her I would definitely not need it and she could have it if she thought it may help her. She assured me she had got plenty of her own and suggested she leave it here anyway, just in case I had the same problem again.

We drank coffee together and during her visit, I went to the toilet twice more. Every single time, the bowel motion had been perfectly normal and I was not at all worried. As I said before, I felt I had four days' worth to get rid of. Caroline went home as she had things to do. I got on with the things I needed to do – between ever increasing trips to the toilet.

By mid evening of that Saturday, the bowel motion was definitely not 'normal'. In fact, although not exactly diarrhoea, it was very definitely much softer. Still, I didn't worry. I figured that this was the result of all the coffee and vegetables and fruit I'd stuffed down myself in an attempt to get the bowel moving again.

At bed-time, I knew I did not dare to fart. If I felt anything at all, I ran to the toilet and this was a very wise move. I began to worry about going to sleep. What if I didn't wake up and soiled my bed? I padded myself out with giant sanitary towels and went to bed.

I need not have worried. Although I woke up and dashed to the toilet once, for the rest of the night I slept soundly. In the morning, practically as soon as I opened my eyes, I had to rush to the toilet. This time it was full blown diarrhoea. I still didn't worry. Loki sat on my lap, apparently oblivious to the terrible stench I had made and purred as loudly as ever.

All day long I ran to and from the toilet. Several times, I nearly didn't get there in time. Eventually, I explained to my sons that they must not use the downstairs toilet at all because when I had to 'go', I had to go right now and I would not make it up the stairs to the upstairs bathroom in time. The boys thought it was rather funny. In fact, they teased me a bit and I laughed with them, assuring them that it was my own fault and due to the excess of vegetables and coffee I'd taken in the need to get going again.

And that was really where it all started. The cancer symptoms, I mean. I had no idea that was what I was dealing with. Why should I? I'd had this before. The only difference was that I had never before in my life suffered from constipation.

Every day thereafter, I spent all morning and most of the afternoons, running to and from the toilet with diarrhoea. It smelled terrible. I had to put air freshener in the toilet just so I could cope with it. That had never happened before either. The late afternoons, evenings and nights seemed to give me a bit of a rest, but in the mornings, very quickly after waking, I had to dash to the toilet.

The first time I didn't make it in time was awful. Fortunately, there is a basin and hot water in the downstairs lavatory. Once I'd cleared up the mess I made and feeling very relieved (for once) that I was actually alone in the house, I rinsed out my underwear, paused only to grab more and some clothes before trotting upstairs to the bath to clean myself up properly.

Whilst bathing, I had to get out twice more to sit on the toilet and explode. I was quite exhausted. And all this before even a cup of tea or breakfast!

Once clean, I made it downstairs before having to rush into the toilet again. In fact, between trips to the toilet, I managed to make myself tea and toast, put the washing on, get spare underwear, clothing and cleaning stuff and put them in the toilet and feed the animals! I counted the toilet episodes on that day. By the time it had stopped, I had visited the toilet twenty three times. I could not understand how one person could have so much shit in them!

Actually, that was by far the worst day. The following days still included running like an athlete to the toilet several times, but never quite as many as that awful day. You may be wondering why on earth I didn't go to the doctor. Well, on the one hand, I didn't really trust any of them. On the other hand, most surgeries opposite my house were in the mornings and I really couldn't go anywhere in the mornings. Wednesday afternoon was the exception. Two surgeries are held on a Wednesday and after a week of running to and from the toilet, I did decide to see which doctor was on duty. I rang the surgery.

Dismayed, because it was the doctor who had mocked me, I very nearly didn't go at all. In the end, I steeled myself and thought it best that I do. He may be able to suggest something to help me, although inside my head I was almost certain he would tell me I was suffering from anxiety again. Actually, I was getting quite anxious – that I may have to go somewhere where there was no available toilet. Anxious that I might get taken short and have an embarrassing and smelly accident in public and quite anxious that this episode would continue for years as had the previous one which caused me to lose so much weight.

Before I attended the appointment, I spent some time on the internet, Googling my symptoms. I'd done this before, of course. The more I searched, the more it seemed to me that I had all the symptoms and signs of Crohn's Disease. Although there is no cure for this, there are ways to manage symptoms and I thought I might suggest this to the doctor. I also fully expected the doctor to give me some grief, or at least patronise me in some way.

As it happened, the doctor was very sympathetic. I told him I thought I may have Crohn's and to my utter amazement, he replied, "Yes, I think that is highly likely myself. However, I am not allowed to treat you for it unless you have the investigations to confirm it. If I refer you to gastroenterology, will you attend this time? Please?"

Reluctantly, I agreed that I would, in fact, attend at gastroenterology, should he make the referral again. The doctor also told me it would do no harm to use Loperamide to control the diarrhoea (although he didn't offer me a prescription for it). I told him I would go to the local shop and get some. He asked after my general health, complained about my 'chaotic diet' as he put it – to which, offended, I pointed out that I did have a poor diet but that it was hardly 'chaotic'. He then told me my whole lifestyle was chaotic, in his opinion. After all, I rarely sleep before three in the morning, get up around ten or eleven and am eating breakfast when most people are considering lunch, lunch when most people are eating dinner and dinner when most people are preparing themselves for bed. I decided not to argue the point, but I thought it quite unfair that he should describe my lifestyle as chaotic. If I had been a shift-worker, for example, my routine would not have been commented upon. People are creatures of habit and my bowel had dictated my habits some years previously and by and large, they had never changed back.

I did go to the shop and buy some Loperamide, marketed as Imodium Instants. That is, there are no pills to swallow; just a tiny little thing which dissolves on the tongue – a much easier option for someone like me, who has real difficulty in swallowing pills at all. I didn't use them a great deal, to be honest; only if I had to be somewhere.

There were one or two occasions where I'd go through my morning and early afternoon toilet rituals and then, believing myself to have 'finished' and without taking the Imodium, I drove into town to go shopping. Several times, knowing there was only one public lavatory in the town, which I would never get to in time, I had cause to rush to a shop worker and explain I had a bowel problem and really needed the toilet most urgently. On each occasion, they were very obliging and showed me to the staff toilets. After a few of these events, I resolved to take a couple of Imodium before trying to do any shopping. Even so, I still had a few events despite this 'wonder-drug'. Other than that, there is a large independent supermarket, 'Stans', up the road from where I live. They have toilets which are both convenient and clean. It quickly became easier to go to that supermarket (although rather more expensive) than to try the trip to town.

The results came back from the scan I'd had. They showed some 'scarring' on my right lung, just as the previous chest X-ray had done. The doctor felt that it was probably the remnant of the pleurisy I'd had, just as the doctor had thought before. I was advised to make an appointment to have a further X-ray done in six weeks time. I did this.

The appointment duly arrived for gastroenterology. I asked Caroline to come with me. Although the appointment was in the early afternoon, I worried a great deal that I would disgrace myself, even though, by that time, the diarrhoea had lessened a lot, especially with the regular use of Imodium. She agreed and made a great many jokes about 'accidents' and other such things. She always manages to lighten a situation for me and make me laugh. For this, I was more grateful than she will ever know.

Between us, we started to tidy up the garden. Although I was not able to do even a quarter as much as I used to do, on account of getting breathless and chest pains, and of course, the obligatory running to the toilet, I felt a lot better than I had done for a while. Sometimes, it takes a good friend to ground and motivate you. She did a hundred times more than me, but we got a fair bit done.

Days seemed to drag at the time, but then, when I look back, I find that the whole year or more has passed ever so quickly, more like a stampede actually. Of course, the day of the appointment arrived and I was most mightily anxious. Very aware of my anxieties, I was so pleased to see Caroline, I could have wept!

I can't recall now whether we went in her car or mine. Even so, we arrived at the hospital and, as soon as we had found the correct department, the first thing I had to do was find a toilet! I didn't have very long to wait, but even so and despite the Imodium, I had cause to rush to the toilet no less than three times – this is in the space of approximately twenty minutes, you understand.

The doctor I saw was an extremely patient man. He listened to my account of symptoms, asked a few questions, not least about the constant heartburn and nausea I suffer and then said that, in his opinion, there needed to be gastroscopy and endoscopy examinations. Immediately, I felt the old familiar panic welling up. I wanted to run away (but Caroline had positioned herself between me and the door, so that was impossible). I explained my emetophobia to the doctor and he appeared to understand. He suggested that perhaps I should like to permit this examination under a general anaesthetic. Again, I refused, citing the fact that general anaesthesia can cause vomiting. He sighed and shook his head, but did not press the matter.

He then went on to explain that he needed me to have a full colonoscopy – that is, a camera which looked at the whole of the large intestine. I expressed my reservations about taking a laxative which would permit this. Before the doctor could reply, Caroline piped up, "Well, you've already got diarrhoea, so taking a laxative can't really make it any worse, can it?" The doctor smiled. He reassured me as best he could and we agreed that I would have this examination.

After studying the notes in front of him for a while, the doctor pointed out how anaemic I was and suggested a course of iron tablets. Rather than dismissing my remarks about being unable to take oral iron, he merely said, "Very well. That's not so unusual. We'll have an infusion instead. I'll get that and the colonoscopy arranged shortly." A little more conversation finished the appointment and I was free – to rush to the toilet again.

Once home, I'm afraid I regarded the whole thing as over and done with. In other words, I really didn't think about it. I was able to chat with my sons and my visiting friends, not to mention a few days where I went up to the local shop and once or twice when I went into town. I took just enough Imodium to stop the diarrhoea, although I was still rushing to the toilet about five to six times a day and most usually in the mornings.

I was also busy writing, although nothing like as much as I had been in the previous couple of years. Those books were finished and I simply had a 'NaNo' novel to edit and another private book about my cat to finish –

although that one involves poetry, which doesn't come as easily to me as normal writing. I got on with those small projects, did my normal minimum amount of housework and very little else.

About three weeks after the appointment with the gastroenterologist, I was sitting at my computer one evening, messing about on Facebook and chatting to Damon. I was most definitely not feeling unwell or anxious. In fact, it was as normal a situation as I can imagine. All of a sudden the feeling of needing the toilet most urgently overcame me. I remember holding my hand up to stop Damon speaking. "Hold that thought," I said, "Toilet!"

I got up and began to trot toward the toilet. Before I was halfway there, however, the bowel contents flooded out – very noisily. I continued, whilst thinking only "Bugger!" because it would mean a cleanup and change of underwear – actually trousers too.

Imagine my shock and fear when I got into the toilet and what had flooded out of me turned out to be blood. Lots and lots of bright red blood! I sat down on the toilet seat whilst still more flowed from me (with added sound effects). I peeled off my trousers and underwear and opened the toilet door. I called to Damon and asked him to find me some more trousers – I already had spare underwear in the toilet.

Psyche-Imp must have made himself tiny and crawled up the plug-hole of the sink, for there he was, sitting on top of the toilet roll holder, grinning from ear to evil ear. He watched me as I waited quite a time on the toilet. Every now and then there was a fart – and each fart was accompanied by some more blood.

Even without Psyche-Imp whispering terrifying things to me, such as that I would sit there and bleed to death, I was, quite simply, absolutely terrified. Damon dropped a clean pair of jeans inside the door and called out to me, "Are you all right, Mum?" I'm afraid I told him that everything definitely wasn't all right at all and that there was blood and a lot of it.

Now Damon, my youngest son, is only fourteen years old. Fair enough, he is sensible, fairly unflappable and tends to treat crises as minor things. Even so, he swore loudly and demanded to know, "How much blood?"

"I don't really know," I replied, "A little bit of blood goes a long way, but a few tablespoonsful at a guess."

Damon swore some more. The other sons were not about, so he took it into his head to call a couple of my friends to see if anyone could come. Caroline said she would come immediately. Damon came back to the toilet to inform me that she would shortly be with me.

Although I cleaned myself up and at first was able to keep reasonably calm, shortly after exiting the toilet and putting my bloodied clothing into the washing machine, mainly due to the fact that Psyche-Imp had climbed up my back and was 'nutting' me in the back of the head, I had a full-blown panic attack. This is not good. I felt sick to the point of retching; I shook – that is, my whole body shook in absolute uncontrolled terror. I kept telling myself that I was fine, I wasn't dead, nothing hurt and I would be all right, but I simply couldn't dispel the panic. I took an extra anti-emetic pill and tried to drink a cup of tea. Psyche-Imp jumped up and down on my abdomen, whispered more terrifying things in my ears and pissed in my tea. I was too far gone with fear to even be able to do anything awful to him.

Caroline arrived and questioned me closely about what had happened. Of course, there was nothing to show her; after all, I'd put the clothes in the washing machine, cleaned the toilet floor, flushed the toilet and so on. What's more, I had cleaned everything with bleach.

Her presence helped to calm me somewhat. Usually, if I was in a panic attack, this particular friend being present would be enough to dispel the panic completely. However, on this occasion, I could not stop the panic. I asked her to stay with me. She said she could stay fairly late, but she had an appointment herself the next morning, so could not stay the night. Besides, she had left her dog at home unattended.

I rang Peter. He said he would come over and stop the night with me. I think I was most worried about having another attack and bleeding to death. Of course, it had to be a Friday, so the doctor surgery was closed and no way was I travelling all the way to Wrexham to see the out of hours doctors. Besides, they would have wanted to do a rectal examination.

So Caroline sat and chatted with me. Damon went to bed. Peter turned up and spent a while chatting to me and Caroline before she went home. Peter is not the best conversationalist in the world; he tends to clam up whenever you demand that he talk to you. However, he is an exceptional guitarist. He had brought his guitar and he played and sang to me for hours.

In breaks between singing, he made endless cups of tea and sometimes rubbed my back for me. So long as I didn't ask him to talk, he spoke a little, but since he is a nurse, mostly the conversation centred around what had happened to me.

Before Caroline went home, having also been, in her distant past, a member of the St. John Ambulance as a medic, she and Peter had decided that the most likely cause of the bleed was the fact that I have had seven children and most probably have haemorrhoids. If one of these had 'popped' this would cause a bleed. They both put the nausea and other symptoms down to panic.

Peter and I were up until at least four in the morning then we both eventually fell asleep on separate settees.

I think I must have slept about six hours when I woke up. I needed the toilet and I was terrified of going in case I bled to death. I woke Peter as I dashed past en route to the toilet. I need not have worried. It was the same kind of bowel motion as I had every morning. Not quite normal and in preparation for the diarrhoea to come that day.

Slightly less panicked, I managed my normal anti-emetic pill and a cup of tea, although nausea still kept sweeping over me in waves. Damon got up and his chatting and Peter's presence soon enabled me to have a cup of tea that I could actually drink. In the end, I had a piece of toast as well, although I didn't enjoy it. I continued to have panic attacks all day. I don't think I was left alone for even a minute. I was terrified that something dreadful would happen to me were I to be alone. So silly now I look back on it, but then, panic is a funny old thing – and of course, externalised into Psyche-Imp, entirely and wholly his fault.

In fact, the whole weekend passed without my being left alone at all which was great. I'm afraid though that I was rather pathetic and needed a lot of input and conversation. I ate a lot of Extra Strong Mints, drank some tea and very little else.

Very gradually, over the next week or two, I began to feel less panicked. I still had the diarrhoea and, if I didn't take the Imodium, I could be stuck in the house for days on end. I also began more and more to dislike being left on my own. Of course, I am a grown up and it is not possible to have someone with you the whole time. I think I must have driven my few friends crazy with my need for company.

The appointment date for the colonoscopy arrived and I read every little piece of paper enclosed with the appointment letter and stared for hour upon hour at the diagram of the procedure. I read the risks section and began to wonder if I would be one of the unlucky ones and get a perforated bowel, for which I would require immediate and urgent surgery. "What Ho!" piped up Psyche-Imp, "Something real and genuine to fear? Of course, it's bound to happen to you, Kat. Off we go with panic again."

I had also been sent two sachets of Picolax and instructions upon what I would be able to eat the day before taking Picolax and how I could drink nothing but water and clear fluids once having taken it.

Of course, I made the mistake of Googling Picolax and its effects. I actually encountered an extremely funny account of Picolax and a colonoscopy by somebody called nothing more than 'Blutone'. As I read it all, my terror mounted, even though I was laughing like a loony at what the man had written in his blog posts.

Caroline was not in the least amused by Mr. Blutone's blog. She said she thought it was 'over the top' and was mortally worried that it would put me off having the procedure. It had put me off. Of course it had, but I thought at the time that I could maybe hang on, failing any other terrible events and symptoms; I would call off the event just with hours to spare. After all, there was nobody here who could sit on my chest and force the damnable laxative down my throat, was there?

In fact, it was at that point that the diarrhoea seemed to lessen off. I still found myself running to the toilet three or four times in a morning, but the motions were normal enough and there was no more bleeding. I allowed myself to be lulled into a (very false) sense of security.

Exactly one calendar month after the first bleed, I had another one. This one felt like I needed to go to the toilet. It was mid-afternoon and I'd been three times that day already. I'd eaten some toast and a sandwich and was feeling pretty good. I rushed to the toilet and managed to plonk myself onto the seat just before the world erupted from my arse. I must have sat there for about twenty minutes with this liquid running from me. It didn't smell, so that was a mercy and I had Loki on my lap purring for all he was worth.

Imagine my panic and distress when I stood up and saw nothing but blood in the toilet bowl. Of course, I completely failed to notice the little blue bastard scratching his crotch and laughing, but he must have been there as I instantly felt sick, dizzy and thought I might faint. Panic completely overwhelmed me. Surely, after having lost that much blood, I was going to die? I somehow staggered out of the toilet, told my son to call Peter, used my mobile to call Caroline and also Lesley, another friend and told them all to come quickly as I was definitely dying.

I'm such a drama-queen. Bless them; they all came as soon as they humanly could. I got myself a basin to keep by my chair because, despite the anti-emetic, I was sure I was going to vomit. Anyone who is familiar with the 'fight, flight or freeze' syndrome of panic will understand that, if I feel sick, due to the phobia, I freeze and cannot possibly run to a toilet or sink. The basin was the best option, even though it would mean that the event would occur in my living room. Not a very hygienic option but the one I was stuck with.

I could not bring myself to drink tea, although I was aware that after such a blood loss, I would need to make up the lost fluid as quickly as possible. I managed to sip at water occasionally, but that was it.

Caroline came first. She sat down and I told her I was certain I would vomit and I was panicking about it. She said something along the lines of "Oh, well. You're probably gonna throw up anyway, so it doesn't matter! Anyway, I'm here now, so you'll be fine." She made a drink, including a cup of tea for me and sat down. She asked me to describe what happened. Then she rang the doctors on my behalf and insisted that a doctor come out to visit me at home.

When Peter and his son, Ryan turned up, they both brought guitars. For a long time, they played and sang and in between songs I chatted to Caroline. Then Lesley arrived and the conversation increased. To be honest, I didn't say a great deal. I focused on their conversation and used it as a focus point. I also concentrated on the songs and the remarks made in between as a further distraction from panic. I think someone eventually sat on Psyche-Imp. In any event, he was absent after a couple of hours.

In the early evening, the doctor called. It was one of the female doctors, the one I particularly liked. I told her what had happened and how bad it had been and about the event the previous month. Just as Caroline and Peter had suggested, she thought I probably had some bad haemorrhoids and that one of them had 'popped'. She said they would find it and fix it when I had the colonoscopy – which was scheduled for about ten days ahead.

The doctor also thought I was 'very wired' as she put it, meaning not only panicked but very prone to panic for the slightest reason. What with the bleed, the anaemia and the panic, she put me on beta-blockers, promising as she did so, that they would not make me sick. She also gave me a prescription for Valium, which was the only anti-panic medicine I was prepared to accept as 'safe'.

As she went to leave the house, I said, "Doctor, am I going to die?"

She replied, "Good, grief. No, of course not! I don't have young patients like you dying on me. You'll be fine. I'm, sure it's nothing serious and is quickly fixable." With that, she left. I felt a lot better and had a cup of tea or two and then Lesley and Caroline together managed to persuade me to eat a piece of toast.

After several hours, Lesley and Caroline left and Peter was saying he needed to take Ryan home. I begged him not to leave me. He agreed to take Ryan home and come back later and stay with me through the night as he had before. All this and he would still have to get up for work the next day!

When he left with Ryan, Psyche-Imp was loitering in the porch outside and did his best to slip through the door and grab me again. However, five milligrams of Valium and Peter's assurances that he would quickly return, meant that I managed to shut the door on the little swine and so avoid the panic for a while longer.

Peter did come back. He brought his laptop with him and set it up on a dining room chair in front of the settee. Using my wi-fi network he got me into Stargate Universe. I'd never seen any of these and I quickly became absorbed by it. Peter sat beside me, tirelessly rubbing my lower back as we watched about five episodes of Stargate Universe into the night.

Eventually, I began to feel sleepy and I lay down on the settee. Leaving an episode on for me to watch, Peter went to lie down on the other settee and was soon snoring. I fell asleep very quickly indeed.

When I woke up, I was alone and Psyche-Imp was peering at the laptop – no doubt wondering how to break it. My first thought was to panic, but somehow, I managed to keep it together and get up to go to the toilet. A normal bowel motion! Buoyed up by this, I made myself a cup of tea and a slice of toast, took all my usual medication and settled down to watch the television. I wanted to save the Stargate Universe episodes to watch with Peter, although in truth, I had no idea how to get them up on the laptop. (I'm a bit of a techno-idiot and need to be shown these things about two dozen times before the information sticks).

Fortunately, Lesley called in after only a few hours and sat chatting to me until Damon came home from school. Damon can talk up a storm and he did so, bless him. In fact, he kept talking until Peter turned up again. He looked dreadful; so tired and pale, but when I queried his state of health, he claimed he was just a little tired and would get over it. He quickly set up the laptop with more Stargate Universe and sat down with me to watch it.

And so passed another night. Once more, we remained awake until late. Again, I was fine so long as I had someone with me. I took the beta-blocker and the Valium and felt as if I could cope – so long as I didn't have to be alone, I would manage. Psyche-Imp, foiled again, slunk under the coffee table and spent the evening flicking at Loki's tail causing the cat to lash the limb backwards and forwards.

I'd already been sleeping on the settee downstairs for several months before these problems began – why? I cannot actually answer that. Suffice it to say I have a number of mental health issues which are not part of but are certainly exacerbated by, this condition. They all got worse; much worse. Not only did I not feel safe anywhere except on that one settee in my lounge, I had come to a point where I could not bear to be left alone for any longer than a minute or two – alone except for a foot high blue guy who torments me horribly that is.

As the days passed, I became panic stricken about going to the toilet; I'm pretty sure Psyche-Imp made his home in the downstairs toilet and always seemed to appear bringing a massive dose of fear with him. I was terrified, even if I only needed a wee, that gallons of blood would pour out of my arse and I might die, right there on the shitter and Psyche-Imp thought this was incredibly funny.

To add to it all, I had no appetite and felt constantly sick – which is cause for panic in itself with this damnable emetophobia. My friends and my sons were incredibly supportive and they all did their very best to ensure I was never left alone for long at all. It's a great pity none of us could really see the Psyche-Imp I knew was there. If any or all of us could have, he'd have suffered some dreadful tortures and I may have been calmer and a lot more relaxed.

The days passed very, very slowly at the time, although looking back now, they passed all too quickly. The appointment date for the colonoscopy was creeping ever closer. I wasn't actually so worried about the procedure, which is strange, especially considering the 'risks' section of the information sheet. I was panicking about having to take the damned Picolax! I think one of my main concerns was that the stuff may make me vomit as well as give me chronic diarrhoea. I won't do anything which may induce vomiting, hence I don't drink alcohol, rarely eat much and avoid any foods which may be even remotely on or past their sell-by dates.

In fact, I got myself into such a state about Picolax and my assumption it may make me vomit that I rang the surgery and asked to speak to a doctor!

The doctor rang me back. It was the other lady doctor this time. I tried to gabble out my anxieties about the Picolax. She quickly dismissed that as insignificant and said she'd never heard of anyone ever vomiting after taking it. In fact, she said she had been led to believe it tasted quite pleasant. She went further, telling me it was the actual procedure and its results which were worrying me more than I realised. She actually said these words to me: "Take the Picolax. You'll be fine. And don't worry about the procedure itself. It's only slightly uncomfortable and it's hardly ever cancer."

"Cancer?" I squeaked. "Cancer had never even crossed my mind!"

She said something like, "Oh, really? Well, everything will be fine, don't worry." She then hung up.

Psyche-Imp was pissing himself laughing at me. In fact, he was pissing in my cup of tea. I considered what the doctor had said and then I started to worry about things I had not been worrying about previously. And then, to Psyche-Imp's delight, I felt sick. And then I started shaking ... and a little while after that, I got diarrhoea again. Big time. Psyche-Imp was curled round his little fat belly laughing like a drain, although I note the evil-minded little git didn't shit himself or lose control in any way like I had done.

In fact, all the above symptoms began to completely overtake my life. In the last few days before the colonoscopy, I ate virtually nothing and in all truth, I did virtually nothing, except run to the toilet. I could think of virtually nothing but this awful upcoming procedure and the terrible Picolax and its possible effects. Psyche-Imp stamped around in my dreams, planting ever more terrifying thoughts into my subconscious mind which would materialise upon waking. It got to a point where I could barely get to sleep before I had opened my eyes again, overwhelmed with another possibility of disaster.

Strangely, on the day before the procedure, I was suddenly calm. When I woke up, I was alone in the house. I had my usual diarrhoea, took my anti-emetic and anti-heartburn medications, had a cup of tea and two pieces of toast (all I ever eat but all I was permitted prior to Picolax), had some more diarrhoea – and then decided to go in the garden and burn some rubbish. I have no idea where Psyche-Imp was – probably out causing trouble somewhere else. Anyway, I took advantage of the fact that I had a little freedom without panic.

I had to run inside two or three times with diarrhoea, but I made it to the toilet all right on each occasion and had at least one cup of tea after each event before going back into the garden.

Lesley had agreed to come and sit with me after I took the Picolax. Since I know her very well and also happen to know that she is an excellent caregiver, this had given me some confidence. At least I wouldn't be alone. Lesley turned up whilst I was still in the garden. We had a cup of tea together and we chatted.

Mainly, of course, we chatted about the stuff I was about to take and how terrified I was. I confided in Lesley that I wasn't actually at all sure I could bring myself to take the laxative at all. She assured me I would take it. We were, by that time, standing in the kitchen. I had about an hour or so to go before I had to stop drinking tea and take the stuff.

The instructions for taking Picolax are perfectly clear and simple: Mix the granules into half a glass of cold water. Stir thoroughly. The mixture gets quite warm; let it cool a little. Drink it down. Follow it with at least one full glass of water. Stay close to a toilet; it can work within a few minutes. After taking it, one can have only black tea or coffee, water, fizzy drinks or cola to drink. You're not allowed to have anything to eat at all with the exception of boiled sweets or mints which you are permitted to suck.

Actually, halfway through my second cup of tea with Lesley, I had to put it down and dash to the toilet. To say that the world fell out of my backside is an understatement. To describe it as 'pebbledashing' the toilet is probably a bit more accurate but really doesn't give the reader any idea of the quantity. I think everything I had eaten for three or four days (albeit not much) had queued up, somehow turned to evil-smelling liquid and saved itself for that one event! It was awful. And to make matters worse, it smelled so terrible that even Loki abandoned me and left me to my fate in the enclosed space of the tiny little downstairs toilet. Of course, Psyche-Imp is not bothered by such disgusting things at all, so he sat on the edge of the wash-basin, pulling faces and peering at the results in the chrome taps. I turned away and tried to concentrate on 'trying-to-prevent-panicking breathing'.

Lesley thought I would be better commandeering the upstairs bathroom after taking the Picolax. She said should I need help or support, it would be easier for her to get to me in there. I realised she was right. The downstairs toilet is tiny and there is the problem that the toilet itself is situated behind the door. In fact, if one is sitting on the toilet, someone can open the door, use the hand basin right in front of them or root through the piles of shoes to their right and take their coat whilst completely protecting the toilet-sitter's modesty – on account of the door is now rammed up against their knees. Definitely, the upstairs bathroom was the best option.

I drank a last cup of tea and began transporting everything upstairs that I thought I may need: bottle of spring water; glass half full of spring water; sachet of Picolax; puzzle book and pen; novel to read; pack of Extra Strong Mints; strip of anti-emetic pills. I checked there were several toilet tissue rolls to hand as well. Eventually, I could put it off no longer.

I mixed the contents of the sachet into the spring water and left it on the shelf at the back of the sink. Psyche-Imp peered into the glass and sneezed as fizzy bubbles went up his nose. He dipped a long, clawed forefinger into the mixture and then tasted it. He screwed up his horrible little blue face and pretended to retch. My stomach lurched in fear as I sat on the edge of the bath and watched the mixture froth and fizz. Lesley sat on the landing making funny remarks. I stared at that glass for about ten minutes. Once or twice, I stirred it again. When it had stopped fizzing, I picked the glass up; it felt warm. I put it down again. I told Lesley I felt sick already. She told me I only felt sick with nerves which did little to dispel the nausea!

Finally, with my heart in my boots, I lifted the glass and sipped at the contents. The doctor had not lied but Psyche-Imp had. It didn't taste exactly pleasant, but it really wasn't vile. I thought I could almost taste oranges – not that I'm a fan of oranges; they tend to give me heartburn.

Nobody was more surprised than me that I actually drank the stuff! Not only that, but in small sips, I managed to follow it with half a bottle of spring water as well! That done, I immediately dropped my trousers and underwear and sat on the toilet, expecting the world to erupt from my arse within the next few seconds! I watched as my mental image of Psyche-Imp clambered up the shower screen and proceeded to hang upside down from the shower hose. I hoped the rotten little swine would break his neck.

Lesley still sat on the landing blissfully unaware that I had invisible 'company' in the bathroom. We chattered and talked. After about ten minutes, I became quite uncomfortable sitting on the toilet. I leaned back against the tank – which was cold. I crossed my legs and picked up the puzzle book, where I then proceeded to read crossword clues aloud to Lesley.

Damon came in from school and called a greeting up the stairs. I yelled one back. There was some fun and silliness between Damon and Lesley and I laughed at them. Still nothing happened. The backs of my thighs were beginning to ache from sitting on the toilet.

An hour passed. Lesley went downstairs and made a hot drink. Of course, she could have a cup of tea (which I would really have liked) but all I could have was black coffee. I'm not a fan of black tea – or black coffee either as it turned out.

Still I sat and still nothing happened. The conversation continued. One talking whilst getting a numb bum sitting on the landing floor; the other talking and getting numb legs and an aching back from sitting on the toilet! Psyche-Imp had clearly become bored because he had vanished. Still nothing happened at all.

Peter arrived. He came up the stairs and sat on the chair of the stair lift. There ensued a merry half an hour or so because Lesley was furious she hadn't thought of sitting upon the chair lift herself. They played about; they teased each other and laughed. And I sat on the toilet and laughed like a loon – but still, nothing happened.

I had more black coffee – I only drank a mouthful or two of the previous one. Now I had two people with whom to converse on the landing. There was laughter; there were joking remarks, there was some serious and interesting conversation, but there was still nothing at all appearing from my back-side.

My back ached. My shoulders ached as well. My legs kept going to sleep and sticking to the toilet seat. I tried every conceivable position, never more than for a few minutes at a time. It never occurred to me though, to get up and move about. Eventually, Lesley came into the bathroom, looked at me and said, "Why don't you stand up and walk about a bit? That might help."

In fact, she had to say a lot more than that, but after a lot of persuasion, I did get up and shuffle backwards and forwards over the bathroom floor about half a dozen times. Then I could feel 'something coming' so I plonked myself back down again.

It was a tiny amount and it was purely water. A very strange sensation indeed! We all cheered that the Picolax was finally working – even though it had taken several hours to do so. I don't know why I was cheering. I was the one who had to stay on the toilet. Although, with hindsight, I now know I need not have done so. I had read Mr. Blutone's account of course and I was determined that I would have no 'Picolax Accidents'.

Several times over the next two hours, a small trickle left me. There was never much, even though I had drunk almost all of the water in the bottle and one cup of black coffee. I'd also eaten about six Extra Strong Mints. I had an iced lolly (permitted) and some more water.

At about half past eleven, Lesley had to go home. She promised to return the next day to see me when she had finished work and before I left for the hospital. Peter took up station outside the bathroom door. He joked and laughed and ran up and down the stairs with black coffee, bottles of water and all sorts of other things. Eventually, when nothing much had happened for an hour or more, he suggested I come back downstairs.

I thought about this. It seemed a better idea. After all, the results of Picolax hadn't been as bad as I'd feared and surely, if I sat on some old towels, it wouldn't even really matter if I had an accident? Besides, Peter is a nurse. He's used to dealing with that kind of thing.

With a little more persuasion and some towel piling preparation by Peter, I stood up. I found it incredibly difficult to walk! I had sat so long on the toilet my legs were both dead and I had backache, pins and needles and felt extremely light-headed. I made it down the stairs somehow and no sooner had I sat on the settee with its carefully piled towels, than I had to get up and rush to the downstairs toilet.

There was more this time. A lot more! Sitting down on the toilet hurt. Everywhere hurt in fact, except, bizarrely, my stomach, which felt fine. I was aware, for the first time in months, of feeling hungry. I wished I could have some toast and several cups of tea – but they were not permitted. At that moment, Psyche-Imp appeared carrying a dish almost as big as himself. He perched on the edge of the hand basin and stuffed his ugly face with every foodstuff I liked; I could almost smell the food! When I was fairly sure that I'd finished that little bout, I went back to my pile of towels. Peter had set up the computer and we began to watch some more Stargate Universe.

Right up until about four in the morning we watched Stargate Universe, punctuated every half an hour or so by my rushing to the toilet. I couldn't believe how much fluid I was losing. I felt very thirsty and so I drank even more spring water. I also felt very, very tired, but I feared disgracing myself whilst sleeping.

In the end, I dozed off in a sitting position with one heel balanced between the big toe and second toe of the other foot. Very strange, but I do sometimes sit like that – probably because I'm mental. In any event, I certainly felt I must have been mental some two and half hours later when the pressing need for the toilet woke me up! I had one dead leg and the other one was stiff. Add to that pins and needles and a feeling of lead in both feet. Psyche-Imp danced a little jig of glee as he saw me struggling to stand up.

I squeaked with urgency as I gimped my way to the toilet and sat down – which made my back and hips protest. And that's when the world really gushed out of me. Actually, it was more like Lake Superior. I honestly thought it was never going to stop! That occurred at six thirty five in the morning and I was scheduled to take another dose of Picolax at seven!

Peter did go and fetch the glass, the water and the sachet of Picolax for me but he expressed extreme concern and thought that perhaps I should not take the stuff. After all, what I had just expelled was almost completely clear. He thought I was pretty much cleaned out.

Determined that, now I had started, I would do this properly, I insisted. As it happened, I only managed about half the second dose as I began to feel quite giddy and sick. I now know this must have been dehydration, but at the time, and with Psyche-Imp's insistence, it simply caused me to panic and fear vomiting. I also think, with hindsight, that I should have heeded Peter's advice!

My appointment at the hospital was at two o'clock. I had to be there twenty minutes early to book in and prepare. Between seven thirty five in the morning and twelve forty five, when Lesley arrived, I went to the toilet thirty eight times!

I felt dreadful; dizzy, faint; hungry and sick at the same time and utterly, utterly panicked about travelling in case I disgraced myself in Peter's car. I was very relieved when Lesley offered to come to the hospital with me as well.

The car was padded out with old towels, I rushed to the toilet one last time, and off we went. It is only a matter of about eleven miles to the Wrexham hospital from my house, but that was eleven miles of absolute purgatory. I hardly dared breathe in case there was more to come out of me. We got there entirely without incident and also managed to park the car (this took some time to find a space) and to walk along about quarter of a mile of corridors before finally arriving in the relevant department.

I presented myself at the desk, but before the nurse could say a thing, I squeaked, "Is there a toilet?" She pointed and I ran – with Lesley close on my heels. I can report that there was a lot less fluid leaving me by this time, but enough that I wouldn't want to have not been sitting on the toilet!

Twice I went back to the reception desk and twice I had to flee back to the toilet. I was entirely unable to give any details at all. Peter had to do it for me! I felt exhausted. I honestly felt I was going to pass out or die or, possibly both.

A nurse came to fetch me for the procedure and Lesley walked with me, supporting me as I was shaky. I must have looked awful. I had tied my hair back but had also left my dentures at home as I cannot bear the impressions they have to take to make new dentures and I was terrified the hospital would somehow lose mine if I wore them! I'd also removed all of the jewellery I wear all the time; I felt entirely naked.

The nurse gave me a gown to put on and an enormous pair of very strange bloomers. These were made of a kind of papery fabric and had a trap-door in the rear secured with Velcro. Even though they were dark blue, (more or less the same colour as Psyche-Imp's imaginary skin) I did not bother about allergy as they were quite clearly not cotton or wool but a man-made fibre. Relieved that I would not have to bare my bottom and lady-bits after all, I tugged them on – and then had to rush to the toilet again!

As the nurse went through the consent form and took my blood pressure, Psyche-Imp whispered terrifying things into my ear in his scratchy voice. I began to get increasingly worried that I would get a perforated bowel. I explained my emetophobia – and for the first time ever, someone understood. That nurse had a daughter with the same phobia! She reassured me that the procedure doesn't make people sick. She inserted a needle-thing (I think it's called a Venflon) in my hand as I had elected to have 'sedation'. When I expressed my concern about a possible perforation, the nurse kindly offered to go and summon the doctor who would be performing the colonoscopy to speak with me. I agreed.

The doctor came relatively quickly to talk to me. What I must have looked like, I have no idea. Definitely *not* a sane and rational person, that's for sure. He agreed there were some risks associated with the procedure; he listened to my symptoms and finally suggested that I have a sigmoidoscopy instead of a full colonoscopy. This would involve the flexible scope travelling just along the length of the sigmoid colon and stopping just below my left ribs, where the colon changes direction and becomes the transverse colon.

I agreed to this and allowed myself to be led through and placed on a trolley. Psyche-Imp sat on my head and farted – in any event, I could smell something unpleasant. Two or three very kind and chatty nurses came bustling in and did whatever it is nurses have to do regarding paperwork and other preparatory procedures. I complained that I felt I needed the toilet and one of them told me not to worry, there would only be a little water left – which would be hoovered up by an attachment on the 'scope'.

I had an injection into the Venflon of about two milligrams of a drug called Midazolam – street name Rohypnol. This would help me to relax and prevent me from remembering anything (apparently). Then my trolley-bed was wheeled through to the room where the machine was located and the doctor too. I vividly recall thinking that it looked like some ultra-modern kind of torture chamber with the huge machine and the screen along with various wires and lights and wondering if the medieval torturers had thought of anything similar by way of tormenting their victims.

I had been positioned lying on my left side. Just to my right was a large screen. Apparently I could watch this screen if I wished to do so. I didn't. I jumped violently as the Velcro-fastened trap-door was tugged open on the bloomers and jumped again as what was unmistakeably a gloved finger was shoved unceremoniously up my arse. The murmured "Just relax," from behind me did nothing to help me relax at all. In fact, the more I tried to relax, the tenser I felt.

The finger vanished and then the anaconda and the film crew were introduced. Clearly, these people had done this many times before. The problem for me was that I had never experienced anything like this before. It wasn't simply 'uncomfortable'. It bloody hurt! Actually, I think what caused the pain was the introduction of air to 'widen the colon' so as to give a good view. In any event, I am a big baby, I was panic-stricken before it began and so it's hardly any surprise that I cried out.

A nurse came and took my left hand and held onto it. I resolutely kept my eyes tight shut. I could hear the doctor reporting what he was seeing on the screen. I heard him mention 'ulcerated' and also heard him say something about 'approximately ten centimetres'. I squeaked some more as more air went in. I listened to the doctor describing a two centimetre polyp and was seriously tempted to open my eyes and have a look at it on the screen. Unfortunately, just at that moment, the blasted man puffed another shot of air into me and I was too busy squeezing my eyes tight shut and squeaking to remember to look.

A few more puffs of air, several more mentions of polyps, and then, all of a sudden, it was over. The film crew and the anaconda had retreated, the lights came up and the nurse patted my hand and told me it was all over. My trolley-bed was wheeled out of the room into a small bay – quite possibly the one I'd been in before the procedure started. The nurse made sure I was warm enough and comfortable, advised me to get a little rest and to 'get rid of some of that wind', drew the curtain across and retreated.

I gave a huge sigh of relief. Well, that was all over with and I hadn't died. I closed my eyes, for what felt like about ten seconds, but which turned out to be closer to half an hour.

The nurse woke me and asked if I'd managed to pass the offending wind. I said I thought I may have done but that I'd dozed off. She laughed. As she bustled about the little room, she suggested that I remove the 'dreadful bloomers' and put my own underwear on. She thoughtfully gave me some wet wipes, some paper towels and a bag to put the bloomers and wipes into and then left me to it. I actually struggled, up on the high trolley as I was, to remove the bloomers, clean myself (just a little blood) and get my underwear on. I had also had the forethought to put a sanitary pad in my bag, so I applied that too as I was still wary of unwanted and unrestricted leakage.

When the nurse came back, she dropped the side-rails of the trolley and helped me down and then led me into a kind of waiting area. There were one or two other patients sitting in chairs wearing dressing gowns; I assumed they'd all suffered similar procedures to me. The nurse offered me a cup of tea and a sandwich. In total dismay, I realised I was, in fact, starving hungry –

but I'd left my dentures at home! Damn and blast! I pointed this out and she smiled and offered me tea and biscuits instead. I agreed all too quickly.

Why hospital tea is so weak and foul I have no idea, but it is. Whichever hospital one goes to, the tea is like ditch-water. They must have someone manufacture their tea bags in an old rope factory or something. I decided not to complain; after all, at least the tea was hot. The meagre three biscuits did nothing to fill the gaping chasm that was my rumbling stomach either. I quickly demolished all biscuits and tea and sat there, wondering what would happen next.

Eventually, a nurse came along and showed me a toilet in the corner of the room. She explained that if I could just go to the toilet and urinate, then I could go home. As I stood up, the nurse hovered, almost as if she expected me to fall down again. Feeling quite steady on my feet, I marched over to the toilet.

I had been unaware that I needed a wee, to be honest. I certainly didn't feel I needed anything else and, probably because I'd been told I was 'full of wind' I did not hesitate to fart too. Unfortunately, that 'fart' turned out to be of the liquid variety and, upon inspection, the liquid was blood. Quite a lot of it. "Bugger!" was my only thought.

I washed my hands and scuttled out of the toilet and back to my seat. After only a few minutes, a nurse came back with Peter and led me into a little side room. We waited a few moments and then we were joined by the doctor who had performed the procedure. The nurse handed Peter some paperwork and began to explain that a 'growth' and some polyps had been found and that samples had been taken for biopsy.

Apparently, I would get the results of these within six to nine weeks. I mentioned the unexpected blood loss to the nurse, but when I described how much it had been, she dismissed it and said it often happened after samples had been taken. She further added that if it continued, or if I was in any way worried, I should ring the department or my own doctor. After that, I didn't really listen. I was dying to simply get out of there, have a cigarette, get home and have a decent cup of tea and put my teeth in so I could eat something.

I followed Peter out of the room, through the rest of the department and outside, where Lesley was waiting. She made some remark about the fact that I wasn't dead, had survived it all and praised me. She then offered me a cigarette, which I accepted most gratefully.

The journey home seemed to take longer than the journey there had been. Perhaps I was just extra anxious for a decent cup of tea. I mentioned the blood I'd passed to Lesley and Peter as we travelled home. I also described my ordeal in probably far more detail than they required. There was a distinct absence of Psyche-Imp in the car on the way home (not that I could mention this to either Lesley or Peter, who would both have thought me even more crazy than they already knew me to be). I remarked that my stomach thought my throat had been cut and I couldn't wait to eat something and we all laughed.

Once home, somebody made a decent cup of tea, I put my teeth in and somebody also made some toast, which I tucked into with gusto. In fact, I seem to vaguely recall drinking about three cups of tea. Then I suddenly felt very tired and weary. With the excuse that I'd been awake practically all night and had been given a sedative which hadn't worked at the time but was more than working now, I laid myself down on the settee and promptly fell asleep.

When I went to sleep, Lesley was sitting on the small settee nearby. When I woke up and looked about, Caroline was sitting at the computer. I demanded to know how long she'd been there and she told me she'd been there a couple of hours but that I'd rudely snored all through her company so she'd commandeered the computer.

Caroline went to make me a cup of tea and I went to the toilet. Unfortunately, I still had the diarrhoea, which surprised me a great deal. However, I did feel hungry and I managed to get some toast before having to go to the toilet again. Caroline kept me good company and later on, Lesley returned and so did Peter. Each of us took a turn at inspecting the paperwork given to me by the hospital.

One of the pieces of paper explained what polyps were and that they could sometimes develop into something more serious called an adenoma. In any event, they need to be removed. This would mean going through the whole procedure again. I felt kind of fed up but not especially dismayed at this. After all, although pretty horrible, the whole affair had been nothing like as bad as I had feared.

The other piece of paper was the report made up by the doctor who performed the sigmoidoscopy. There was a diagram of the colon and drawn on it were the locations of these polyps and a line indicating how far the colonoscope had gone. At the bottom was written something along the lines of "Approximately ten centimetre growth, ulcerated and bleeding. Needs staging."

Completely unfamiliar with any of the terms, other than 'ulcerated', I assumed this ten centimetre growth was an adenoma which had ulcers all over it which were bleeding. I peered at the third piece of paper which detailed how the polyps would be removed. Apparently, they were looped with a wire and sliced off. They would then be dissected by the pathology people. Call me thick, if you like. I certainly wasn't worried, merely relieved that the whole process was over until such time as I was called in to have the polyps removed.

Considering I still had diarrhoea, this prospect did not fill me with glee. I wondered if the diarrhoea would have gone by the next day as I drank endless cups of tea and ate quite a lot more than usual.

That night, I asked Peter if he would mind staying on the other settee again, just simply because my tummy still felt very peculiar and I didn't want to be alone. Although he had to go to work in the morning and that settee is hardly what can be described as comfortable, he agreed that he would stay.

All night long I kept waking up and trotting to the toilet with diarrhoea. I did not feel in the least bit ill. In fact, since there was no blood or anything, it didn't even seem worth waking Peter up to tell him about it. Each time I woke and ran to the toilet I had trouble getting back off to sleep again, mainly for fear that next time I needed the toilet I may not wake up in time to avoid disgrace.

Over the next three days, the diarrhoea increased. I have to say that, after that first day, I also felt extremely sick all the time and so I had stopped eating. Even so, although I consumed only Extra Strong Mints and cups of tea, the diarrhoea got worse and worse. In the end, on the Friday, I called the surgery and asked for a doctor to visit me at home. There was no way I could attend, I explained to the receptionist; I simply could not stay away from the toilet for long enough.

It was actually the senior partner who arrived, later that afternoon, to see me. I was surprised because I thought he had retired. I said as much and the doctor smiled ruefully and replied that he had semi-retired due to heart problems.

He listened carefully to what I told him; I thought I was still feeling the effects of the Picolax after three days and I wanted him to give me something to make me feel better and make the diarrhoea stop. I showed him the report from the colonoscopy. He read it and gasped aloud.

"My God!" he exclaimed, "That's an enormous growth in your bowel!" I nodded vaguely. "I'm not going to give you anything to stop the diarrhoea, my dear," the doctor went on. "The colonoscopy only looked at a small portion of your colon and found this enormous growth. There could be several other growths further along. You may, in fact, be almost completely blocked up and that is why you have the diarrhoea. It's called paradoxical diarrhoea. I'm particularly sensitive about this kind of symptom. I had another patient a few months ago who complained of diarrhoea and I prescribed something to stop it. Sadly, he died because he had an intestinal blockage."

Appalled, I looked at the doctor with great concern. Did that mean I might die? I didn't dare to ask. Psyche-Imp popped into existence again and sat on the arm of the settee cackling at my fear.

After enquiring about my diet, which I admitted had been only Extra Strong Mints and cups of tea for three days, the doctor said, "Soup. That's what you need. Nothing with bits in it, just soup."

"Tomato soup?" I asked.

"Yes, yes, that would do. Nothing solid. If you don't eat anything solid, then there is nothing to add to any blockage you may have, you see."

"But I cannot possibly be blocked," I protested. I took Picolax and was on the toilet before the procedure till I was completely empty and have still been on the toilet ever since. Anything I eat just goes straight through me!"

Just for a few minutes, the doctor looked doubtful, but then he rallied. "Best not to take any chances. Once you've had the results of the biopsies, then you'll be able to eat properly again." He then went on to chat, in a most friendly manner, about the family (none of whom he'd seen for several years) the pets and life in general. I let him out, went to the toilet (again) and returned to my place in the living room.

What he'd said had in some ways sounded bizarre and rather silly. On the other hand, it also sounded no less than terrifying. Even though I knew for certain that the Picolax had entirely cleaned me out, I began to feel fearful that I had a major intestinal blockage and might die. This was all the worse because I had two books to finish writing. I tried to sit on the panic which was mounting in me but I failed due to the fact that Psyche-Imp sat on my shoulder, took hold of my ear and whispered over and over again that I would shortly die and the children would come home to find a corpse. I really did try to dismiss the little bastard but he wouldn't go away. Unsurprisingly, I ended up on the toilet again!

I was so pleased when Caroline arrived. I told her what the doctor had said and she shrugged. "Well then, you may as well have some soup hadn't you? I mean, you've only eaten mints for three days and you've still got diarrhoea, so soup won't make it any worse, will it?" I can always rely upon Caroline to bring me back from panic with something as simple, straightforward and logical as that remark.

I had a can of Heinz Cream of Tomato Soup in my cupboard. It was heated up and poured into a large mug. I sipped at it. At first, I thought I might be sick, but after a few more sips I began to enjoy it and drank about half the mug. I asked Damon to go to the local supermarket up the road and buy me some more soup so I would have something to eat over the next few days.

Later in the evening, when Peter arrived, he found me perusing the colonoscopy report. Knowing him to be a qualified nurse, I thrust the blue paper under his nose and pointed at the remark, 'needs staging'. "What does that actually mean?" I demanded.

Peter confessed that he honestly did not know. He added, however, that he could find out easily enough. He sat at the computer for around fifteen minutes before he returned to the settee and sat next to me. He explained, quite matter-of-factly, that from all he could discover, it meant that the 'growth' was some kind of cancer and would need to be graded to see what stage it was at.

Strangely, I was not alarmed by this. I had already read and re-read the leaflet on polyps and adenomas and had decided, in the privacy of my own (somewhat befuddled) head that the growth was an adenoma. (Things ending in 'oma' were cancer, weren't they?) I had also decided that I would probably need to take the wonderful Picolax again and experience another colonoscopy whilst a loop was passed into my colon to snare off the offending thing. In fact, I believe I said as much to Peter.

Not knowing very much about cancer at all, let alone cancer in the colon, Peter nodded agreement, although, now I look back, I'm pretty sure he had a kind of sick, anxious look on his face at the time which I, of course, completely ignored.

Panic dispelled, for the moment anyway, I settled down to watch television. That evening I drank a great deal of tea and even risked a couple of biscuits. By the next morning, when I woke up and went to the toilet, as always, I was the least panic-stricken I'd been since before the colonoscopy. To my surprise, although the bowel motion was not exactly 'normal', neither was it diarrhoea!

Delighted, I dashed out of the toilet, fully expecting, of course, to have to dash back again – but I made myself two slices of toast and a cup of tea. I managed to scoff the toast and drink the tea without having to rush to the toilet too!

Once a couple of hours had passed and I hadn't needed to rush back to the toilet at all, I began to feel extremely pleased with myself. I made myself some more toast! Within an hour I had decided that, although in my opinion the doctor who visited was a little daft, he had been absolutely right about the soup; so I had some more tomato soup – and some bread and butter as well.

The rest of that day was spent in a feeling of utter bliss tinged with slight anxiety that the relief from dashing to the toilet would soon return. Fortunately, it did not. I felt a lot better in myself. With hindsight, this was probably due to the fact that I had actually eaten something!

The weekend passed with only a few toilet trips, and none of those were accompanied by the usual feeling of extreme urgency and neither was there any bleeding. Psyche-Imp had apparently vanished and gone back into the dark recesses of my mind somewhere. By Monday morning, I was able to go to the toilet and pass a perfectly normal bowel motion. However, I didn't quite feel confident enough to go out anywhere – after all, the symptoms might return all of a sudden without warning and it would be terrible to be 'caught short' somewhere.

I was sitting on the settee drinking (and enjoying, thank you very much) some toast and a cup of tea, when the phone rang. Irritated, I let it ring and did not answer it. This is one of my little idiosyncrasies; I hate being disturbed by the telephone or someone banging on the door first thing in the morning. Of course, it was actually about half past eleven, but it was first thing in the morning to me! My personal routine was still much the same; sleeping at three or four in the morning and rising at half past ten or eleven o'clock in the morning.

An hour or so later, when I was curled up on the settee avidly reading a book, the telephone rang again. This time, still irritated (why do I have this damned thing if it only irritates the hell out of me), I answered it.

The lady on the other end of the line announced that she was from the hospital and that I must come to the hospital urgently the following lunch-time. I said no. In fact, I said "No. Absolutely not. I cannot be away from my house at all. I need to be near a toilet. You'll have to leave it a few weeks."

There was great urgency in the lady's voice as she insisted I had no choice and absolutely had to attend the following day. She changed the appointment time to two o'clock to accommodate my need for a toilet in the mornings, but she insisted I had to be there and it was vitally important that I attend. At this point, Psyche-Imp began tapping me on the shoulder. I ignored him. I pointed out to the lady that it would be much easier for me to come to the hospital in say, a fortnight or two or even attend at my own doctor's surgery. I demanded to know why it was so imperative I come back to the hospital. In the end, the lady merely said, "You had a procedure recently. We have your test results back from the lab and you must come to see the doctor immediately."

Psyche-Imp, by this time was jumping up and down on my shoulder, pulling my hair and screaming into my ear-hole that I was a stupid bitch at best and a bloody idiot at worst. I brushed the evil little sod away and moaned at the woman again. "Can't it be next week? Honestly, I've only had one day or so free of diarrhoea. I'd like to be able to enjoy it a few days longer before they start sticking film crews and equipment back up my arse!"

To her absolute credit, the woman joked back, "No, honestly, no film crews, no snakes or anything like that. You seriously just need to see the doctor. He's a very nice man and won't do anything to you at all. I promise."

"Oh, very well," I grumbled. "What time was it? Two o'clock? Tomorrow you say?"

I hung up and picked the book up again. Psyche-Imp did cartwheels from shoulder to shoulder, yelled in my ear, pulled my hair, kicked me in between the shoulder-blades and, after a fruitless hour or more, finally came round to the front of my face, took an ear in each clawed hand and smartly stuck the nut right between my eyebrows. I put the book down.

"Oh, for fuck's sake!" I said, to the room in general. Both dogs looked up at me. Loki appeared from apparently, thin air and crawled into my lap purring apologetically. Absent mindedly, I stroked the cat and looked at the dogs.

"Those test results were supposed to take six to nine weeks," I muttered. "It's been a week. Hmmm." I stood up, carefully pushing Loki onto the settee. I stepped over the dogs and went into the kitchen. On auto-pilot I put the kettle on, poured away my semi-cold half cup of tea and made another. I thought I should be panicking wildly and rushing to the toilet. I wasn't and I didn't. Psyche-Imp rode my shoulder in silence and didn't even try to spoil the tea I was making.

As I walked back to the lounge with the cup he whispered, in his crackly, spiteful little voice, into my ear. "You can't ignore it you know. It's cancer and you know it. What's more, for all those years you've spent going to the doctor moaning about diarrhoea and belly ache and other weird symptoms, the cancer has been growing inside you. Getting bigger and bigger and bigger. And nobody took any notice. Awww ... poor Kat – you weren't making it up and it wasn't in your mind, it was real but nobody believed you!" Then Psyche-Imp began to laugh. In fact, the little bastard didn't just laugh, he cackled like an old Shakespearian crone. All the way back to the lounge, I knew the little sod was rolling about on my shoulder, killing himself laughing.

I stepped over the dogs, moved Loki, put the cup of tea down and sat down myself. Then I picked up my cigarettes. For a few moments, I stared at the pack. "Bet it was the fags, Kat! You've literally smoked yourself shitless!" cackled Psyche-Imp. "You can't smoke one now, ha-ha, ha-ha, ha-ha!"

I took a cigarette out of the packet and lit it, sucking a deep draw of smoke into my lungs. "Bugger!" I said. And that was all. I smoked the cigarette, drank the tea and picked my book up again.

I think I may have sent a text to Peter after a little while. In any event, he did as he always did. He rang me. Just when I don't want to talk and would have much preferred to read a bland text, Peter rang me. He does it all the time. He doesn't like texts; he prefers to talk person to person so he can pick up on inflexions and nuances of speech. A lot of the time, I prefer to text. Except when I'm panicking – that's when I want someone, anyone, everyone to talk at me so I've got a focus other than Psyche-Imp to overcome the panic.

I told Peter about the phone call and the following day's appointment at the hospital. He is a nurse. He's also not in the least bit stupid (although he's very good at pretending to be so). "I'll get the afternoon off and come with you," he said. In fact, he didn't really say very much else. He asked what she'd said and I told him and that was that. I hung up.

I picked my book up again; then, I put it down and picked up the colonoscopy report and the leaflet about polyps. Adenoma – a cancerous polyp. Fine. Right. Very well, how bad could it possibly be? They'd give me more Picolax and have to take the cancerous polyp out in stages I told myself. That's all. So I'd need probably half a dozen wonderful trips to Picolax heaven and then I'd be better. That's all right then. I carefully folded the paperwork and tucked it down beside the settee and picked my book up again.

I'm pretty sure I told Damon (and Uther, my older son, who was at home at the time) about the next day's hospital appointment. As far as I recall, the only remarks made were along the lines of "That was quick." I couldn't tell Zakh because he was on holiday in Spain with his friends. I had no doubt he was drinking too much alcohol and behaving in a way which I'd rather not know about. I certainly had no intention of spoiling his holiday.

As I laid down to sleep that night, having stuffed a good meal of garlic chicken, peas and rice down my neck earlier (and thoroughly enjoyed it), I found I couldn't sleep easily. That's an under-statement. I never find it easy to go to sleep. I absolutely couldn't sleep at all. After a few hours, I got up, rummaged about until I found the Valium and took one. Then I went back to the settee, pulled the cover up to my shoulders ... and passed out.

When I awoke the next morning, I still didn't have diarrhoea. It was a bit looser than it had been the previous day, but nothing to be alarmed about. There was no blood or anything either. I had tea and toast and several cigarettes. Then I needed the toilet again. That one was almost diarrhoea. I decided to dig about in the cupboard and look for some Imodium.

I took two Imodium Instants. These literally tiny tablets melt away to nothing on the tongue so there is no swallowing involved. Then I had some more tea and several more cigarettes.

When Peter arrived, he looked quite concerned, but he didn't say anything scary. In fact, he was very tactful. I chatted away merrily, keeping an imaginary hand over Psyche-Imp's mouth, and the conversation in all honesty did revolve around the 'growth' in my colon and a lot of questions Peter couldn't possibly answer. I resolutely did not panic.

When we arrived at the hospital, we were directed to a part of it where I had been only once before. There were not many people there waiting and there seemed to be even fewer medics on duty than usual. We must have sat there, making insignificant small talk for about twenty minutes. Eventually I was called into a room. I jumped up and Peter trailed after me.

The room contained a desk with a white-coated doctor seated at it, two chairs close to it and a few other items of furniture. Along the back wall there were two more chairs and seated in these chairs were two nurses. I believe there was a small table between them. I remember noting the particularly bland, vertical blinds in the room, between the slats of which I could see a small, rather untidy piece of hospital garden.

The doctor stood up and introduced himself politely. I can't remember his name. He was quite young and very pleasant. I'm sure he also introduced the two nurses as well, but I hardly noticed.

"I already know what you're going to tell me," I said as I sat down and completely failed to introduce Peter at all.

Before the poor young doctor could say anything very much, I launched into an absolutely ridiculous speech about not giving a damn what happened from here on in and they could do whatever they liked – just so long as nothing made me vomit. I went on to explain my phobia and to point out that it controlled my life absolutely and was incurable. I was dimly aware that Psyche-Imp was in the room with us all, but he was busily poking about in a drawer and ignored me totally.

When the doctor could finally get a word in edgewise, I believe he asked if Peter was my partner. I replied that he was my ex-partner and was with me that day for no other reason than that he is terminally stupid and had nothing better to do. One of the nurses (the blonde one, I think) grinned when I said that. The other one, the brunette, looked very serious and she also had this kind of pitying expression on her face. So I ignored her totally.

The original doctor had ordered an iron infusion for me to combat the anaemia. I explained to this doctor that I'd had an anaphylactic reaction to an iron infusion back in the nineteen eighties in a London hospital. He crossed out the infusion ordered and wrote something else whilst telling me that I would have to have the iron, but this particular one he was ordering had a much less chance of giving me anaphylactic shock than the one he'd crossed out.

He rattled on about scans being needed and queried the allergy to Iodine. The young doctor asked me what happened with Iodine. I told him I'd only ever used it externally but had swollen up like a balloon and gone very red and sore. "Yeah. That'll do it," he remarked, striking something through on his paperwork and writing furiously.

He then went on to say I'd have to have surgery. I said something along the lines of "Not a sniff of that happening." He told me I had no choice. I wanted to cry. Every general anaesthetic I've ever had (admittedly, there have been only two and they were when I was a kid) has made me vomit. I was totally preoccupied with the fact that these people were planning to do things to me which would make me vomit! I didn't give a toss about the 'C' word which had been mentioned about forty times by then.

The doctor told me I'd definitely be having surgery and further, I'd not see him again. The next person I would see would be the surgeon! I must have gone pale or something because he hastily added that there were ways of doing surgery these days which would ensure I neither felt sick nor vomited. He shook first my hand and then Peter's and left the room.

The brunette nurse came and sat down at the desk. I have no idea what she said. I decided I didn't like her and that further, it was none of her business. She ended up telling Peter that scans and things would be arranged for me to attend. I think I may have interrupted her to tell her not to bother with morning appointments as I don't get up before half past ten – or something equally as ridiculous and rude. Psyche-Imp had shuffled off somewhere and was mysteriously quiet. In fact, the whole of my mind and being was mysteriously quiet. Hadn't somebody just said 'Cancer'?

Peter drove me home. I know I worried about putting anything on Facebook – just in case Zakh accessed the social networking site from Spain and saw it and so ruined his holiday. I got my mobile phone out and sent a text to ten random people in my phone list. Quite simply, the text read: "It's Cancer."

Psyche-Imp crawled out of somewhere and in a hoarse whisper said something to me along the lines of the fact that I had nothing to worry about as I was already dead. Completely unpanicked (which must have pissed him off no end), I nodded my head and agreed. I stared out of the car window at the impossibly green trees and the fluffy clouds, noted birds flying, cars whizzing by and wondered that the world was still continuing. How could that be? My world had apparently, quite suddenly, stopped completely. There seemed to be no point in going home. What was home, after all? Bricks and mortar rented from a Housing Association; a couple of dogs and a few cats; some 'things' and some personal 'stuff' but nothing really important. Certainly nothing whatsoever of any worth or value; except my sons, but they'd still be sons even if there was no 'home' wouldn't they?

Bugger! It hit me hard; the youngest son, Damon, is only fourteen. That's too damned young to lose your mum, even if she is a largely useless mum, poor as a church mouse and in no way worthy or successful. Actually, Zakh is only nineteen, which is also too young. And then, upon reflection, the next son up, Uther, is twenty three.

I put it out of my mind. I'm lying. I didn't. I did try to put it out of my mind, but there it was, right there, in giant, Neon letters right in front of my face: YOU'VE GOT CANCER! And, to add insult to injury, bloody sodding, bastard little Psyche-Imp was sitting on the top of the sign waving at me and grinning widely.

I can barely recall what it was like to get home and tell the boys. Every part of the memory has a vague, dream-like quality – as if none of it were really true or real at all. Uther was appalled, even though I think he'd been expecting it. He put his arm round me and hugged me and said lots of comforting things. That made me grizzle a bit – not proper tears you understand. I haven't been able to cry properly for years. I rarely cry or get upset when people are mean or nasty to me, but I nearly always have a brief snivel when people are kind to me. (Something weird going on there)!

Damon listened to the news and went quiet for a little while. Then he shrugged and said something along the lines of: "It's only a bloody disease. You've had much, much worse in your life. You'll beat it and everything will be fine, Mum." He hugged me too and I grizzled some more, which was absolutely what I was supposed to do.

Actually, that was the worst part of it all. The diarrhoea had stopped and I *felt* absolutely fine. In fact, just at that moment, apart from feeling a bit weird in my head and my mind, I felt physically better than I'd done for years. I went rather quiet, which is another very unusual thing for me. I think what I was trying to do, was sort it all out in my own head. But this thing was big; really big. How the hell do you deal with stuff like this? I had no idea.

My few friends all either came to visit or telephoned, they were all so sorry. Everyone was upset and worried and I seemed to be floating somewhere above it all as if I were watching it – and it was just like some badly scripted soap episode. Maybe I was already dead and was now a ghost. Were they all mourning my passing? Did I actually *mean* something to some people? I turned further inward.

Psyche-Imp was right there, inside, waiting to pounce. He laughed at me. He pointed his long, spindly fingers at me and stuck his horrible little black tongue out. Then he laughed some more. I knew I richly deserved this. After all, hadn't I been a horrible, worthless person since the day I was born? I knew I had been. Hadn't I done lots and lots and lots of terrible, dreadful things during my fifty three years? And I'd smoked too. I lit another cigarette and thought some more.

Actually, it seemed to me, the more I thought and tried to ignore the hateful little blue guy doing a joyful jig across my brain, that I had done nothing at all in my life but fight battle after unwanted battle. I'd battled to stay alive through emotional and physical abuse; battled to be believed when I told the truth; battled to be accepted – usually without success; more battles for me whilst everyone else was having fun. True enough, a lot of the problems and wars I'd had to fight had been brought about by my own actions, but surely, life wasn't supposed to be *this* hard – all the time?

Suddenly I wished I'd paid attention to the doctor and that brunette nurse I'd decided I didn't like. What had they actually said? Where, exactly, was this growth?

What surgery was it? They were going to cut out half my large intestine; that would mean having a stoma bag. I thought they'd also mentioned other things, but I hadn't paid attention. I started to ask Peter millions of questions. I never gave him a chance to answer any of them either, I just kept them coming. I think I was simply thinking aloud.

One thing I knew for absolute certain. I didn't want to be alone at all *ever* again. Not for a second. I had cancer and that obviously meant I was going to die, and it could be any minute now. In fact, what had happened – which I can see more clearly now was this: I'd been told I have cancer. In my mind it was a death sentence and no matter what drivel the medics spouted, I would die. And because of all that, I immediately began to fear living.

I was afraid to be alone at all. I was afraid to eat or drink and I was afraid to go to the toilet – even for a wee. I suddenly became terrified of going upstairs for any reason, a truly bizarre and unreasonable fear. The prospect of taking a bath in a room where there was no-one else put the fear of the gods into me. As for going out of the house – no, I didn't want to do that either. In short, every tiny bit of self-confidence and belief I had so painstakingly built up over my troubled life was stripped away from me during that afternoon. In my own mind I was useless, a worthless a piece of shit; I wasted the air I breathed – it would do better keeping someone worthy alive. I gave up. The more I thought, the more I came to believe that I not only deserved this disease, I also deserved to die. What's more, I decided I was actually as good as dead already and I didn't want to fight.

Call me selfish if you will. I call myself selfish. Even for the love of my beloved lads and my cats and dogs, I could see no reason whatever to do battle with something else. I didn't even want to do the daily battle of waking and living what little remained of my life. If I was an animal, I would have taken me to the vet and had me put gently to sleep. I could only wish for that. Psyche-Imp laughed so hard he made me wet myself. No chance of an easy way out for this old bag, oh no, not this one.

I took Valium that night or I would never have slept at all. Peter stayed on the other settee, but although he tried really hard, he could not stay awake. After all, the man holds down a high pressure, full-time job. He managed to stay almost with it until about one thirty in the morning and then he simply passed out, mid-sentence. I trawled the television stations, I watched lots of stuff but I didn't actually take any of it in. I picked up the book I was reading, read a few chapters but didn't absorb that either.

I wandered out into the kitchen and stared at the sharp knives. Too messy; I didn't want to be in pain – bleeding to death hurts like crazy.

In total denial, I lit yet another cigarette, drank some more tea, took another Valium pill and dozed off to sleep at about half past four in the morning.

When I woke up, my first thought was "I've got cancer!" My second thought, hot on its heels was, "Why am I still here? Gods I've got to do this for another day." I hauled myself into a sitting position, took my anti-emetic pill and with the shakes beginning already, went to the toilet. Perfectly normal. Loki came to sit on my lap but I disappointed him; I'd finished almost before he arrived. I made a fuss of him anyway and went to make a cup of tea.

With tea in one hand, cigarette in the other, I sat on the settee I'd just slept on and had a massive panic attack. I couldn't breathe. I felt sick – the pill hadn't had a chance to work yet so I would obviously be sick as well. (I'm never sick, so this is stupid). My chest began to hurt. It felt as if an elephant had come along and sat on me – even though I was upright in a sitting position. Psyche-Imp turned cartwheels on the floor in front of me before turning round and miming sticking his fingers down his throat.

Loki crept onto my lap. Willow, one of the dogs – a Border Collie, sat on my feet and leaned against my legs. Clipper, the other dog – a Lurcher, lay on the floor close by. They all paid very close attention to me as I gasped for breath and shook so badly I spilled some of my tea onto my own legs, although I managed to miss both Loki and Willow.

Damon appeared; he'd over-slept. I'm afraid that, rather than tell him off for over-sleeping and not being at school, I asked him to stay with me and talk to me – about anything but cancer. He needed no further encouragement. He quickly dressed, got himself a drink and then sat down on the other settee and began to talk.

I can tell you now, dear reader, that were it not for Damon that morning, I may well have got into the car and driven off the nearest high bridge, which is only a mile or so down the road. Having said that, I was too terrified to go outside the door! What a lot of nonsense I talk! As it was, Damon talked to me and continued to talk to me all day. He also made me endless cups of tea and talked some more. I didn't ring the school to explain his absence; I just let him be with me and talk. After all, I thought to myself, I might not be here tomorrow for him to talk to. In fact, I think I was hoping that, if this kind of fear and panic was all I had to look forward to, I would not be here tomorrow for him to talk to. What a selfish cow I am!

At no point did it occur to me to feel pleased or relieved that my symptoms appeared to have suddenly disappeared and to realise that I actually felt well in myself. By lunch time I had begun to have a little diarrhoea. I remembered they'd said something about taking medication to squash the symptoms and so I took some Imodium and it stopped. I felt entirely unable to do anything. I couldn't put the washing on, hoover the floor or do the dishes. The thought of getting into the car and driving anywhere absolutely appalled me.

Peter telephoned twice during the day; the first time he apologised for having gone to work and left me sleeping! Lesley called in. I'm afraid I let my friends do all the silly, stupid little things that, had my brain been in its right place, I would have realised I was perfectly capable of doing for myself. After all, I was ill, wasn't I? I had cancer. That meant I was, basically, utterly stuffed. Psyche-Imp deliberately knocked over ash-trays and waste bins, spilled cups of tea and generally made a nuisance of himself.

Bless them. All of them. Everyone rallied round and they all did everything they could possibly do to make me feel better, but none of it worked. I didn't tell them that of course. I let them all keep trying and I did thank them sometimes, although most of the time, I whined: I felt sick; I was scared; I couldn't do it; I didn't want to do it – and that was even before I had any clue as to what it was that I would have to do! What an utter wimp! Disgusting!

"Yes, utterly disgusting," agreed Psyche-Imp. "See; I told you that you were worthless and useless and not able to do anything about it." I'm sure that evil little bugger was the thing stopping me from doing everything. Powerful thing, the subconscious, because that (I've decided) is what was holding me back. I didn't know much about cancer except that it killed people; so clearly, if I had cancer, I was dying and so I was scared. Don't get me wrong. Not of being dead per se, but of the actual act of dying. Would it involve vomiting and pain and all the scary things I was dreading having to face? Of course it would. All of those things and some more I hadn't thought of too. Psyche-Imp rolled into a ball, clutching his little blue sides with mirth – and fell off my shoulder. I glanced down and kicked the little swine across the room. To my utter satisfaction, he banged his head and so I had some peace for a bit. The panic eased somewhat.

I decided I had to be very careful. I couldn't put my status on Facebook (and gain even more sympathy from distant 'friends' – some of whom I've never met) because Zakh was still in Spain on holiday and although I am the world's most selfish woman, I'm not so selfish as to ruin a holiday he'd spent ages working and paying for. So I maintained 'Facebook silence' for the few days before Zakh came home. I had no idea how to tell him either. I put it out of my mind for the moment. I was far too busy anyway; I had to panic and feel sorry for myself, after all.

Every single morning after that, my first thought upon waking was "Oh. I'm still here," and followed immediately by "And I've got cancer," along with a pressing need for the toilet. I began to have the odd 'accident' where I didn't quite make it, no matter how fast I tried to move. I began to wear incontinence pads. This didn't stop the accidents of course; it merely made cleaning up a little easier and saved my undergarments and clothing (for the most part).

I never knew which it would be when I woke up. The feeling was the same. On some days, I would tear to the toilet with great urgency and have a perfectly normal bowel motion. On others I would tear to the toilet, either make in time to explode or not make it. Mornings became increasingly difficult.

Not only the first one of the day either. Sometimes, there may be only two or three trips to the toilet. On other days, I would hardly have time to make a cup of tea or sip at one once made between the frequent toilet runs. (Pun there, folks).

Of course, I didn't want to go anywhere at all – in case of shaming myself by having an accident more normally associated with someone aged either under two years old or in excess of eighty! In that regard, I had to rely on family and friends to fetch shopping, money, cigarettes and anything and everything else I needed. It was a pain and a nuisance – not least to the people I constantly pestered. Psyche-Imp, always the perfect little git, made sure that, whenever I asked someone to go to the shop for me, I left the most important and pressing thing I needed off the list. That way, people either had to go out twice or I had to do without whatever it was.

For some reason, I rarely took Imodium. When I look back now, I feel I should have eaten the damned things like sweets and got on with being alive as best I could.

The thing was, I didn't know anything about cancer of the bowel or its symptoms, whether one was permitted to 'control' them with drugs or not. There is plenty of information on the internet, but at that time, I also avoided the computer like the plague. Now and again, I would ask Peter things – and then either disregard his reply or do the opposite of what he advised! I'm sure Psyche-Imp was in control at those times.

Chapter Four: The Treatments

After a few days, something else began to occur which irritated me no end. I really didn't want to hear from the hospital at all, or the doctor. I was happy in denial and after all, I'd dealt with having diarrhoea before. I thought it best to forget all about it all. Unfortunately, the brunette nurse I had decided I didn't like had been assigned to me. Her proper title was 'Colorectal Nurse'. And she began to telephone me regularly and talk about stuff I didn't want to talk about – or even think about. Her name was Alison.

I'm one of those people who have trouble sometimes, in getting around a name. A few years previously, a woman with the same name had befriended me and then hurt me so appallingly I had never quite got over it or forgotten it. Sadly, due I think, to Psyche-Imp mainly, I associated the name Alison with Very Bad Things. Also, added to that was the fact that the nurse had sat there at the desk after the doctor had left and had, quite obviously, disregarded my phobia. She was trained to talk about and nurse this kind of cancer and that was what she intended to do – never mind any silly little phobia which might be getting in her way – and never mind what her total disregard of the thing which mainly ruled my life might do to damage me further either.

Also, the infernal woman would ring up and, when I answered the phone with "Hello?" She would always begin the conversation with, "Karin (emphasising the 'in' of my name), it's Alison here." As if I wouldn't recognise her voice.

Now, that's another thing which irritates the hell out of me. People who do not know me personally have no right whatever to use my forename. They should address me as 'Ms. Ward' and not by my forename. Those people who do know me fairly well, and who have been invited to use my forename (almost non-existent) may do so. Friends call me, simply, 'Kat'. Had this woman called me 'Kat' I think I would have screamed at her. She was, via my blinkered view, in no way any friend of mine!

She always said things like "and how are you feeling today, Karin?" And I always replied, rather rudely, "All right." No matter how I really felt.

The first time Alison rang, she told me she was arranging for me to have the required CT scan, MRI scan and iron infusions. I replied with something like "Oh. Right." She rattled on for a bit about goodness alone knows what – because I wasn't listening. That first day I took the telephone to the toilet with me whilst I exploded and made no apology for the sound effects she must have endured. She did 'shit' for a living anyway – what difference could it make? Oddly, whilst I felt aggressive toward the woman assigned to help me, Psyche-Imp slunk away, probably to pick fleas off the cats or something.

The second time she rang, she told me the dates when my iron infusions would begin and explained it would be every Monday and I had to be at the outpatients day clinic for nine in the morning. I replied, very rudely, "Im not doing anything at nine in the morning except sleeping. Then I spend three hours shitting. So it will have to be afternoons or not at all."

To be honest, I cannot have been the nicest patient Alison had ever had to deal with but she never got rude herself which, I suppose (grudgingly) was very professional of her. She also rang with dates for the scans – these were in the morning as well. I refused them point blank and hung up on her.

She rang me straight back. I felt she was patronising me when she said we must have been cut off! She said she would rearrange the appointments. I said 'good' and hung up again.

I had an appointment with a social worker from the mental health team. Sadly, Arne, my regular Community Psychiatric Nurse had left suddenly and not been replaced – a fact which upset me a great deal. Just when I really needed some support it seemed to me, all support was withdrawn. Oh well, this is the National Health Service and for the most part, it also seemed to me, the word 'Service' meant nothing at all.

The Social Worker came to my house and was wishing to speak to me about a 'care package' which would be funded by the Council and thus help me to cope with life in general, not least the cleaning, self-care and other things. During the conversation, the woman happened to mention that she'd been contacted by Alison who thought perhaps I was somewhat 'not all there' because I had refused immediate treatment and put off the scans and did not, apparently, understand the seriousness of the situation in the least.

I was enraged. How dare that woman think me potty? I let my anger show to the social worker, although I had met her before, she was very nice and I did not direct the anger at her personally. I told her I disliked the Colorectal Nurse intensely, that the woman was patronising and then I explained that, as far as I was concerned, I had already waited some twelve years to get a diagnosis, so a few more weeks couldn't possibly make all that difference. The social worker explained that the Welsh Assembly had decreed that the hospital had, by law, to do certain things once cancer had been detected and do them within a certain time-frame. If they did not, then the hospital would get into trouble. I replied along the lines that, in my opinion, they would simply have to write on their paperwork or schedules, 'patient refused to comply' and they would be off the hook.

I further asked the social worker if she thought I was daft in any way. She replied that she thought I was perfectly sane and she could see and understand my reasoning. She asked if I was frightened. I told her, truthfully, that the only things I was afraid of were vomiting and pain and that, if I could have a guarantee that there would be no vomiting at all and very little pain, I would be happy.

Everyone is scared of pain so that's not unusual, but the vomiting thing had controlled me all my life and was very significant. I said I didn't give a damn for schedules or orders, reminded her that I was a human being and things would be done in my own time or not at all – and that was that. The woman said she'd pass my views on to the Colorectal Nurse and that she could explain my reasoning and thought processes, which seemed very sane to her. I was mightily afraid actually of suddenly finding myself committed to a mental hospital, where all choices and views would be completely disregarded. Once again, suicide started looking mighty good. Damn and blast that bloody Psyche-Imp, I hadn't noticed the little creep slinking up on me whilst I was talking to the Social Worker!

The day Zakh came home from his holiday was traumatic for the whole family. Uther was at work but texting me regularly throughout the day. I had several texts from Zakh too. He was at the airport. He was en route home. I replied to them all with my heart sinking into my boots. Why had he had to be away? If he'd been here at the time, it would have been so much easier. I wouldn't have had the awful news to break to him. I knew I couldn't do it. He would be on a high, having just had the time of his life and I could not bring myself to burst his little happy bubble. Psyche-Imp laughed himself sick and lay on the floor, his pot-belly rising and falling. I stamped on him and he disappeared.

I'm afraid, this coward sent a text to Uther and told him he would have to do the deed and break the awful news. There was a long pause before finally, a text arrived which said, simply, "OK."

Zakh arrived home and greeted everyone with huge smiles and hugs. I tried to smile but I must have looked as if I were trying not to heave. I tried to brightly chatter to him, but found it very difficult. I managed things like "Was the flight back all right?" and "Have you got some souvenirs?" And then, his mobile phone rang. He sat down and answered it with "Hello," nothing more.

I watched as he went deathly quiet. I crept closer, my heart pounding. He hadn't said a word. Just as I got close to him, the phone fell from his fingers and he burst into tears. I sat down and put my arms around him. He sobbed just as he had done when he was a small boy and the dog had been put to sleep. A few stray tears trickled from my eyes too – not tears for me, you understand, just tears because one of my babies was so terribly sad.

I cannot say how long Zakh cried. I kept saying, over and over again, "It'll be all right." Who was I saying it to? Him? It may have been for both of us. I don't know. Finally, Zakh's tears subsided and he turned to me and said, "When did you know?"

"Last week," I replied. "I've been so careful. I didn't put it on Facebook or anything, just in case you went on your mobile internet and saw it and your holiday was ruined.

"I never did. It was too expensive."

"Oh. Well. I'm really sorry you had to come home to this, boy."

There followed a great many questions, most of which I had no answer for. Then Zakh took himself off to his room, leaving me and Damon sitting looking at each other.

"That could have gone a bit better," remarked Damon. "I expect you want a cup of tea now?" I nodded.

I received a text on my mobile and opened it. It was from Uther. It read simply: 'That was the hardest thing I've ever had to do in my life. Is he OK?'

I replied and thanked him, adding that Zakh had gone to his room, probably to talk to Charlotte, his long-time girlfriend, on the phone and cry some more.

Later on, Zakh talked to me, hugged me and said some very supportive and kindly things to me. He told me I was the toughest person he knew and that I would beat this thing. And without batting an eyelid, I lied and said I would.

So now everyone in the family knew and all I had to do was fight. I didn't want to. Not in the least. I felt like crap and as far as I was concerned, I was already a dead woman. A woman still breathing, walking about and shitting (oh yeah, still doing plenty of that), but dead nonetheless.

The days passed, one after the other, as days tend to do. Every day for me was quite similar and every day I should have seen as a blessing, but instead I saw it as a curse. For me, rather than another blue sky or fat raindrops, or funny, furry things or wonderful boys who should be the reason I would fight this thing tooth and nail, every day was another miserable dawn of gloom and doom and to be resented. What a bloody fool I was.

Ensuring I had someone with me – it was Lesley the first time – I went off to the hospital to the day-case unit for the initial iron infusion. This unit had very obligingly told me I could arrive any time in the morning, right up until lunchtime and that the infusion would take a couple of hours.

I actually felt scared to death on the way there. I'd been to the toilet about twelve times that morning and reached the stage where I was passing simply water. I became terrified that I would soil poor Lesley's car and then began to feel sick as well, which of course brought with it even more panic. Looking back now, it was all Psyche-Imp's doing. He jumped up and down, from shoulder to shoulder and whispered terrifying thoughts into my head. What if I had another anaphylactic shock reaction to the iron? What if I shit myself whilst wired up to the drip? What if? What if? What if? Had I been mentally stronger, I would have strangled the little sod into silence and added murder to my list of lifetime's wrong-doings.

It was a lovely sunny day when I had that first iron infusion. The day-case unit where I was to be treated was a broad airy room which had eight large, comfortable recliner chairs evenly spaced around it. The back doors were wide open and there was a television on. Some of the chairs were occupied by other people who, as I inspected them beneath my eyelashes so as not to appear to be rude and staring, seemed to be having everything from something white and unidentifiable to blood dripped into their veins. Most of the people had drinks and sandwiches or dinner plates on the tables beside them.

The atmosphere was calm, friendly and relaxed. Even so, I still felt tense and frightened. I'm not scared of needles at all. At least, I never had been in my life before, but all of a sudden, the prospect of having one shoved into a vein in my arm was not something I could face calmly. Lesley chattered to me about everything from the great weather to what was on the telly. I silently chided myself for foolishness. Psyche-Imp again – clearly, he'd hitched a ride to the hospital with Lesley and me.

The nurse showed me to a chair and made sure I was comfortable and then went off to get what she needed. Another lady came – a health-care assistant. She offered both Lesley and me a cup of tea or coffee and asked if we would like a sandwich. We both said yes and thank you.

The original nurse came back, easily slipped the needle painlessly into a tiny vein on the top inside of my right wrist and attached the bag of brown stuff which had to be dripped into me to a pole beside me. I noted it was on wheels. I asked what I should do if I needed the toilet and where the toilet was located in relation to the room I was sitting in. The nurse told me to unplug the machine, drape the electrical lead over the big box on the pole – which would bleep – and wheel the whole pole with me to the toilet which was just a foot or two outside the entrance door.

I was very relieved. I hadn't got even as far to go as I had at home. I should be fine. I then explained that I'd suffered an anaphylactic reaction to an iron infusion in the past and felt worried it may happen again. The nurse smiled and explained that the type of infusion which could sometimes cause that was not what was being used on me. She further added that she would start it slowly and keep checking that I felt all right and that I was not to worry.

Best of all, she addressed me respectfully as Ms. Ward – until I decided to tell her she could call me 'Kat'. She wrote that down on my notes too – something no-one else had troubled to do up to that point.

Lesley and I drank tea together and ate our sandwiches. I hadn't thought I was hungry at all, but I managed to eat most of it. The tea wasn't as foul as hospital tea generally is either. I learned the supplies came from the League of Friends shop. This probably explained the better quality.

I had no reaction at all, only a slight headache for a little while, but I'm pretty sure that was simply Psyche-

Imp slinking off. He always kicks me in the temple before he skulks away.

That first infusion took just about three hours including arrival and setting up. During that time, I chatted to Lesley, watched a bit of television, even though the channel was not to my usual taste, remarked on the weather and drank two more cups of tea. I got up and went to the toilet twice. Both occasions it was only wind, but even so, I was glad I'd not stayed in the room. How embarrassing it would have been to fart, really loudly, in the company of several strangers.

On that day, none of the other patients spoke, either to me or Lesley. Some of them were talking on their mobile phones; one was doing a crossword; one was asleep. Their infusions or transfusions completed, they stood up, straightened their clothing, collected their belongings and left. That day I was the last to finish and leave.

I hadn't actually missed my cigarettes whilst sitting in that room; Lesley had popped outside once or twice but even that hadn't bothered me. Even so, as soon as we got outside, both Lesley and I lit one up and then smoked another in the car on the way back. I felt no different to how I'd felt when I went there, which surprised me. For some stupid reason, I'd thought if I could just get some iron into me, I would instantly feel better! Silly woman!

I did very little for the rest of that week, except my obligatory toilet dashes of course. I stayed home, inside the house and did nothing but sit on the settee, watch television without paying it that much attention and read a very little.

I think Alison phoned twice. On neither occasion did I want to speak to her. I grunted and made the odd remark here and there, none of them pleasant. She kept rattling on about these scans and how important they were.

On the Thursday of that week two letters arrived from the hospital. One appointment letter came in a very large envelope indeed and was very heavy. Upon opening it, I found two or three small bottles and a long list of instructions. This would be my 'bowel prep' medicine. I was to modify my diet and eat only the things on the list allowed for two days prior to the scan. Then I had to drink one of the bottles of medicine, continue to eat only things on the list the next day and take the second bottle and then on the third day, eat nothing at all but drink the bottle of medicine.

I opened one bottle and sniffed at it. It smelled of aniseed. I noted the date and time of the scan. It was for mid afternoon the following Thursday.

I opened the other letter. This contained two sachets of Picolax with all the same instructions as before. It was for a colonoscopy! It was also scheduled to take place on the Monday following the scan and was to be first thing in the morning.

I looked back at the other appointment. Yes, this was definitely for the Thursday. So I would be restricted to eat only things on the list Tuesday and Wednesday, nothing on Thursday, have this scan thing and then go home. I would be able to eat for the rest of Thursday – but I noted the warning that I may well be subject to two days or so of acute diarrhoea. Then I must eat only a few things Saturday, nothing at all Sunday, take Picolax and present myself Monday morning for the anaconda and film crew to take their trip into the depths of my body. As soon as I'd undergone that procedure, I would have to go down to the day-case unit for my iron infusion! Bugger that!

I read the proposed scan instructions carefully. Apparently, this 'bowel prep' would show up my insides better on their scan. They also planned to have some delightful person standing close by with an air hose, which would be stuffed up my arse so I could be filled with air! I recalled the extreme discomfort which had made me cry out during my colonoscopy. That was 'only' air too. Then I noticed that they also intended to put a needle into my hand and inject me with Iodine so that my blood vessels all showed up beautifully as well. This, with a total disregard for the fact that I am allergic to Iodine! Now, wasn't that great? How very thoughtful of them. The bastards! Psyche-Imp sat on my shoulder rubbing his ugly little hands together and cackling like an old crone. Why he found the prospect of me being subjected to all these horrors so fascinating I have no idea, but he happily began to whisper terrors in my ear immediately so that I could barely think straight at all.

I turned my attention to the colonoscopy appointment letter. This was clearly some kind of mistake. I'd already had the damned colonoscopy. I certainly didn't want another one and if anyone thought I was going to have one they could most certainly go somewhere horrible and pro-create.

I rang the colonoscopy unit to cancel the appointment and explain how they'd made a mistake. The nurse told me there was no mistake. I was to have a full colonoscopy of the whole bowel and a polypectomy into the bargain. I told her, very firmly, "No, thank you. You'll have to cancel it. I'm not coming." I then hung up.

"Bloody stupid people," I muttered. "Of course" replied Psyche-Imp, appearing from wherever he'd been hiding causing some mischief or other. "No-one ever listens to you, do they? You may as well go and camp out in the hospital grounds and never eat again. I mean, going there every week for iron means you virtually live there already." I agreed with Psyche-Imp. (It was easier than arguing). I then telephoned the X-ray department to remind them that I am allergic to Iodine and had no intention whatever of taking their foul bowel prep stuff. I already had diarrhoea and I didn't intend to suffer any worse, thank you very much.

When the X-ray department answered their phone, I explained to what turned out to be the receptionist. She passed me to somebody else – to whom I explained it all again and then she passed me on to some man. I told him he could go whistle if he thought anyone was sticking anything up my back-side. And furthermore, if he thought I was deliberately going to restrict my already very limited diet or take his foul medicine and that, should he intend to kill me, carry right on with the Iodine.

It must have been very difficult for that particular health professional to deal with someone so angry and, frankly, abusive on the telephone. However, I think he recognised fear when he heard it and he did his best to reassure me. I still refused. He told me he had struck out the Iodine but advised me to take the bowel prep and that it rarely gave people diarrhoea. I insisted it would give me diarrhoea, which I already had. I also said it was too soon and I wasn't ready to tackle things.

I was just busy trying to get iron into myself and had to come to the hospital once a week already.

He was very sympathetic. I honestly have to admit he tried everything to persuade me not to cancel the appointment but he failed. I did cancel it. I told him I had no intention of doing anything at all until I was ready and the bullying colorectal nurse could get as cross and as patronising as she liked. I think I also pointed out that I had been declared sane by a mental health worker and that further attempts to have me certified as mentally deficient and hauled away would not succeed. With a sigh, the man agreed to cancel the appointment and try to rearrange it at a more convenient time without either bowel prep or Iodine. He said there would have to be air introduced no matter what. I told him nobody was going to sodomise me with an air hose or anything else, thank you very much. I hung up.

I felt quite pleased with myself. "Yes," agreed Psyche-Imp. "You did really well. You certainly put those interfering buggers in their place, didn't you? Fancy wanting to treat you for cancer! Whatever next? Anyone would think they were trying to kill you before you die horribly of your own accord anyway." I swatted the little sod away and told him to shut up. Then I went to the toilet and spent a panicked half hour feeling sick and with almost constant diarrhoea.

I got my come-uppance the next day when Alison rang me. Not only did she ring at stupidly early o'clock in the morning when I was still sleeping (and so had to wake up, answer the phone and immediately rush to the toilet) but she opened her conversation with the usual irritating 'Karin? It's Alison' emphasising the 'in' of Karin again.

Whilst the world fell out of my nether regions – odd because I'd eaten nothing at all the previous day except lots of Extra Strong Mints and one slice of toast – Alison told me off about cancelling the appointments and told me she had reinstated them!

I'm afraid I was extremely rude to her. I shouted at her. I called her an interfering busy-body and that no amount of bullying would force me to do anything I didn't want to do for myself in my own time. I think she was somewhat taken aback by my tirade. The woman insisted that things had to be done quickly and in a certain order. She realised, she said, that it wasn't always convenient or comfortable or pleasant but that they simply had to tackle the cancer quickly and at once.

I found my mouth took over. It was not, in any way, connected to my brain. Besides, I think my brain was currently floating in the toilet bowl at the time. I told her no-one had even bothered to ask me if I wanted treatment. They'd assumed and taken things upon themselves without so much as a by-your-leave. I didn't want treatment, I told her. She could go forth and multiply. Actually, I'm pretty sure I said "You can fuck off, that's what you can do, and leave me the fuck alone!" I mean, you can't actually get much ruder than that, can you?

Doggedly, the infernal woman ploughed on regardless. She said things like "You're so young. You *must* have treatment. We can fix this." And to everything she said, I said something rude or negative back to her. She may well have reinstated those appointments, but I wouldn't bloody-well be there and then they'd be wasted. I suggested she cancel the appointments again quick-sharp and give them to someone who enjoyed being sexually abused. Then I hung up.

Loki was on my lap. He still purred like a traction engine and didn't seem to mind in the least that I'd been shouting or that I'd sworn every other word. I'm pretty certain that Psyche-Imp was sitting on top of the toilet tissue with his legs crossed, inspecting his finger-claws and looking inordinately pleased with himself – the little swine.

A tear trickled from the outside corner of my eye. I wiped it away and decided I must have started a cold – no doubt caught from that vile hospital. After all, that's where you go if you want to catch something, isn't it? A hospital. That's all they were good for. Psyche-Imp nodded his head in satisfaction and then jumped into the toilet. Gods alone knows why, but it was the best place for him anyway.

With Psyche-Imp flushed away, for the moment anyway, until he found a way to return to bugging me, I sat down and rang the mental health team. I *really* needed some support, I told them. They said they simply didn't have anyone available. I got irritated and pointed out that I had been referred by my doctor, had been receiving a service with a community psychiatric nurse, who had left. This was no fault of mine. I further pointed out (in my most snooty tone) that they were duty bound to provide a service and it wasn't my problem if they had funding and staffing problems. They still had to provide the service. They said they'd look into it.

When Peter arrived that evening after he'd finished work, I regaled him with my grievances. I didn't want all these scans and colonoscopies and whatever treatment they had planned; they'd better involve me or I'd simply refuse. He was supportive, in a quiet sort of way. I think he was becoming somewhat overwhelmed with the enormity of what he'd taken on by telling me he'd stand by me and help to care for me. I asked him heaps of questions about scans and he answered as best he could, sometimes even going to the computer to check the internet to make sure what he was saying to me was accurate.

I sat up very late that night. I simply could not get to sleep or even unwind to the point where I felt able to try to sleep. I watched Pirates of The Caribbean through three times. Peter had agreed to stay again and was snoring on the other settee. I knew he was there; if anything happened or I felt as if I was going to die or anything, I could have woken him up. But, apart from a couple of trips to the toilet – Loki came too – there was nothing I could say if I did wake him up. I felt more alone and miserable than ever. Eventually, I took a Valium and lay down with my book, but whatever I read I couldn't tell you. The words may have gone in my eyes but it certainly didn't arrive in my brain!

Peter left in the morning without waking me. This was probably just as well because it had been very nearly half past five in the morning when I'd taken the Valium and so must have been after six when I finally fell asleep. It was actually getting on for midday when I awoke. As usual, my first thought was, "Oh. I'm still here; and I've got cancer."

For once, I was able to put the kettle on and take my anti-emetic pill and anti-heartburn medication before needing to go to the toilet. I brightened up considerably. Perhaps, after the first iron infusion, I was already getting better. I made the tea and sat drinking it before I needed to go again and it wasn't too bad. Loki came as well, bless him. That fat, ginger cat had taken it into his furry little head that I should never have to endure going to the toilet without his support; and I cannot find words to explain how grateful I felt for it.

I made more tea and managed to drink it all before I had to go again and after I'd been (and washed my hands), I made toast and ate that. For the first time in weeks, I actually began to think about both the disease and the possible treatment.

I didn't like those thoughts. They were very frightening. I realised that Psyche-Imp had returned from his (well-deserved) trip through the local sewers because I felt true fear. Mind you, this time, I was actually able to identify the fear as being 'fear of the unknown' and 'fear of fear itself'. At least, I managed that much before the panic attack overwhelmed me.

I felt sick. I shook from head to toe and I had one hand on Willow's neck and the other tightly curled around Loki's furry body. I began to talk to the dogs and cats. I said silly, inane things. Willow cocked her head from one side to the other and lifted her ears. Clipper sat up and listened intently. Of course, I knew they couldn't understand 'human' but they were listening and I'm absolutely certain they understood fear.

Very gradually, the panic attack subsided. By the time Damon came home from school to regale me with silliness, I was relatively calm. I allowed myself to be transported into the world of the teenage boy without protest. It was a great distraction.

The diarrhoea wasn't too bad over the weekend. It may have been because I ate a little more than usual but I resolutely avoided all vegetables, fruit and fibre. A terribly unhealthy diet of white bread, chicken, white rice and garlic seemed to have the best effect. I decided to try to eat at least that much daily.

What also helped, I am quite sure now, was the fact that there was a lot going on over the weekend. Friends visiting, kids in and out, always somebody here, doing stuff, chatting and so forth. It enabled me not to think about being ill. I even managed to put some washing on, do a few dishes and tidy the lounge up a little.

The second and third times I went for an iron infusion I went with far more confidence. Now I was sure I would have no nasty reaction and therefore I felt less nervous all round. Unfortunately, on the third occasion, the nurse who tried to put the needle into the back of my hand managed to miss the vein completely and caused an enormous, painful bruise. Another nurse came and used the same vein in my wrist as before.

I always had someone come with me to these infusions. I was perfectly capable of driving and being there and driving home, but at the time, my confidence had deserted me completely and I truly believed I could do nothing alone. The very thought of going anywhere in the car on my own filled me with terror. Again, I look back now and know it wasn't me; it was that spiteful little Psyche-Imp working his wicked ways and stealing away all the confidence that I had gradually and painstakingly built up over a lifetime of disasters and stress.

By the Wednesday following the third iron infusion, the diarrhoea had definitely lessened, although not disappeared altogether. Hope began to creep back into my mind, albeit haltingly. Maybe I could get control of this and the symptoms and so would not need all these scans and procedures. Even though I knew I could 'do' the Picolax now and probably would not vomit or even feel sick, I still dreaded the removal of the polyps. Surely, that would hurt?

Alison rang me just once more. She had re-arranged the CT scan and an MRI scan for after the iron infusions had finished. She told me she had also arranged an appointment for me to see the surgeon. I just happened to be in a reasonably good mood when she rang that day. Also, it was mid-afternoon so largely, the diarrhoea had abated and I was feeling more awake than whenever she rang me first thing in the morning and woke me up.

The CT scan would be in the afternoon after my last infusion and the MRI scan would be in the late afternoon a couple of weeks later. Apparently, this was against hospital policy and they had 'missed' their deadline for treating cancer patients by a couple of weeks. I was to see the surgeon on third of August.

Alison explained he was a very kind man and very experienced in the field of colorectal cancer and I had nothing to worry about; he would see me all right.

Even though I was in a good mood, I found her irritating by the end of the conversation and was glad to put the phone down. I'd noted down the times and dates and put them in the calendar part of my mobile, even though Alison had assured me that letters would be sent out to confirm the appointments.

I felt able then to actually forget about the cancer altogether and concentrate just on the iron infusions. I thought if I could just take one step at a time, I would be fine. Psyche-Imp tried to fill me with fear again, but that day, I swatted the little tyke so he flew from my shoulder and actually vanished altogether for a few hours.

It wasn't until later that evening, after I'd eaten more than usual and felt over-full and rather sick, that he returned to taunt me with terror again. Damon and Peter had a hard time that evening; I needed to be talked at for hours. Every time conversation stopped, so the nausea returned, the panic overwhelmed me and exacerbated the nausea and off I went into shaking panic attack again. Of course, I ended up taking Valium.

When I say I took Valium, one thing I haven't said is that the doctor had prescribed five milligram tablets which were supposed to be taken three times a day. I was taking them infrequently and only half a tablet at a time. I say this now because that night, I had to take the other half about an hour later before the panic subsided. I then took a further half tablet when I wanted to go to sleep.

Rosemary, my best friend of thirty-five years, who I've already mentioned and who lives miles away in Woking came up to stay with me for a week. She was present on either week four or week five of the iron infusions, I really can't remember which. She told me I looked a lot less ill as soon as she arrived. This gave Peter a whole week's break from having to play nursemaid to me. He needed it by then; the poor man was beginning to look extremely tired and haggard.

Rosemary took up station on the other settee. We sat talking and laughing just like the old days, late into the night and we slept late in the mornings as well. Rosemary herself suffers from Irritable Bowel Syndrome and has had similar symptoms to me for many years. She, however, has been thoroughly investigated with many of the same procedures and found to have nothing wrong that a few pills and some fibre won't help – but not cure. She's recently been diagnosed with Type Two Diabetes, so now she has to eat more regularly.

Funny, in the whole week that Rosemary was with me – and we were together day and night, either yapping, laughing, simply sitting quietly, watching television or asleep, I only had one small panic attack. I have come to the conclusion that Psyche-Imp is scared of Rosemary and just stays well out of her way. I ate better during that week than I had for many months and I actually fell off to sleep without requiring any Valium at all.

In the one small panic I had, Rosemary chatted to me like a person who needed therapy for being unable to stop waffling and I quickly became absorbed by the conversation and completely forgot to panic!

During that week, I actually got out of the house too and not just to attend the hospital for my infusion either. We first went to the local supermarket up the road. Then we went to the pet shop for animal supplies. Once or twice, I actually drove and Rosemary was a passenger. On the day of the infusion, I drove and she just came along for company. During the week, I also did a little housework, washed dishes, sorted through and did the washing and one or two other little jobs. I felt much more like my old self and quite confident with Rosemary around. Of course, she has her own life and a very understanding husband (thank goodness) but she always comes when she's needed.

Literally ten minutes after Rosemary had left at the end of her stay, Psyche-Imp reappeared and the panic came back big time. I was alone. I shook from head to toe, rushed to the toilet with the diarrhoea – about four times – and wished she could simply have stayed for always. My common sense knew that was utterly stupid of course.

I noticed Psyche-Imp everywhere I looked. When I sat down to distract myself by reading a book, there he was, in the middle of the page, picking his horrible long nose and flicking the bogeys at me. I shut the book and paced up and down the living room. I ended up sitting at the computer checking emails which I hadn't done for ages. Psyche-Imp vanished somewhere and so did the panic.

Rosemary had purchased a laptop whilst she was here and I'd shown her what little I know of computers (which, in all honesty, is not a great deal as I treat the thing as a glorified typewriter). By the time she went home, she could connect to the internet, check her new Facebook account, read and send emails and access other things on the web. She needed to add the Office programme in order to be able to do some stuff, but the computer was a pretty good one which came with everything she needed to get started. I was pleased with myself.

I sent Rosemary an email, thanking her for coming and for her support and promising to ring her the following weekend for one of our two to three hour conversations. Then, again for the first time in simply ages, I accessed my own Facebook account and spent a merry couple of hours playing games, replying to messages and other inane things. It seemed one of the ways of avoiding panic had been right there in front of my face and I'd completely ignored it. Naturally, that was Psyche-Imp's fault and I knew it.

I had something to eat that evening, greeted Peter with something closer to a smile than I usually managed and went back to the computer. This time, I looked up Macmillan Cancer Support.

In actual fact, I was at the computer for hours. I read loads and loads about cancer and my type of cancer in particular. A lot of what I read filled me with fear, but I managed the fear and read on. I even joined their online community and chatted to a few other cancer sufferers before the internet crashed.

After that, I sat and talked to Peter about what I'd learned. I had the insane urge to ask him to play a game of cards with me, but he was clearly tired so I said nothing as he sat down on the other settee. I didn't ask if he was staying, he'd already demonstrated he intended to do so.

I did need a Valium – well, half a Valium – that night to get off to sleep and as always, I dozed off with Pirates of the Caribbean playing on the television. I was gradually learning the script off by heart in my sleep.

The last two weeks of iron infusions went without a hitch. Lesley came with me to the fifth one and Peter came with me to the last one. On both of those occasions, the patients were mostly women and so there was conversation as we sat in our recliners with various substances dripping into our veins.

One lady asked me what my illness was and why I needed the iron. I told her it was bowel cancer and I was afraid of having to have chemotherapy because I had a vomit phobia. She was much older than me and she was surprisingly, very reassuring. She told me that she herself had suffered from and recovered from breast cancer many years ago. She also said she'd had chemotherapy and had not been sick with it. Her worst symptom of chemotherapy, she told me, was that afterwards, she often felt tired and weary and just needed to rest and sleep a lot. This information buoyed me up a great deal.

As the lady left the ward that day, she stopped by my seat and wished me luck. She then patted my hand and advised me to take all the treatment I could get and that I would recover and live a long and happy life. I almost felt I could believe her too.

After the last infusion, Peter came with me to the other end of the hospital to the X-ray department to present myself for the CT scan. I had to change into a gown (a white one this time) and wait for about ten minutes before being called in.

It was a man who summoned me in. He called me 'Ms. Ward' and offered his hand. Apparently, this was the man to whom I had spoken on the telephone (and to whom I had been so terribly rude). Humbled by his politeness, I felt embarrassed by my previous outburst and apologised to him. He waved the apology away, telling me it was entirely un-necessary.

The scan was almost the same as the scan I'd had some months before. I was required to lay flat on my back on the couch-thing, which moved forward into the doughnut ring of the scanner itself. The man did warn me that the machine would 'speak' and give me instructions. When to breathe in, when to hold my breath and when to breathe out as well. He also reassured me that he and his colleagues could see me at all times and, although alone in the room, I only had to raise my hand and they could stop and come to attend to me.

I am never entirely comfortable lying flat on my back, especially not upon a hard surface. This is due to numerous back problems I've had over the years. Getting into position is awkward (and hardly decorous); once there, I am fine as long as I am not required to move.

The scanning took around ten minutes in total. Nothing horrible was done to me. No Iodine was introduced into my veins; no-one pumped air up my bum and I'd not been required to take any bowel prep either.

Getting up from the flat position was even less decorous than getting into it! I flailed about like a beached whale and made rude remarks about myself which had both the man and the other nurse laughing. I hurried to get dressed and return to Peter. At no time had I felt any kind of pressing need for the toilet and I was feeling very happy about that indeed.

On the way home, we stopped at MacDonald's and I ate a fish-burger and an ice-cream. I felt more relaxed than I had since Rosemary went home and felt hopeful and confident that I only had the MRI scan to go before seeing the surgeon. I wasn't exactly happy about what the Macmillan site said would be done to me, but I was also secretly hoping that the scans would reveal that the cancer was only small and would need no operation at all.

I can be incredibly stupid sometimes and convince myself of ridiculous things, both good and bad. I swing from thinking the absolute worst to thinking the absolute impossible.

One of the things I haven't yet mentioned is the fact that the week before Rosemary visited, Damon conspired to hurl himself off his roller blades and had broken his arm – which was in plaster. Uther had taken him to hospital and been the 'responsible adult in loco parentis' on my behalf.

Just a few days after my last iron infusion, Damon had to return to the hospital to have his cast removed and an X-ray to see if his scaphoid had healed. Uther took him once again. Although my diarrhoea had lessened to almost nothing, I still often had to run to the toilet at odd times and I did not feel confident about sitting around for several hours at the hospital.

The boys were gone for hours and I was worried. Eventually, I received a telephone call from Uther. He felt he had to phone me to tell me that the scaphoid had not healed at all. In fact, the break was worse than it had been to start with. The doctor they had seen had first asked Damon if he smoked and then, when he discovered that his mother smoked, blamed the non-healing on that. I was appalled. Uther then went on to say that he needed to ring me and tell me because he thought I may not believe him if he waited till they got home.

I felt terrible. I have always smoked in the house with absolutely no regard for anyone else's health at all. I believe I have already said, several times, that I am an inherently selfish person. Suddenly, for the first time, I felt incredibly guilty. I waited for them to get home so

I could apologise to Damon and I resolved not to stop smoking ... but at least to smoke outside the front door.

Peter arrived before the boys did and I told him what the orthopaedic doctor had told them. Peter scoffed at it and said he'd never heard of anything like that at all. In fact, he went to the computer to check it out and could find nothing of the sort. There was plenty of evidence that smoking can cause cancer, is bad for your heart and lungs (as is passive smoking) but absolutely no reference to broken bones not healing because of passive smoking. I still felt awful.

By the time the boys got home, I was standing outside the front door with Psyche-Imp on my shoulder as I smoked my cigarette and feeling like a criminal. Damon went straight off out but Uther stopped to tell me that, in his opinion, the break not healing had far more to do with the fact that Damon had continued to roller-blade (and had fallen over several times) had also continued to lift weights (with his arm in a cast) and numerous other silly things. He told me not to beat myself up about it and it was probably rubbish anyway.

As I finished that cigarette, I thought about what Uther had said and found I did have to agree. It did seem more likely to have been caused by teenage idiocy than by my cigarettes. Even so, I still felt guilty. Out of the corner of my eye, I noticed Psyche-Imp creeping through the cat-nip trying to murder bumble bees. Little bastard, I thought to myself. Now I have a guilt-trip to contend with as well!

My health had improved no end. I could actually do quite a lot without suffering chest pains, breathlessness (despite the smoking) or exhaustion. Obviously, the iron was just what I needed. I still had to go every now and then to the surgery to get a B12 injection, but I really did feel a lot better. My confidence began to return a little and I was able to drive up to the supermarket and once or twice, I even gave Damon's friend, Zeke a lift home to Chirk. Things were looking up.

On the day of the MRI scan, I felt more irritated than anything else. Yet another trip to the hospital; it seemed I could never get away from the damnable place! Peter took me. I reported to the X-ray department and was shown to the MRI suite. I had actually been there before with Damon, so it wasn't entirely unfamiliar. However, I found anxiety building as I waited, sitting there in my hospital gown. I hadn't thought I was particularly claustrophobic, but the idea of going into the tunnel head first was not pleasant.

A nurse came with a check-list and asked hundreds of questions. I answered them all truthfully and in no time at all, I was shown into a large, bright and airy room with an enormous machine in it. The extremely heavy, lead-lined door closed behind me and the two health workers – who may have been radiographers, but they may equally well have been nurses.

Once again, I had to lie flat on my back. I felt very grateful that both of these nurses were female. I was so undignified, scrambling up and turning over with grunts and wheezes of effort. One of the nurses asked me if I suffered with heartburn. I agreed that I often did but that I was on medication for it. She offered me a tablet and a glass of water. Of course, this would mean sitting up again to take it. Besides, I would have to chew it up as I am pathetic and cannot swallow a pill. Fortunately, the other nurse stopped the first one, pointing out on my file that I have angina. The tablet was contra-indicated in angina. Instead, the second nurse told me to breathe as normally as possible and hope that I didn't get heartburn.

Apparently, I could stop the scan at any point by raising my hand, but, if I did so, then they would have to begin all over again. I swallowed hard. Psyche-Imp had appeared and was jumping up and down on my abdomen. I'd felt fine before they mentioned heartburn, but now it had been mentioned, I could already feel the familiar burning in the back of my throat beginning. Psyche-Imp was determined to make things as difficult for me as possible. With him jumping up and down on my stomach, trying to induce the 'possible' heartburn I began to feel rather 'over-full' at the other end too. I sincerely wished I could murder the little git.

I told myself I'd had no heartburn with the other scan and that I would be fine. Psyche-Imp kicked me in the throat. I fought down the urge to panic as the nurses left the room and closed the heavy door behind them. They probably weren't nurses, I told myself. I expect they were radiographers or something.

I'd been positioned so I would travel into the tunnel feet first, which was a big relief. It meant that I could look at the beautiful pictures artfully displayed on the walls and go through the script of Pirates of The Caribbean in my head in an effort to keep Psyche-Imp at bay.

The machine made a lot more noise than the CT scanner and to be honest, it was pretty scary being in that big room, sliding into that tunnel and knowing I was all alone. All alone except for blasted Psyche-Imp of course, who tried absolutely everything to get me to move or stop the scan. He caused a tickle in my throat meaning I wanted to cough (for which I would need to sit up to avoid pulling stomach muscles). He jumped up and down on my stomach again and again. He even crawled down the tunnel and did something to my nether regions so I was certain I was going to lose control of my bowels – even though I'd taken the precaution of taking several Imodium before I left the house. I breathed carefully; quite shallow breaths really but careful, concentrated shallow breaths, so I neither panicked nor succumbed to any of the things Psyche-Imp was doing.

At last, the couch I was lying on slid out of the tunnel, all noises stopped and the nurse came back in and helped me to first sit up and then get down in quite a dignified manner. I felt total relief. In fact, I thought I might even stop at the hospital cafe for a cup of tea on the way out!

Peter was not where I'd left him, outside the scanner. I got dressed quickly and took myself off to the main waiting room, where I found him. I smiled and spoke brightly that it was all done and we could go home. Peter gave me a strange look. I'm sure that poor man thinks I'm daft sometimes.

In the end, we didn't stop for tea at the hospital cafe. I felt desperate for a cigarette and we came straight home. I did feel hungry though. How odd that all traces of diarrhoea and heartburn had magically disappeared as soon as I left the hospital. I began to wonder if some of my doctors hadn't been correct after all; most of my symptoms quite possibly were able to be put down to anxiety.

Anxiety or not, they had caused me to be investigated and they'd found the cancer, which would never have been found had I not continued to plague my doctors with my incessant, seemingly unrelated symptoms. I found I was looking forward to my meeting with the surgeon on third of august. I would probably get to see my scans and discuss all possible treatment options. He'd listen to my fears of vomiting and think of brilliant and novel ways to do what he needed to do to avoid them.

In fact, I was so much more relaxed that Peter was able to take a few days' break here and there so he didn't need to be with me every minute. He promised however, that he would attend with me at the meeting with the surgeon.

Lesley and I went with Peter on the Friday of that week to 'music night' which is held in a pub some distance from my home. Several amateur musicians get together in a tiny, cramped little room and play and sing.

The place was packed. I felt acute anxiety as I squashed tightly onto a bench with Lesley beside me and Peter and his guitar beside her. I thought I might need to rush out, but it would mean picking my way through musicians and onlookers, probably knocking drinks over as I went. The chap to my immediate left had part of a drum kit. He was very friendly and chatty. After about five minutes, I noticed there was a closed door behind him. I asked where it went. Once the fellow had said I could get out that way if I needed to, I completely relaxed and thoroughly enjoyed the evening. The three of us stopped out late and I marvelled at what I'd been missing. I hadn't been out for the evening for many months, possibly even a whole year!

I slept that night without needing any Valium at all and I slept well too. In the morning, I think that was the very first time I'd woken and not immediately thought, "I've got cancer and I'm still here." What I actually thought, when I woke up the next morning, was what a wonderful time we'd had the night before and I went to make a cup of tea before going to the toilet at all!

The day passed without any panic attacks and I went to the local garden centre, had some coffee and watched as Peter actually bought himself some new clothes (they are a garden centre but they have other shops in the building too). I enjoyed my day. I'm pretty sure Psyche-Imp was still playing in the MRI scanner at that point, probably terrifying other patients, for a change.

There was only a week or so to go before the surgeon's appointment, and Damon had an appointment at the fracture clinic well before then. I decided I would take him and Uther offered to come too. As luck would have it, Alison phoned and said she needed to speak with me. I had agreed, on that very first day of meeting her, to take part in a Macmillan study of cancer patients. She needed to give me the first questionnaire and speak to me about my treatment and how I felt. She suggested I come to the hospital to see her. I told her of Damon's appointment and said I would be there that day anyway. She suggested I arrive half an hour before his appointment and meet her in the hospital cafe. I agreed.

We arrived in plenty of time and I went to buy snacks and drinks. We sat down at a table next to the corridor so that Alison would see us as soon as she approached. After some fifteen minutes, I made my way to the reception desk and asked the gentleman to bleep her to let her know I was waiting. He agreed to do so.

We waited another ten minutes. By this time, it was nearly Damon's appointment time, so Uther took him off to the fracture clinic and I remained in the cafe. I was feeling quite irritated. Why on earth would the woman ask me to be there at half past two if she had no intention of seeing me until three o'clock?

Alison arrived, somewhat breathlessly, plonked herself down in the chair beside me and gushed something about having been held up. I said it was fine as Uther had taken Damon down to his appointment. She had a pile of paperwork with her and I watched as she rummaged through it and took out a pack, which she pushed across the table at me.

"This should have been given to you on the day of diagnosis," she said. "I can't believe you never got one." Before I could reply, she flipped the pack open to a page where there was a diagram of the bowel. She pointed at a roughly marked asterisk which had been drawn in with blue biro. "That's where your cancer is, see; in the rectum." Again, I could not reply before she turned the page and pointed at another page. "This explains all about it. I'm sorry, I really haven't got much time. I need to go to pick my little boy up from school you see," she glanced at her watch. "You'll have a good look through this when you get home, I expect. There's a page here about the ward you'll be on," she flipped the pages over, but before I could look at them, she flipped them again. "This is the operation you'll be having." Then she closed the pack and took a large manila envelope from under her arm.

I drew in a breath. "But ..."

Alison interrupted me. "I'm sorry. I really do have to go. You know how it is with little ones. I can't have him standing at the school gates and there's no-one there for him. This is the questionnaire; you're still happy to fill it in are you?"

I nodded my agreement. "Yes, but, I ..."

Again, she interrupted. "Right, you just need to fill it in and send it back to me at the hospital here. There is an envelope enclosed in here; it's got a stamp on it so it won't cost you anything. After that, the other questionnaires will all be sent to you by post. I'm the Macmillan nurse for round here you see, so it has to come to me, but only the first one." Again, she checked her watch. "I really have to go. I'm sorry. Maybe we could meet up again at another time? Although I'm on holiday next week and the week after. Maybe I'll see you after that. All right, Karin?" She stood up.

Bemused, I stared at the pile of paper in front of me. As I opened my mouth to speak, she leaned forward and patted my hand. "Everything will be fine, you'll see. Oh. I forgot to ask. How do you feel about having a stoma?"

"What? Well, I am none too happy about it, to be honest," I replied, preparing to launch myself into at least ten minutes of objections and express my fear of the unknown and the known (I'd dealt with someone else's years ago).

Alison turned to leave. Over her shoulder, she looked back and smiled at me. "Don't worry, Karin. You'll be fine. You'll soon get used to it. I must dash! See you again. Goodbye." With that, she hurried out of the cafe and out of the hospital.

I watched her go, a mixture of resentment, fear and perplexity building within me. I glanced at my own watch. If I didn't hurry, I would miss my own son's appointment. I stood up, gathered together all the papers and left the cafe. I hurried so much I was a little breathless by the time I got to the fracture clinic. Damon hadn't yet been seen. I sat down to wait with the boys and complained bitterly to Uther about Alison and the fact that she had arrived half an hour late and was far too busy to bother with me. I felt slighted in some way. Maybe this was her way of getting back at me for all the rudeness I'd displayed. I wondered if I'd asked for it. I probably had. Even so, it did nothing, admitting that it was my own, stupid fault, to make me feel any better about things.

I didn't have time to take a look at the cancer patient pack because Damon was called in. His cast had been removed and his arm washed because I'd had the forethought to bring a wet flannel and plenty of kitchen paper with me. Uther had warned me how badly Damon's arm smelled last time the cast was removed.

The doctor came in, said he could not do an X-ray because there was a big delay at the moment. He asked Damon several questions, examined the hand and arm and pronounced him free to go. Damon was delighted. He had really feared being put into yet another cast. We all left the hospital immediately.

Later that evening, once Peter had arrived, I carefully went through the cancer patient pack. There was a great deal of information in there, not least about the planned operation (in great detail and with diagrams) and the 'support' I would be getting as a cancer patient – none of which I'd had because the pack had not been given to me on the day of diagnosis as it should have been.

My first thoughts, (mainly because Psyche-Imp had clearly found his way back from the hospital and was probably sitting on my shoulder reading everything too) ranged from utter terror through to stomach-churning disgust at the proposed operation.

How absolutely *vile*! I would have to deal with a stoma bag – and it would be connected to my *small* intestine. I know enough anatomy to be aware that it is the large intestine which absorbs fluids from the 'waste' in the body. Therefore, if this were not being used at all, I would be dealing with bags of liquid shit for anything from eight months to three years.

I've not got a very tough constitution. I don't 'do' shit. I've always said it. Actually, what I've always said is this: "I cannot do sick and I really hate shit. Cat poo is fine as it's generally small and I can hold my breath, but dog-poo and people-poo is a no-no." The very prospect of having to not only 'do' this kind of poo (I can't keep saying shit) but to have it actually upon my person almost made me retch. Alison's parting words, "How do you feel about having a stoma?" rang in my mind. The fact was, had I been given the cancer pack on the day of diagnosis – as I should have been, I'd have already had some two months to get used to the idea. Alison had not given it to me. She was there. It was her job and she hadn't done it. In fact, I thought, she hadn't really done anything at all for me except try to have me committed as insane and bully me into doing whatever she wanted me to from a distance.

As for 'support', there had been none that I could think of. Not from the hospital or any of the professionals in any event. The few times I'd had questions and had thought to ring Alison, I'd got an answering machine. Mostly, I'd hung up; no-one likes talking to a machine and saying something to a machine like "I'm scared to death," is not the most normal message in the world to leave on one. Mental health services had let me down. Despite my remarks about duty of care and all that rubbish, nobody had been allocated to me and no support forthcoming. They had sent the office manager out to see me but he rattled on about their lack of funding, the fact that almost everyone was off on long-term sick leave and had been less than pleased with my reply: "Not my problem. I am a patient and you have a duty of care. Sort it out and support me. Please."

Psyche-Imp was absolutely delighted with this turn of events. Here was Kat, sitting at home with a plastic pack full of absolutely terrifying information and with panic building exponentially by the second. The little bastard had a field day.

Before I quite realised what had happened, I was in a full-blown panic attack. I had to run to the toilet first. The diarrhoea, which had stopped altogether in the last weeks of iron infusions, returned with a vengeance. As I sat there with Loki on my lap and the whole universe falling, it seemed, from my behind, I also began to feel sick. Now, I'd already taken my usual anti-emetic pill, so it had to be 'nerves' right? I tried to tell myself (and Loki) that fact. But Psyche-Imp was swinging on the towel-rail from one long, clawed hand and miming sticking his other clawed fingers down his throat. I was convinced I would vomit. I began to shake violently. "I'm not going to be sick, Loki" I said out loud (hoping that by uttering the words aloud they would somehow be true).

"Yes, you are!" howled Psyche-Imp. "And once you've started, you're never going to stop. Not ever. You'll puke and puke and you'll shit and shit and then you'll die! You'll choke to death! You won't be able to eat anything again, ever and you're going to die. Right here. In a minute."

I believed him. I actually retched. Loki turned his head and regarded me with his orange eyes. I expected him to jump off my lap, but he remained where he was. The shaking got worse. Poor cat! He was being jiggled mercilessly by my shaking legs. I tried to stroke his head, but in truth, it was probably more like being patted than being stroked. Still he didn't jump down. If anything, he snuggled closer; he closed his eyes and gave me his very best "I love you, Mum" kitty smile and the purring increased in volume.

I can't tell you how long that episode lasted because I can't actually remember. All I know is that it was absolutely awful and seemed to last a lifetime. Neither can I recall what it was that actually got me moving again. Yet I did come out of the toilet. I know I brought Loki with me and I went back to the lounge.

Peter was clearly alarmed. I must have looked pale. I was certainly sweaty. In a most unusual move, Loki remained sitting on my lap when I sat on the settee. He never usually does this. Lap-sitting is reserved exclusively for either the toilet or for when I am sitting at the computer writing. Peter moved to sit beside me. He talked and he rubbed my lower back.

I'm almost sure that both Damon and Uther were there that time too. They also talked and distracted me. At some point in the evening, the panic subsided a little and I was able to drink half of a cup of tea. Psyche-Imp slithered under the closed toilet door and scuttled, like a four-legged spider, into the lounge, where he crawled up the side of the settee and sat on my cigarettes. He tapped his fingers on the packet, drawing my attention to them. I couldn't face one. Not right then. Psyche-Imp laughed fit to bust.

Peter had the right of it. He talked about what he knew. And he did know about patients with operations and stomas because he'd worked with them for a while. Every question I asked he was able to answer confidently and with candour. He didn't pull any punches either. He told me the truth – which was what I needed to hear, even if I didn't like it much and it scared me. Yes, the operation was a really major one. Yes, I would be in pain; I would be hardly able to move afterwards, but I *would* recover in time. The stomas were horrible, he agreed, but I would get used to dealing with it and it would never be quite as bad as I feared. I'd be able to control what I ate and so what came out of the stoma.

We talked very late into the night, probably until about four in the morning – which was pretty unselfish of Peter, seeing as he needed to be up to go to work at seven. I calmed down enough to drink two cups of tea and I finally smoked a cigarette (much to Psyche-Imp's disgust) and it didn't make me sick. I'd taken another anti-emetic shortly after coming out of the toilet (one extra won't do any harm, Peter had assured me) and I also took a whole Valium tablet at about half past three. In short, when I went to sleep at last, I actually passed out.

Now, one is not supposed to dream if one is taking Valium. It is one of the side effects of the drug and one of the reasons why they are so bad and damaging in the long term. People *need* dream-sleep to remain healthy. Most of us don't remember most of our dreams, just the odd one ... and of course, sometimes, we recall in livid detail, the nightmares. As did I that morning.

I woke, with a start at about half past nine. I had a pain in my chest and another in my stomach. I sat up and tore the cover off to inspect the 'leaking' stoma I had expected to find. It wasn't there. All I saw, when I lifted my thin tee-shirt, was the smooth skin of my abdomen and my small rolls of post-menopause blubber. I nearly wept with relief. And then I realised I needed the toilet.

Completely missing the fact that I was alone in the room at the time, I dashed to the toilet. As if by magic, Loki appeared from somewhere. He mewed an enquiry before following me into the toilet. With panic rising, I sat down and the cat jumped onto my lap. Psyche-Imp must have still been asleep, dreaming up new forms of torture for me because although I was shocked and a bit shaky from the dream, I was not panicking. To my utmost surprise, I passed a perfectly normal bowel motion! I made a big fuss of Loki, washed my hands and went back to my bed.

I dozed on and off until Damon appeared in the room. He'd been great. All through the summer holidays he'd made a point of being there for me in the mornings, chatting and being silly, doing all the things he does to entertain his deranged mother. I'm not sure if he does it on purpose. Perhaps it is just an innate ability. In any event, he's very good at engaging me and making Psyche-Imp slither away to hide.

After several cups of tea and some toast, I was able to pick up the cancer patient pack again and look through it. I'd already learned enough, through Macmillan online, to know that if I didn't take the treatment, then the cancer would metastasise around my body and I would get more and more ill until I died. Back when they first told me – or when I went to see them and already had worked it out – I had toyed with the idea of suicide. Now (I'm sure Psyche-Imp had something to do with this) I began to think about the Swiss company Dignitas. I knew it cost a great deal of money to go there, but I also knew, having watched a documentary on it, that they could help one to die. On the documentary, it was about fifteen thousand pounds. I began to daydream about getting fifteen thousand pounds together and taking myself off to Switzerland and having that final drink which would finish me off entirely.

Psyche-Imp changed his tactics. Actually, maybe he didn't he's just got several tactics and uses whichever will be most disruptive. "You can't raise fifteen quid never mind fifteen thousand," he whispered. "I can appeal online and to everyone who knows me to chip in," I replied aloud. (I was alone in the room at the time). "You've never flown before," prompted Psyche-Imp, "and you're terrified of flying." I thought about this for a while. "No. I'm not terrified of flying; I've never done it before. How can I be terrified of something I've never done?"

Hating to give the little blue bugger any credit for trapping me within my own reasoning (which he had very effectively, done), I added – after further thought, "Well, I've never had an operation before either but I'm scared of that, more scared of that than I am of flying. Anyway, I'd only have to fly one-way. It wouldn't matter if I didn't like it. I'd be coming back in a box."

"Right. And you're going to do that all by yourself, are you? You can't even go to the toilet by yourself!

You're such a wimp. You need a cat to hold your hand to take a dump – and you think you're going to pack up your stuff and get on a plane and go to Switzerland, just like that and die? Grow up. You're living in a dream-world, you stupid cow!"

Psyche-Imp pissed in my tea and disappeared. I drank the tea anyway. I smoked several cigarettes. I looked through the cancer patient pack again. And then ... I got angry.

Why had that infernal woman not given me this when she should have done? How is it that I had suffered weeks of panic and uncertainty when the pack assured me I would be 'supported all the way'? Where was my support? Why hadn't anyone done anything they should have done? And was this how it was for all cancer patients? The Macmillan television advertisements seemed to imply that everyone got support from both Macmillan *and* their hospital, but so far, I'd had none. What about the mental health service? I was already a patient and, just when I needed them, they'd completely abandoned me!

All right, it did occur to me that I may get more support from, say, Macmillan if I telephoned them as the television adverts say you can. And perhaps I was relying on an outdated, under-funded, rather useless mental health service when any fool could see they couldn't help, even if they wanted to. And I was being supported. Peter, my boys, Lesley, Caroline, Rosemary; everyone was doing everything they could for me. How did they feel? What must it be like for the boys to hear that their mother had cancer and further, that she was too much of a coward to take the treatment? I lit another cigarette and smoked it, thinking about what an evil, selfish woman I am.

At no time did it occur to me to support myself. I look back now and think that Psyche-Imp did a really good and thorough job on me; he prevented me from seeing anything positive; he encouraged my panic attacks and feelings of uselessness and worthlessness and he resolutely refused to allow me to do anything normal. Damn my subconscious mind!

I had a telephone call one day from an entirely different social worker in the physical disabilities team. She made an appointment to come out and see me, explaining that the social worker from the mental health team had gone off on long-term sick leave and that the process of a care package would have to be started all over again. I was a little confused, but I agreed to the appointment with her. I knew I would be going to see the surgeon in a couple of days anyway and get a chance to discuss just how bad things were. Then, I would be able to talk with the social worker and tell her just what I was dealing with and upon what timescale.

The day of the surgeon's appointment dawned. I was to be seen at two o'clock in one of the outpatient departments by a man called Mr. Billings. Peter had taken yet another afternoon off work (my gods, but his employers must have been getting sick of his time off) in order to come with me. He drove me to the hospital and we went to the waiting room where we sat, completely unable to see the obligatory television properly because there was a large pillar between the seats and the screen.

I didn't feel particularly nervous that day. After all, what was to be nervous about? I would be ushered into a consulting room with Peter. We would sit down and be shown the scans and then we would discuss the treatment options and I would be treated with respect and as a human being. I felt sure everything would be fine and then I could really get to grips with what I had to face. (I must have left Psyche-Imp at home for the moment. Perhaps the little blighter was busy running up the A483 because he hadn't been in the car with Peter and me).

Well, we sat there. And then we sat there some more. I watched people for a while. I noticed a few patients who waited a while and then they went off somewhere. Nurses came and went and Peter began to tap his foot. When it was getting toward half past two, Peter stood up and approached a harassed-looking nurse. He spoke to her for a while and she turned and walked off down a corridor.

"I moaned about the long wait," Peter informed me. "She's gone to see what's going on."

The nurse came back and came over to us. She explained that the clinic was running late and that I would be the next patient called in. At this point, a little nervousness began to creep into me. I scuttled off to the toilet.

Now, on that day, not only had I had no diarrhoea, I hadn't, in fact, 'been' at all. I felt rather 'bunged up' in truth. Even despite being in the hospital toilet, all I could manage was a wee. I'd not taken any Imodium either. This was quite a novelty and for the first time in ages, I felt pleased about a trip to the lavatory. I went back to the waiting room and sat down.

We waited a further twenty minutes or so before another nurse came into the waiting room and called my name. I stood up and let Peter get up and go after the nurse ahead of me. We went a short way down a corridor and the nurse opened a door. Peter was just in front of me but I could see into the room.

About twelve feet square, the room contained an examination couch, a trolley, which had something on it which resembled a giant syringe with added hose and pump – more like a torture device from the Spanish Inquisition (had they had telescopes and plastics back then) and two chairs.

Peter went to step into the room but I baulked at the door. My heart began to thud painfully in my chest and I found it rather hard to breathe. The nurse patted my hand and said, "Are you a little bit nervous, love?" I scowled at her. She sort of shepherded me through the door ahead of her and closed it as soon as Peter and I were safely inside. That's when I noticed there was another door, right next to the one we had come through and, at the end of the examination couch, another chair.

I believe I said something about not having expected this. I sat down on one of the chairs, crossed my legs firmly and held onto my handbag on my lap, hugging it as if it would somehow protect me from something terrible. My eyes drifted to the trolley which was positioned just beneath the small window. Psyche-Imp appeared as if by some kind of dark magic and whispered into my ear that there were probably bars on the window and that the door I had just entered by was probably now locked as well. (That horrible little fiend had obviously had no trouble at all in finding his way both to the hospital and to me). I felt like I wanted to retch. Panic crept upwards from my knees, making my stomach clench and my legs shake. I also felt decidedly light-headed – as if I might faint.

I'm almost certain I spoke to Peter – or he spoke to me, but I cannot actually remember now. All I can really recall is the feeling of utter panic. This was *not* how it was supposed to be! Where was the well-appointed office? Where were the comfortable chairs and subtle pictures on the tastefully decorated walls? Where, in fact, was the surgeon himself?

These questions were not answered. The nurse had disappeared through the other door, which now opened and three people squeezed into the cramped space of the room. A man in his early sixties, a woman of about thirty and a nurse, who I thought I may have seen before. I glared at them. The man sat down on the chair at the end of the couch and the thirty year old woman went back to wherever they had all come from and procured a chair for herself and then sat on it.

The man was holding a file in his hand. He opened it before greeting me. He introduced himself as Mr. Billings, the Colorectal Surgeon. I don't recall the thirty year old woman being introduced at all or the nurse, for that matter. Mr. Billings then went on, saying something about my colorectal cancer and that I'd had a partial colonoscopy and they had found both the cancer and some polyps, which, he said, he intended to remove as soon as possible. He also said he intended to do another 'proper' colonoscopy to check that there were no other patches of cancer anywhere else in my colon.

He was pleasant enough, but the way in which he delivered this information made it absolutely clear that these things had already been decided and furthermore, that they were nothing to do with me!

"I've had a colonoscopy. It hurt a lot and I'm not having another one," I said, defensively. I clutched my handbag tighter to my chest.

Mr. Billings drew in a breath and smiled. "Yes," he said, "But we didn't get to have a look at the whole of your colon. I understand you were anxious about perforation or something and refused the procedure?"

I nodded. It was true. Psyche-Imp chattered in delight. Something horrible was going to happen and he was loving every minute of it.

Mr. Billings went on, "The next person you will see is the oncologist who will decide what chemotherapy and radiotherapy you will need before the operation. We need to have done this polypectomy before then. Right now, I need to get a look at the tumour myself. Just pop up on the couch and ..."

I had been staring at the instrument on the trolley. After all, it was right beside me. It resembled a rigid white pole which had markings in centimetres along it. I have to say it was marked to twenty centimetres; it wasn't a little thing. I'd already noticed it had a light on the end. Coming off the end of it were some wires, a black box thing and something I could not identify. There was also a tube of lubricant positioned next to it and a box of gloves. As Mr. Billings spoke, it occurred to me that he thought he was going to ram this thing up my arse – in front of this lovely audience! Not only had I not been to the toilet at all that day, I was beginning to feel the intense urge to 'go' building up as he spoke. Also, I consider any kind of interference with my nether regions as abuse – abuse because I don't want *anyone* looking at, touching, groping any part of me or anything else. I'd only gone ahead with the previous colonoscopy because I'd been given the giant bloomers to protect my modesty and I'd already suffered the bowel prep of Picolax.

I interrupted him. "No. No, you're not doing anything of the sort. Why haven't I been shown my scans? Why do you think you can get me into this room and then sexually abuse me in front of all these people? Who the hell do you think you are?"

The poor man fell silent and stared at me in open astonishment. Psyche-Imp jumped up and down in obvious excitement. In Psyche-Imp's book, *this* was true, hard-core entertainment. I'm sure the little swine was clapping his hands and dancing a jig.

"I am a surgeon. I most certainly have no intention of abusing anyone, madam," Mr. Billings replied frostily. "I need to see this tumour for myself so I can plan what surgery you're going to need, that's all!"

"Well, you're not sticking anything up my arse," I almost shouted. "You haven't even asked me if I *want* treatment or surgery or anything else. I'm just another piece of meat for you to do with as you please. No-one has proved to me that there even *is* a tumour."

I turned to the blonde nurse, suddenly recalling her face. She'd been there that day with the infernal Alison. "No-one told me this was going to happen," I snarled. "I was told I would be seeing the surgeon. Silly me! I thought I'd be treated with respect and be able to see my scans and discuss treatment options. I didn't think I'd be confined in a cell and be sexually abused by some man with a load of people watching!" I stood up. "You can stuff your treatment. I don't want it."

Peter put his hand on my arm. The blonde nurse had blushed. "With all due respect," Peter addressed both the surgeon and the nurse. "Anybody would be upset at this. I mean a person without a background of sex abuse or anything would be upset at this kind of thing. I mean, Karin was simply told she'd be seeing the surgeon. It's not unreasonable to be upset to discover that she is to be intimately examined with no forewarning at all. It's very bad practice, you know." He turned to the nurse herself. I could see her name badge now and she was also a colorectal nurse. "Why didn't that other colorectal nurse, what's her name ..."

"Alison," I supplied.

"... yes, Alison. Why didn't she let Karin know what to expect?"

The nurse looked acutely uncomfortable. She mumbled something about my not having been told what to expect because Alison had anticipated that I would refuse the examination and treatment had I known.

Peter pointed out again that 'best practice' had not been applied in this case. I made as if I was going to the door. The thirty-year old woman was sitting right in front of it. I would either have to ask her to move or physically shove her out of the way. She looked interested in the proceedings, nothing more.

"I don't want any bloody treatment," I repeated.

"You've got cancer, woman!" the surgeon interjected. "It's cancer! It's not going to just get better and go away!"

I hesitated. "All my symptoms have gone," I replied.

"They'll come back," Mr. Billings sighed and indicated the chair I'd vacated. "Please, sit down again. Let's talk about this some more."

I did sit down again, and in the same huddled position with my handbag as guard. At least I listened to what Mr. Billings had to say this time. I wouldn't get to see my scan results. He told me what he'd seen which was, basically, a thickening of the colon wall around the area of the tumour, and that it was actually located in my rectum itself and in the beginning of the colon. Ten centimetres, for a tumour, is apparently, simply huge. He was curious as to whether or not I felt pain when sitting down and surprised when I stated I did not.

I needed to see a man called Simon Gollins, who was the oncologist. I would be required to undergo a treatment of chemoradiotherapy prior to any operation. I explained, with help from Peter, about my emetophobia and the fact that I *would* actually rather die than vomit because the phobia was so powerful and had affected me for decades. I think Mr. Billings had never encountered this before. He'd certainly not demonstrated any familiarity with it as he listened, an expression of incredulity spreading across his face. He reassured me that there are some very efficient anti-emetics in use for patients on chemotherapy and then, rather than tell me I would be seeing this oncologist, actually asked if I would agree to see him. I said I would.

Much to my surprise, Mr. Billings then asked if I would be prepared to come back to the hospital the following Wednesday afternoon for the examination he had planned for that day. At least I'd have a week to get my head round the idea. Reluctantly, I agreed to that as well (with Psyche-Imp telling me, in his scratchy little voice, that by the following Wednesday, I would have offed myself anyway and so I could tell whatever lies I liked).

Consultation finished, I was able to escape. I followed Peter out of the hospital, stopping at reception to get a form to prove I had attended so I could reclaim my travelling expenses. I'd got about twelve of these forms saved up to take to the hospital office.

Peter said he needed to visit Whitchurch to speak with his employer about something or another and that it would be easier to go direct from the hospital. I didn't exactly agree to that, I just didn't object.

During that car journey, I didn't speak. Neither did Peter. I was thinking hard. Actually, that's a complete lie. Psyche-Imp had taken over my entire thought processes and was thinking hard for me. I would need to find a fail-safe way to commit suicide. I had to be realistic; I couldn't raise the money for Dignitas and I couldn't drive my car into anything or off anything – there was no guarantee it would kill me. With my luck, I'd just hurt myself badly and have to be treated for that as well as cancer. I trawled through all my memories and everything I'd ever read or seen about suicide. I had no gun – anyway, I might 'miss' and simply lobotomise myself. I dislike guns anyway. Unrealistic to think I could get one in this country. Had I lived in America, it would probably be a piece of cake to acquire such a thing; in fact, I'd probably already own one. Whichever method I chose would have to be completely reliable with no chance of intervention and absolutely zero possibility of vomiting.

Peter didn't seem to notice my silence – which was actually quite silly of him with hindsight. He should have known something was very definitely wrong. Perhaps he had noticed but decided to refrain from commenting about it. Just before we arrived at his employer's house, Peter asked me what I was thinking. I told him, honestly, I was thinking about suicide. He replied that he'd thought as much.

I had to make small talk with Peter's employer, an animated and bubbly woman who knew about my phobia, but clearly did not understand it. She advised me to take the chemotherapy anyway. After all, she reasoned, I may as well have a reason to feel and be sick if I already felt sick so often already. I agreed and smiled and said all the things expected of me. Inside, I was roiling with the urge to run away and die. I hadn't given a thought to my children or my friends or my animals. As I said before, I am a selfish person.

When we finally got home that day, I ranted about the hospital and how badly I had been treated. I hated that colorectal nurse for a start. Although Uther didn't actually say much, I could see he felt I was a fool for not having allowed the examination to take place. The fact that I see every kind of intimate examination as sex abuse is something nobody seems to be able to understand. It's probably all Psyche-Imp's doing anyway.

Having told the boys of my ordeal and that I would be going back to the hospital the following week, I fell silent. Very silent.

In fact, I was so uncharacteristically silent Uther noticed and asked me what was wrong. I could not tell him at first; I couldn't have told anybody because I wasn't entirely sure myself. I did something I'd not done for several months; I sat down at the computer and wrote a post on my regular writing site, which I'd been avoiding. I wrote it directly onto FanStory.com; usually I write in Microsoft Word and then copy/paste it on to the site.

In short, it was about five or six thousand words of why I hadn't been on the site for months – the illness and the diagnosis of cancer and a long-winded and selfish account of my feelings of wanting to kill myself for a perfectly treatable cancer. I rambled on and gave my reasons for wanting to die as having had enough battles to fight already in life. The reasons I gave for not wanting to take the treatment boiled down to simply fear: emetophobia and fear of the unknown; fear of pain too – also an essentially foolish, incomprehensible fear of being alive. I finished writing, did not bother to check for spelling and typing errors and hit the 'post' button.

Uther badgered me for nearly a week and I still did not want to talk – another very unusual thing for me. I really couldn't say now – or even back then – what I was actually thinking at the time. I've pretty much had my finger on the 'self-destruct button' all my life. At least, in my own opinion, being such a rotten piece of crap all my life, I've caused most of my own miseries and battles. That I've let fear rule me most of the time I've lived here in St. Martins proved to me that I am entirely worthless; a waste of space, of good air that someone worthy could breathe and put to good use. If I'm totally truthful, I was giving serious thought and consideration to the possibility of killing myself quickly and cleanly. For once, it wasn't just Psyche-Imp in control. This time, it was me and I wanted out with such a firm finality it took my breath away and caused my fear to fade somewhat.

Rosemary came to visit again – and offered to stay long enough to attend the hospital with me for the awful appointment and stay with me through it all. Strangely, at the prospect of Rosemary being there with me, almost all the fear (and Psyche-Imp) disappeared completely.

I'd been wondering who, if anyone, I could ask to help me to kill myself successfully. Rosemary had been one of the people on a very short list indeed. Once she arrived however, I knew, without a doubt that I could not ask her to do such a thing. Furthermore, I knew what her answer would be: no. In fact, it would be more than just a simple 'no' but a resounding and very firm refusal to even consider it. Why would she want to lose her best friend?

My feelings of wanting to die did not go away even though Rosemary was there. I tried, one evening after the lads had gone to bed, to explain my feelings to her. She listened; she always listens to me, even when she thinks I'm being utterly stupid. She commented several times that, in her opinion, I'd been badly let down by everyone and had not had the support and encouragement I needed, most particularly from the Mental Health Services. Lastly, she told me that she knew I could do it and beat this thing. All I needed to do was view it as part of life's rich tapestry and another little hurdle and stop being so afraid of everything – which she added she knew was not an easy thing.

I nodded and agreed, although I knew that Rosemary knew my heart was not in it. I told her I couldn't think clearly and could not bring myself to talk to Uther, Damon, Zakh or Peter about it. Caroline could not understand my fears at all since she'd never had a panic attack in her entire life and Lesley already had too much going on in her life without me making things worse. In short, after several hours of conversation, the only agreement we'd reached was that I never used to be this frightened and cowardly all those years ago when we lived close to one another. Rosemary told me that I'd lost my 'Joie de Vivre' and no longer enjoyed life at all because I'd been depressed and lived a lonely and panicked existence for so many years – which my doctors had not treated. She said that, in her opinion, continually sending me away with "It's just anxiety," but doing nothing to treat the anxiety meant they'd let me down badly as well. That mental health services had started well and allocated me a CPN who had then left suddenly in mysterious circumstances and not been replaced just compounded the lack of support I should have had from medical and mental health services. She felt furious with Alison, the Colorectal Nurse assigned to me who had failed to provide me with the cancer pack on the day of diagnosis, who had gone on to try to get me classified as 'potty' because I refused scans and treatment without any support and many other failings too. I listened as Rose raved about how angry she felt on my behalf.

I spent hours trying to remember what it had been like to have fun, enjoy life, laugh and joke and do normal things. I could not remember anything of it at all. When I considered my life, I felt as if I'd always been flat and felt little, except for deep misery and despair. Rosemary assured me that was not in fact, the case. When I'd lived in Woking years before, even when really dire things happened, I'd been vivacious and determined, busy and full of energy.

Rosemary also pointed out that back then, I'd cried whenever things got really difficult and had her to lean on, not to mention numerous other friends and acquaintances. I'd also not spent much time at home; I'd always been out and about. She felt that I'd become depressed quite soon after moving here and had not recognised it. True, I'd had a breakdown and things had been addressed so I learned to deal with life again – and that's when I'd met Peter. Rosemary admitted that she dislikes Peter intensely and she actually added, that night, that she blamed him entirely for my current state of mind. She pointed out that shortly after I met him I went from active, up-beat and my normal self (thanks to the input of the psychologist at the time) to a reclusive, depressed, lonely person. She blamed Peter for 'chasing away' all my friends except her and told me that, in her opinion, I should tell him to get lost altogether.

I pointed out that if I did that, I would have no support at all. Rosemary disagreed. She thought that if Peter was no longer around, I'd get more support from Uther, Zakh and Damon and be better equipped, within myself, to fight. She also thought I'd see a lot more of Lesley and that other friends would begin to drift back.

Looking back upon that conversation now, I wonder what exactly Rosemary thought Peter had done to me. That he disapproved of my boys and felt they did not support me enough was obvious – he'd made no secret of that opinion. Yet, we were no longer a couple and he really had always been there whenever I needed him and for whatever reason. I kept those thoughts to myself, I'm not sure why; perhaps I didn't want to argue with Rose and lose her friendship too. In that regard, she was right. I'd never have let fear of losing her friendship keep me silent about something so important all those years ago when we lived close to one another. I silently pondered what Rose had said. In all truth, it wasn't completely Peter's fault. I'd met him just as I came out of a complete mental breakdown and, even though I knew I wanted no relationship whatsoever, I was too weak to avoid it – and it was an unmitigated disaster. I couldn't blame Peter for my choices; after all, I could've simply told him to go away and leave me alone and that would've been that.

Even though Rosemary was staying, I was still a lot quieter than usual and Uther in particular continued to ask me why I wasn't talking as I usually did.

Eventually, I got FanStory up on the computer screen, found my page, the recent writing, pointed Uther at the computer and told him, "Read that, then you'll know what I'm thinking and why I'm so quiet."

He read it. I saw him frowning. He was getting angry. He was, in fact, quite fed up and cross – and who can blame him? After all, he'd just read a load of rubbish which showed his selfish mother had given up even before she'd started!

Uther then questioned me, somewhat angrily. He remarked that I was being stupid, that the disease was treatable but I was letting fear get in the way of living. When I demanded if he'd take the treatment – especially if he had a phobia like mine, he replied, "Hell, yeah." He then went on to explain that he could think of no reason not to stay alive (despite problems or illness) and further, that it was a survival instinct to remain alive at all costs.

During this heated exchange, Psyche-Imp did cartwheels, jumped up and down and rubbed his clawed hands together with glee. He was thoroughly enjoying this. As far as Psyche-Imp is concerned, any trouble for me is good news for him.

Of course, I ended up needing to cry and also able to squeeze out a couple of tears because Uther said something unexpectedly tender in the middle of all the shouting. He'd also pointed out that the company Dignitas would not accept me, even if I raised the money, because my disease was treatable.

Far from making me think better of wanting to die, this only served to make me all the more determined to do it. Worse, it meant that I could no longer talk to either Rosemary or Uther about my feelings or intentions because they both resolutely refused or were unable to appreciate my feelings and thought processes.

There were two other people on this planet who I know for certain, if I asked them, even if they didn't like it, might help me achieve my goal. Again, this was totally selfish of me. I cannot say who they are in this writing (of course) but I found, at that point in time, I fully intended to ask one or both of them anyway.

Later that day, I did ask one of them. To my surprise, the reply was something along the lines of "Yes, all right. But I would feel a whole lot better about it if you would at least try the treatment first. Just a little. If it doesn't work or you can't do it, then I'll help you."

I considered this. Psyche-Imp was picking his nose with one set of claws and scratching his back-side with the others; he watched and listened intently. "Is that an absolute promise?" I asked. "Absolutely," was the reply.

"Done, then. I'll try. If I can't do it or it gets too painful, pukey or shitty, then I'll off myself and you'll help me. Right. I can do that." And that's where that conversation was left; unfinished but with a strange finality to it.

Yet somehow, that small, abrupt and intense chat had kicked me in the bum and made me want to actually give it a try. I don't think the boys had any idea how or what had made me change my mind and give it a go. They didn't ask and I didn't tell them. In any event, Psyche-Imp sulked horribly. He did lots of nasty little things over the next few days: pissing in my tea was a given (I was so used to it, I didn't notice); he hid appointment letters and other important documents – some of them in the bin; he irritated the cats so they bickered and fought; he opened the fridge door so everything inside got warm and lots of other annoying things.

For a few nights, I didn't need the Valium to get to sleep. I still felt frightened and panicky and had no idea at all really of what was going on. Life had suddenly swept me off my feet again and I was being carried who knew where at a too fast pace.

Once Rosemary had arrived, Peter gratefully retreated for a few days, earning himself some early and undisturbed nights of sleep. Usually, when Rosemary came, Psyche-Imp slunk off to hide. This time, he was a little bolder. My chat with Rosemary had made him think he could do as he liked and torment me again. With Rosemary around, even though Psyche-Imp was about, I was once again calmer and began to do a little more.

Rosemary never puts any pressure on. There is something about her which makes me calm – even if I'm panicking and Psyche-Imp is laying it all on thick. On those occasions, she chatters, I listen (or not) but in just a few minutes, the panic subsides (personally, I think she can actually *see* Psyche-Imp and that she stamps on him until he passes out for a while).

Full of trepidation, I went with Rosemary and Peter to the hospital on the tenth of August. Mr. Billings was as polite and charming as ever. In fact, he actually smiled and remarked that this was not the most pleasant way to spend a Wednesday afternoon, but it had to be done and would not take long. We were in the same examination room as before; this time, the thirty-something woman was not present. It was simply Mr. Billings, a colorectal nurse, me, Rosemary and Peter – who left the room for the actual examination.

Now, in my brain – as always, I had expected far worse. I didn't actually have to get undressed, just lie on my left side and slip my trousers down a little – not even so far as all my lady-bits would be in view. Rosemary stood at the head of the examination couch and hugged my shoulders tightly.

Nothing at all like the colonoscopy, the instrument did not hurt and only went inside a little way. I heard Mr. Billings say something like, "Yes, I see it. It's probably about, oh, eight to ten centimetres and is ulcerated only a bit, but there is evidence of healed ulcers." The instrument was removed and I was able to sit up. *Was that it?* It was. I cursed myself. All that stress and panic over something which took a couple of minutes and wasn't really that bad at all. Damn Psyche-Imp!

Mr. Billings then went on to explain that he personally would do the colonoscopy and polypectomy. As the surgeon, he wanted to have a good look at the whole colon himself so as to know what to expect before surgery. I agreed, even though I thought of how horrible it would be; still, I'd done it once, I could do it again.

I also agreed to see the oncologist with a view to chemo and radiotherapy. I'm sure it was only because Rosemary was there with me. As I said before, I always seem so much calmer when she's around. My blood-test results had been returned during the week and Mr. Billings said they were fine. Even my haemoglobin (always low throughout my life, so I was anaemic to one degree or another) was perfectly healthy. I felt very pleased. In fact, I asked if that may have something to do with the lessening of the diarrhoea and Mr. Billings agreed it could be so, particularly as the tumour had ceased bleeding for the moment.

I did ask him how long it had been there; after all, I'd been complaining of symptoms for years to doctors who thought it was all in my mind. To my surprise, he said, "I don't know. In fact, no-one will know until we've cut it out and had a really good look at it. But my best guess would be a few months only."

This reply surprised me greatly. Mind you, I had no idea how long a ten centimetre tumour took to grow, but I had expected the surgeon to say a year or two at least.

I gratefully left the hospital in company with Rosemary and Peter. I felt free – at least for a couple of weeks. I could pretend that everything was all right again. In actual fact, things felt pretty all right as we travelled back to my home. Psyche-Imp looked pale and depressed. He sat on the dashboard of the car and nodded his head this way and that much like one of those ornamental dogs.

It goes without saying that I really relaxed and enjoyed Rosemary's company whilst she stayed a few days. Psyche-Imp made himself scarce – well, except for one brief visit whilst Rosemary was upstairs. The little git jumped on my head, and me all unsuspecting, instantly panicked. Rosemary took one look at my face when she reappeared in the lounge and asked, "What are you panicking about?"

I answered, absolutely truthfully, "I have no idea. It just swept over me all of a sudden. I feel sick, dizzy and I need the toilet." I fled and let the world explode for a few minutes. Loki, as usual, arrived at the toilet door at the same time as me. He stuck his 'pins of pleased' very painfully into my knee as he hauled his huge, ginger bulk onto my lap. With hindsight, he was probably seeing off Psyche-Imp. Everybody knows cats can see things that people can't. In any event, after the (very unpleasant) explosion and a brief trip to hysteria, which lasted all of thirty seconds, the panic disappeared as suddenly as it had arrived.

Of course, when the day came for Rosemary to go home again, depression settled on me like a thick, floor-length cloak -- almost before her car had turned onto the main road. If only she lived closer. When I lived in Woking, true, we were on opposite sides of the town, but any visit or support we each needed was easily achieved by a rapid walk or a short bus-ride. Looking back, it's always been Rosemary supporting me. I must be like a weight around that poor woman's neck. This realisation did nothing to lift the depression at all. I think, had I been able to simply cry and feel genuinely sorry for myself, the depression would have passed quickly. However, as I mentioned before, ordinary things don't make me cry. Generally I only cry when someone is kind to me or does something especially thoughtful. On that day, life at the mad-house I live in resumed as per usual and so I never released my sorrow. Psyche-Imp was delighted.

Despite the fact that someone stayed with me at night (I was still terrified to sleep in a room alone, and the dogs and cats, much as I love them, did not quite fill the need for a human person), I had trouble sleeping. When I did sleep, crazy and revolting dreams woke me in a cold sweat and shaking terror. None of these dreams had anything to do with cancer; they were all bizarre, bloody and more like something out of a 'B' rated horror movie. I began to wonder where my brain got such awful images; I think I convinced myself I'd gone completely mental.

My next appointment at the hospital was scheduled to be another colonoscopy and a polypectomy – which I was not dreading as much as I thought I should be. After all, the surgeon himself was doing the procedure. I'd reassured myself by looking Mr. Billings up on the internet and knew him to be an expert in his field; what could I possibly have to be concerned about? Apart from having to take Picolax again and the fact that I was 'first on the surgeon's list' that day and so had to be at the hospital at ridiculously early o'clock in the morning.

Now, I'm pretty sure I've already mentioned that my 'symptoms' had, largely, disappeared by that time. I just had the occasional bout of usually very predictable diarrhoea; all the nausea and heartburn were still present, but anyone who thought they would stick a camera down my throat to investigate that could think again. I ate the anti-emetics regularly, every eight hours, took the heartburn medicine every morning and my (very silent and hidden) mind continued to hope I didn't have cancer at both ends as it were.

Once again, I was to have the support of Lesley, Damon and Peter through the workings of Picolax. Last time I took the stuff I sat for hour upon hour on the toilet – and then suffered over the next few days with horrendous backaches and worse. I resolved not to allow that to happen again. To that end, I went to the supermarket up the road and purchased some puppy training pads which I covered the settee with. I also bought the heaviest duty incontinence pads I could find.

Due to the procedure being in the early morning, I was permitted to eat a light breakfast the day before it and scheduled to take the first sachet of Picolax at three in the afternoon. I had the usual piece of toast, several cups of tea and a couple of half litre bottles of water during the morning. As it turned out, I also had diarrhoea that morning too.

Bearing in mind that last time I'd also had diarrhoea, I took careful note of this and thought seriously about whether or not I would need the second sachet of treatment, which was scheduled for nine in the evening. Maybe I would not need it at all?

I sat on the settee and took the first sachet just a little after three. Lesley stayed with me and we chatted for an hour or more before the laxative began its work. I hurried to the toilet; there wasn't much. I quickly returned to the settee.

Lesley went home for her tea and to sort her family out. By that time, Peter had arrived. I sat, miserably watching Peter and the boys eating, suddenly feeling very hungry indeed. This illusion was quickly dispelled by another trip to the toilet. Loki came too and I think even the fat, ginger cat was faintly perturbed by the awful smell I'd somehow managed to make; it was not pleasant at all. I used air-freshener in the tiny room and bleach in the toilet and returned to the settee yet again.

I only went three or four more times during the early evening. I also continued to sip at bottles of spring water and kept myself a lot better hydrated than I had on the previous occasion. Certainly, it was a lot more comfortable sitting on the settee watching television than it had been confined to the bathroom.

By nine in the evening, (sorry, I have to describe this) the fluid I was expelling was completely clear and only a faint yellow colour – much like urine. I deduced from this that I was more or less completely 'cleaned out'. However, to be on the safe side, I mixed half a sachet of Picolax into half a glass of water – and drank just half of it.

By about two thirty in the morning, the whole process seemed to have halted and I was able to doze, somewhat fitfully, secure in the knowledge that, if I leaked, the leather settee would not be ruined as I was lying on puppy training pads. I need not have worried.

In fact, in the morning, I had one or two trips to the toilet and everything appeared to have settled down. I was, however, very thirsty but knew I was not permitted even any more water. I took the anti-emetic and left the anti-heartburn medicine until later on.

Once again, Lesley appeared and we went, the three of us, me, Lesley and Peter, to the hospital. My nerves were beginning to have an effect upon me. Now and then I shook a little, but each time (which I now recognise as Psyche-Imp doing his 'terrify Kat' thing) I managed to overcome it.

There were no problems booking in to the department this time. At least, I didn't have the continual, uncontrollable urge to go to the toilet as I had before. Also, this was different altogether; different staff and taken on a different route, via a different waiting area where I changed into a gown and the dreadful 'colonoscopy bloomers' and went to the adjacent toilet 'just in case'.

The nurse allocated to me to fill in the relevant form had clearly had a bad start to her day; she was not in the least welcoming or friendly toward me. She asked questions in a bored, dull tone of voice and, when she could not understand me as I told her of the emetophobia (because, once again, I'd left my dentures at home) causing me to repeat the word more carefully, accused me of 'being abusive and sarcastic' toward her. I was stunned.

"Pardon?" I said.

"I'm not having you use your snooty, sarcastic tone with me. I don't have to put up with that sort of thing," the nurse snapped.

"I'm very sorry if you took offence," I replied. "You may not have noticed, but I have no teeth in; I left them at home. I was merely trying to enunciate the word more clearly so that you could understand me. I had no intention of being rude and certainly not abusive. How is the word 'emetophobia' in any way abusive?"

"Well, how am I supposed to know what it means?" she scowled.

"It's a phobia of vomiting. And it controls my life absolutely. I also suffer panic and anxiety disorder."

She didn't reply to that. I did notice she scribbled something out which she had written down and scrawled something else in its place. I don't believe she spoke to me after that, except to say 'follow me'.

She left me sitting alone in a very small room wearing the enormous colonoscopy bloomers, a hospital gown, my dressing gown and slippers and with my bag of clothing beside me.

I sat there. I tried to distract myself by reading all the wall posters but, apart from the headings, I couldn't see them properly because I'd also left my spectacles at home. It must have been around fifteen minutes I sat alone in that room. Of course, Psyche-Imp made his appearance almost as soon as the door closed. He taunted and tormented me relentlessly all during the wait; I began to sweat with a hot flush. I suddenly felt very nauseous and realised there was no toilet anywhere close by. In fact, in the maze of the hospital, I had no idea where I was or where the nearest toilet might be. This led on to a feeling that I needed the toilet more and more urgently.

As I said, it was only about fifteen minutes, but it felt like a week. How would you like to be stuck in a strange room deep in a maze with nothing for company but a psychopathic anthropomorphic creature bent on tormenting you to madness in as short a time as possible?

When the door finally opened and a very fresh-faced and cheerful looking nurse summoned me, I practically ran out of there!

As soon as I had people around me again, the nausea began to subside and also the pressing need to go to the toilet too. I mentioned this to the nurse as she led me into a little side-room down a corridor and helped me onto the trolley. This nurse reassured me; it was probably only wind and I shouldn't feel worried. After all, they had all the gadgets and equipment with which to vacuum up any little accidents. She invited me to relax.

Psyche-Imp was dancing about on the adjacent counter, sticking his long nose into everything he could find; the nurse didn't notice him at all. I presented my hand for the Venflon to be inserted, tried to avoid noticing things sliding off the counter to the floor (as kicked there by Psyche-Imp, no doubt) and listened as the nurse chattered about mundane things such as the weather and the fact that Mr. Billings had just arrived so I wouldn't have to wait long.

Once I was prepared and lying down on my left side, Mr. Billings came into the little room. He smiled warmly and told me he was looking forward to ridding me of my unwelcome polyps and that I had nothing to worry about; everything would be over and done with in short order. He retreated back into the operating room.

The nurse checked one or two things, stooped to pick up the papers which had mysteriously fallen to the floor and then another nurse arrived. Together, these ladies wheeled me through the doorway into the room where Mr. Billings waited by a monstrous-looking machine. I tried not to look, but Psyche-Imp was already on it, tugging at hoses and wires and pulling faces at himself in a reflective bit of chrome.

Mr. Billings came to stand beside me. He had a syringe in his hand. "Just a shot of Pethidine, my dear," he murmured. I snatched my Venflon-equipped hand away and waved the other hand with the red plastic bracelet dangling from it.

"I'm allergic to Pethidine!" I squeaked.

"Really?" Mr. Billings checked the bracelet. "And so it says here, you are." He turned to someone behind us that I couldn't see. "Morphine please, nurse. About, let me see ..."

I interrupted and waved the bracelet again. "And morphine too. I'm allergic to it."

Mr. Billings paused and peered down at me. "Are you sure?"

I nodded vigorously, still keeping my Venflon hand out of reach.

An expression of interest crossed Mr. Billings' face. "What happens if you have morphine?"

"I vomit." My reply was firm and convincing.

Mr. Billings waved his hand. "Oh, that's not a problem at all. We're quite used to that kind of thing here. The nurses deal with it all the time."

I made as if to struggle to a sitting position. "It's a very big problem for me," I replied. "My phobia; remember, I told you about it? I absolutely cannot vomit. I want to go home."

Mr. Billing looked down at me. He frowned. "Oh. Yes, now I remember. You do realise that this can be an extremely uncomfortable procedure, do you? I mean, to have it without pain relief ... I, er, I wouldn't recommend it. No, not all!"

I nodded. "I know. It hurt like hell last time. I'm dreading it," I replied. Psyche-Imp leaped from the machine on to the end of the bed and crawled up the light blanket covering me. When he got to my neck, he pulled my hair and began kicking me repeatedly in the ear. I shook my head. "I can't have anything which may make me vomit. Please understand."

"Fine. Well, no-one can say I didn't offer you pain relief," Mr. Billings turned to a small trolley I hadn't noticed. He lifted another syringe and showed it to me. "Do you intend to have the sedative I've prepared for you?"

Psyche-Imp fell off the trolley. "It didn't work last time I had it," I began.

"Yes, I know. This is a larger dose. Do you want it?"

I shoved my Venflon-hand toward the surgeon. "Why not? Knock yourself out," I replied.

"Actually," said Mr. Billings as he emptied what I'm almost certain was four millilitres of the sedative into the Venflon, "I'm rather hoping it will knock *you* out!" He smiled.

As before, as soon as the cool liquid sedative rushed into my veins, everything shot into sharp focus. I became aware of some classical music playing in the background, which I had not noticed before. I cannot say what it was, but that's because I'm only familiar with the extremely well-known classical pieces; I didn't recognise it, but it was pleasant all the same. I noticed the screen and various implements and machines, as before. I also noticed silly, little things like the way the nurse closest to me to me had secured her hair and a faint crack in the ceiling near the door.

With Mr. Billings at the helm, the beginning of the procedure was not as unpleasant as it had been the first time. Of course, that may well have been simply because I knew what to expect (and the fact that Psyche-Imp, bored with my failing to panic had slunk off under the trolley to pick his long nose in peace). However, when the first 'puff' of air was introduced, I squeaked, as before. I must be extra sensitive to the stretching of the bowel I thought as I squeezed my eyes shut and tried to remain still.

Because of that, I didn't see the actual tumour, although I heard Mr. Billings describing it. When the film crew and anaconda went a little deeper and I heard Mr. Billings mention a 'large polyp' I actually opened my eyes and looked at the screen.

The little, dark coloured 'thing', which resembled a tiny grape, didn't look particularly large to me on the screen. I watched as it was removed. This didn't hurt at all but it did leave a mark on the inside of my colon – it looked like a small burn. Back in went the anaconda and another polyp appeared on the screen. This one was a bit bigger. I gasped and squeaked as the air went in, but even despite the pain, I couldn't tear my eyes from the screen. This unwelcome guest also disappeared.

There were seven polyps in total, all of which were removed with what appeared to me, to be very little effort. They were all in the sigmoid colon. I actually asked to see the last one. When Mr. Billings obligingly showed me the thing, resting on a small, cotton swab, it looked even smaller than it had on the screen and was a horrible, dingy purple colour.

I'm afraid I squeaked and yelled rather a lot as the anaconda went back in and, with the addition of what felt like about six hot-air balloons-worth of air, turned the corner into the transverse colon. Of course, Psyche-Imp leapt up, scrambled from beneath the trolley and climbed up to see what mischief he could cause because I was clearly suffering discomfort. I'm sure it was him which caused me to think I was going to vomit. I cried out in pain and added, "I'm going to be sick!"

A small, grey paper kidney dish arrived beside my mouth and one of the nurses laid a hand on my shoulder. "Nearly done now," she murmured. "It's fine to be sick if you need to be. We're all quite used to it."

Ah-ha! Just what Psyche-Imp needed; he jumped up and down on my shoulder and spent a good three or four minutes kicking me in the throat, so I very nearly retched. A particularly sharp pain just under the right ribs caused me to shriek again and I forgot all about being sick. I also forgot to look at the screen. The pain had my full attention.

A nurse came to my shoulder and spoke to me. Under her persistent instruction, I managed (eventually) to

stop screaming and breathe the way she told me to –
slowly, in through the nose and out in little puffs
through the mouth. By the time I had this under control
and could hear what Mr. Billings was saying again, I
realised I had been asked to roll over onto my back.

This manoeuvre sounds simple but is not, in fact, easy
to manage at all if you have about two yards of
anaconda and camera inside you with all their various
equipment hanging out of your rear end. The pain had
eased to almost nothing and I had to be helped to turn.

Mr. Billings pressed on my lower right abdomen and
nodded. "Yes, there we are, right at the end of the large
colon. Take a look at the screen." I looked up. "There
is your appendix."

"Really?" I stared at the blurry image of purply-pink
interior flesh. It didn't look like much to write home
about.

"Yes, really, it is. And the procedure is all over now.
You did very well, my dear, particularly since you had
no pain relief." Mr. Billings allowed the nurses to roll
me back onto my left side. "And," he added, "I'm
pleased to tell you that there were no growths, polyps or
anything else untoward in the rest of your colon."

It seemed a matter of minutes only for the devices to be
removed and for me to be covered once more with the
light blanket and wheeled, trolley, Psyche-Imp and all,
into the recovery area. The pretty, friendly nurse
invited me to have a short nap and to try to evacuate all
the excess wind inside me. She told me she would
leave me for the moment and come back to check on
me in a few minutes.

The previous colonoscopy, which turned out to be just a short investigation of my sigmoid colon, had not resulted in any wind at all that I was aware off, although in truth, I had fallen asleep after the procedure. I nodded, thanked the nurse and closed my eyes.

Unfortunately, due to the double dose of the sedative which doubly didn't work, I opened my eyes again almost immediately. I lifted my head to look at my surroundings. I was in a small cubicle with the curtain left open onto the rest of the department. Sadly, even this small movement caused me to fart, long and loud.

Appalled – I never usually suffer from loud wind – I lay my head back down and hoped no—one had heard. Psyche-Imp, totally fed up that I was not panickable at that time, crept away, leaving me in peace. I thought I should try to sleep, but I didn't feel in the least tired. In fact, I was acutely aware of being extremely thirsty and, after another loud evacuation of wind, hungry too – something I'm also not renowned for feeling.

I think I remained in the cubicle for the best part of an hour, farting occasionally, but wide awake. Once, the nurse peeped around the open curtain-edge and asked if I felt all right. I complained of being very thirsty and she kindly brought me a cup of ice-cold water.

When a completely different nurse came along and invited me to put my underwear and dressing gown on and make my way to the patients seated recovery area, she made the mistake of giving me my bag. There was nothing whatever to clean up like there had been on the previous occasion. I dressed myself awkwardly due to the fact that I was still sitting on the trolley. It's awfully difficult to get knickers and trousers on when lying down! The nurse returned and made no comment on the fact that I was completely dressed. She let the safety rail down on the side of the trolley and I got down and stood up, pausing only to put my shoes on.

I'd left my dentures at home again, which was annoying me because I could have eaten a whole loaf of bread and a pound of butter at that point. I was only offered tea and biscuits, which I'm afraid to say, I guzzled and scoffed in record time. Now I had to wait to be told I could go home. I remembered I would need to see someone and be given a report and that I would also need to urinate before they would allow me to leave.

Upon that thought, I had a sudden and pressing need to urinate. Unfortunately, there was already another lady in the one toilet available. I crossed my legs and sat, watching the door of that toilet, hawk-like in my intensity. Psyche-Imp clambered off my shoulder and proceeded to dance upon my abdomen, right over my bladder. If that lady didn't come out of there soon, I thought, I'd wet myself!

There is little more to tell. Lesley and Peter were waiting for me. Actually, Lesley was outside the hospital, having a crafty smoke when Peter and I walked out of the unit. I immediately demanded a cigarette for myself and we travelled back to my home with pleasant conversation and a lot of laughter. Now and then, just to make things interesting, Psyche-Imp kicked me in the gut and I farted!

I'd been given a report which had a diagram upon it as before. As soon as I got indoors, I perched my specs upon my nose and read it. I had counted correctly; seven polyps removed, the tumour was now estimated at around eight to ten centimetres ... and I had ... what was this? There, on the written report was a diagnosis: Diverticulosis. I pointed it out to Peter and Lesley. This certainly explained away years of intermittent symptoms like diarrhoea and discomfort.

Peter left to return to work and Lesley settled down to 'watch over me' fully expecting me to sleep as I had done the time before. I wasn't tired in the least. I did lie down on the settee and try to close my eyes, but I felt full of energy and still very thirsty. Instead of sleeping, I sat with Lesley, chatting, smoking and drinking endless cups of tea for two or three hours.

I had no unpleasant effects at all after that colonoscopy. No diarrhoea and no nausea either. In fact, I felt quite hungry and ate well. I chided myself for being foolish enough to be frightened at all and preened to myself that I had been correct to only take a dose and a quarter of Picolax. The report showed that it had completely cleaned me out to the surgeon's satisfaction.

It was a very short couple of weeks until my appointment at the hospital with yet another doctor. I felt more well than I had done for years; I had more energy and certainly more inclination to do things, although I was still mildly concerned about a sudden onset of unexpected diarrhoea, so I still disliked being far from a toilet. Even so, padded out with large incontinence pads, I even managed to drive the dogs to the local nature reserve a few times and let them run about whilst I shuffled along with my walking stick, not daring to move too fast or too much in case I aggravated either Fibromyalgia or Diverticulosis!

The next appointment was to see the oncologist. As the days passed, I became (much to Psyche-Imp's delight) more and more nervous. I'm not sure what my tortured mind thought this man was going to do to me, but I feared that appointment equally as much as I had feared that first colonoscopy. I kept telling myself not to be a fool but it didn't work.

On the morning of that appointment, I suddenly developed diarrhoea again. I took an Imodium, but I still felt as if I may need to 'go' at any minute. I did not feel at all comfortable as Peter drove me to the hospital. He'd taken yet more time off work to attend with me.

The 'Shooting Star Unit' at the hospital is designed to be as open-plan and friendly as possible. Unfortunately, they do not seem to have many toilets. I only found one and it was close to the reception desk. Having used it, I had to go and wait in a very small area which was packed with people. I thought it strange that the rest of the unit was so open and un-cluttered and yet, the waiting area was so small and claustrophobic.

Many of the other patients waiting were elderly and one or two were clearly very ill indeed. Of the rest, most people appeared to be entirely healthy and I found it difficult to tell who might be the patient and who the companion. I suspected people were probably looking at me and Peter in much the same way.

I was sent to have blood drawn. Once again, in a short space of time, I had about a dozen little vials-worth taken from my arm. The phlebotomist this time was a cheerful woman who laughed when I asked where my cup of tea and biscuit were. She remarked that I must have had at least two pints taken over the previous few weeks and, in her opinion, deserved at least a chocolate biscuit.

I was then led off to an area of corridor where my height and weight were carefully taken and recorded. I recall feeling somewhat surprised that my height appeared to have shrunk by three quarters of an inch; I wondered if I'd simply not stood up straight enough. I'd gone from five feet nine and a quarter inches to five feet eight and a half inches. My weight had dropped about three pounds since the last time anyone weighed me at the hospital – but that had been many months ago and I was not surprised; after all, I'd barely been eating for months. I didn't feel as if I'd lost weight. I'd never really got used to the extra stone I'd put on with menopause anyway.

We waited for about twenty minutes, during which time I hurried back to the Reception area to the toilet. I was appalled when I went into the toilet room. Obviously, someone had recently vomited in there; not only did the room reek of vomit, there was a faint 'scum' still floating in the toilet bowl. Desperate, and with no other toilet to flee to, even had I had the time, I was forced to use it. I tried to hold my breath, so as not to 'catch' any horrible bug or disease.

Whilst I sat miserably on the toilet, Psyche-Imp had a ball. He danced about in front of the large mirror (which someone had thoughtfully placed right opposite the toilet itself), making the motions of sticking his fingers down his throat and retching. Panic began to build. I had to breathe, but the smell of vomit in the room made me retch. Full-blown panic swept over me and I shook from head to toe. I *had* to get out of there! Of course, due to what had to get out of me, I was unable to flee so the panic got worse. My chest hurt – holding my breath clearly was not helping that – and I felt the distinct stirrings of nausea gnawing at my own gut. Surely, I couldn't be affected by someone else's bugs so quickly? Psyche-Imp jumped up and down and nodded his head vigorously.

I finished what I had to do and, taking one last, shallow breath, washed my hands industriously, knocking the taps on and off with my elbow. Then, I fled back to the waiting room, all the time trying to control the way I was shaking.

Peter noticed the state I was in; he questioned me. I explained that someone had vomited in the toilet and that this had caused me to panic. He took hold of my hand and squeezed it whilst making sympathetic noises at me and adding reassurances to which I was completely deaf. All I could think about was that I'd come to this hospital for help in dealing with my own foul disease and felt sure I was now affected by someone else's equally or more foul disease.

Being called through to see the doctor did not really distract me. He was going to inject me with some poisonous chemo drug and then I would have to vomit. The panic swelled and my knees shook as I stumbled toward the little room the nurse was indicating. Psyche-Imp whispered horrible threats in my ear and suggested I run away now, before anyone had the opportunity to hurt me or terrify me further. I'm not sure how I resisted him.

Of course, all my fears were completely groundless. The nurse first spoke to me and told me that I would speak to the oncologist and ask any questions I may have and that he would then want to examine my rear end – but only with a gloved finger. I shook my head in utter refusal. No way was I going to subject myself to that, particularly with the fact that I was suffering with diarrhoea! The nurse didn't seem fazed by my refusal;

she nodded and led me through to the dreaded oncologist whilst explaining I would be required to sign a form consenting to treatment after everything had been explained to me.

Mr. Gollins was a charming man, although he looked rather weary. He stood up and shook my hand before indicating seats for me and Peter to sit. He asked who Peter was and I tried to explain the complex fact that, although he is my ex-partner, he was all I had, apart from my kids – and that he is a qualified nurse. This was accepted. Mr. Gollins began to talk about the treatment, which was to involve both chemo and radiotherapy.

Now, I had all manner of pre-conceived ideas about chemotherapy, not least that it was delivered intravenously. I was amazed to hear that my particular chemotherapy would be in the form of tablets, which I would take at home. Straight away, with Psyche-Imp prompting me (actually, he was kicking my ankles furiously), I explained that I couldn't possibly take such a drug because of the emetophobia.

Mr. Gollins smiled. He didn't ask what emetophobia was; maybe he'd already had some other patients who suffer similarly. What he did explain to me was that, due to the nature of the way the chemotherapy would be delivered, that is, orally, it would not be a smart thing for the manufacturers to make a tablet which would cause people to vomit – otherwise how would the drug attack the cancer?

I paused to think about this. Of course, Psyche-Imp was not satisfied; not at all. He took control of my mouth and I sat there, taking up this doctor's valuable time with lots and lots of reasons why I shouldn't be given the tablets. All of them involved me vomiting and the fact that I could not permit this to happen and would, in fact, rather die. At no time did the oncologist stop me or interrupt me. In fact, he allowed me to rattle on until I sort of dried up of my own accord. He then reassured me that I could be given very strong anti-emetic drugs – much stronger than the ones I already took and, if at any point I found myself to be feeling as if I couldn't cope, I could stop the treatment.

Faced with this reasonable prospect, even I could find few objections, although Psyche-Imp did whisper to me that it would be a bit late *after* I'd already vomited. In fact, Psyche-Imp kept trying to interrupt as the oncologist continued explaining what side-effects, if any, I might experience.

Apparently, the most common side-effect by far was the 'palmar-plantar' response, which meant that my hands and feet could become excessively dry and sore. Emollient creams would be prescribed to help with this. I could expect an increase in diarrhoea with both radiotherapy and chemotherapy, but again, I would be prescribed medicines with which to control it. The only other significant side-effect was tiredness. The drug was well-tolerated and was being used successfully in many patients without any nausea or vomiting at all.

To my total surprise, I found a couple of tears trickling down my face. I gasped and looked at Peter. Then I leaned my face on Peter's shoulder and whispered, "I might be able to do this!" Peter patted my hand and then squeezed it.

Mr. Gollins asked if I would sign the consent form to agree to chemotherapy. I wiped the tears away and nodded. He handed over an A-three sheet which was printed with an awful lot of tiny writing. I did not have my spectacles with me, but the attending nurse explained that all Mr. Gollins had said was printed on the form and that I would get a copy of it. I signed.

Then there was the radiotherapy, which would be administered at the same time as the chemotherapy. The whole treatment, both chemo and radio would take six weeks and be Monday to Friday, with the weekends free. He'd already said as much about the chemotherapy.

What took me totally by surprise however was the fact that the treatment would not be delivered at this hospital, but at the Cancer Centre for North Wales, which is at Bodelwyddan near St. Asaph – a journey of some fifty miles. I was appalled. The prospect of travelling fifty miles every weekday for a treatment which would apparently only take a few minutes seemed ludicrous. I asked why I couldn't be treated locally.

The explanation was that the local hospital did not have the facilities to deal with cancer treatments. The X-Ray department was already working at maximum capacity dealing with all other demands. Besides, the cancer centre was designed specifically for treating cancer. The nurse pointed out that there was a hostel available for me to stay at, should I wish it.

Psyche-Imp immediately had an absolute field day. I felt sick; I began to shake. How could I possibly leave my home and be in a strange place Monday to Friday every week? I would never sleep; I would be alone, I'd have no television, no pets, no Loki to sit on my lap in the toilet. It was too far. The family would not be able to visit. The objections were apparently endless.

Both the nurse and Mr. Gollins tried their best to reassure me that I did not have to stay in the hostel and, if I travelled to and from the cancer centre daily, my costs would be refunded. Eventually, in a daze, I signed the consent form. Yet my mind was racing still; all manner of objections to the treatment plan; the place I'd have to go to receive the treatment; the possible side-effects; the effects on my family. In fact, what was really going on, I now believe, is that Psyche-Imp was having some kind of mental attack himself. All I recall is that new objections and stumbling blocks continued to cascade into my mind. There was absolutely no escaping this now. I'd signed the forms; I'd admitted I'd got cancer and would be forced to face it and deal with it – and Psyche-Imp didn't want that at all. If the little bastard had his way, we'd have gone direct from the hospital to the cemetery where I would have dug my own grave bare-handed and slithered into it.

Before we left, Mr. Gollins asked if he could examine the tumour. I refused, of course. He didn't seem to mind. In fact, I'm sure he said something along the lines of that he quite understood.

The nurse asked me if I'd like her to contact the Cancer Centre with a view to my staying there during the week. I simply wanted to escape. I replied that it wasn't necessary yet. I'd need to think about it and I would let her know. This seemed satisfactory. Peter and I left.

As soon as I left that room, I immediately began to worry about the vomit in the toilet again (I'd forgotten all about it in my terror about chemotherapy treatments). I tried to remain calm, but as we walked past the Reception desk, I shook from head to toe. I wanted to get home and wash my hands again. I resolved not to eat anything at all for at least forty-eight hours, just in case I'd caught some bug.

Of course, when I say I'd eat nothing for forty-eight hours, I mean actual food, rather than nothing at all. I consume Extra Strong Mints by the multi-pack load whenever I stop eating food. After all, they dissolve in my mouth and don't, somehow, count as food.

By the time we got home, I'd largely forgotten about the vomit because Peter kept talking all the way. I drank tea and was about to make myself a piece of toast before I remembered I wasn't going to eat anything. Generally in such situations, I manage forty-eight or even seventy two hours without eating. I put the loaf back in the cupboard and popped a mint into my mouth.

Later that evening, I did eat some toast, although as soon as I had finished it, Psyche-Imp caused me to ponder upon the possibility of being ill and so very quickly, I felt sick. I took some Valium a little while afterwards and felt better. It helped that everyone was talking to me and asking a great many questions.

As always, Uther was the most optimistic of all. He told me that it would be fine for me to go off and stay fifty miles away Monday to Friday for five weeks. He went on to reassure me that everyone would visit every day and furthermore, they would take care of the home and the animals. I still didn't want to do it. When questioned as to when this would happen, I could only tell everyone that I would be contacted when it was time, but it would probably be a couple of weeks.

It is barely worth mentioning to you, dear reader, but I didn't catch anything from that horrible toilet. Of course I didn't. I think Psyche-Imp was a bit peeved by that. Although I can't claim that I suddenly began eating really well, I certainly didn't go without food for very long and in fact, several times, actually managed to eat almost a proper meal.

The diarrhoea became intermittent. One thing the oncologist had informed me was that it was perfectly fine to use as much Imodium as I needed to control it. Over the next couple of weeks, I actually managed to get out of the house a few times; I even did a little shopping on my own.

There were calls from Alison now and again, generally with progress on how much longer I would have to wait. During one call, she told me she thought I was rather unusual because most patients were champing at the bit and wanting everything to get underway very quickly indeed. I, on the other hand, wanted everything to slow down so I could think and feel it all through.

I had a visit at home from the Mental Health Team Psychologist – who doesn't actually 'do' home visits. Bless her, Isabel is a very thoughtful woman and had taken the time to come to my home. I welcomed her sincerely. I've always found I can get along very well with psychologists – they don't have the same judgemental attitudes as psychiatrists!

Isabel told me that her office manager, who had visited me some weeks before, had returned to the office in some despair. In his opinion, the only 'help' I needed was some anger management!

At first, we laughed about this together and then I began to think about it. "You know, Isabel, I actually am quite angry, now I come to think upon it." I said this slowly, wondering what she'd say.

To my surprised relief, Isabel replied that I had every right to be angry and that this was really the only appropriate response to having been let down by all parties. She told me much the same as the office manager had done. There really was no-one available to send out to me, hence, Isabel's visit. Apparently, problems with the Mental Health Team were more than simply financial; they had long-term sickness to work into the equation too. Clearly, you can't fire someone and replace them because they are ill!

There is one support which I haven't yet mentioned. This, from a quite unexpected source: Damon's school. The counsellor there, a lovely lady named Ann, had telephoned me several times and knew about the cancer and the things which were going on. She rang me frequently and chatted. I found this to be most helpful, especially if I was alone at home. At no time did she in any way judge me and seemed to understand when I vocalised my fears.

Almost everyone thought that travelling fifty miles a day would be terribly difficult, but, as the days wore onward and my symptoms were not so troublesome, I began to think that perhaps it would be possible. I didn't think I'd be able to drive myself; "Why would you, you're ill aren't you?" mumbled Psyche-Imp sulkily. I asked my few friends if and when they were available and questioned whether they would be prepared to drive me now and then. I thought maybe if I could spread it out, I may not have to stay at the hospital at all.

A social worker called to visit. She began the form-filling all over again for 'care and support' through the council. I told her all the possible side-effects of treatment and that I expected to be quite incapacitated by them. I also went on, at some length, to explain that all the support I'd been led to believe would be available turned out not to be so at all. With hindsight, I wonder what, exactly, I expected anyone to be able to actually 'do' that they were not already doing.

A letter arrived from the Cancer Centre. There would be a 'planning' scan and appointment on the sixth of September and, a week later, treatment would begin. I arranged with Uther to drive me to the planning appointment because he had some time off work. This didn't mean I was happy about it – of course not. Psyche-Imp saw to that; the little sod kept prodding me and kicking me in the ear. Every time I nearly relaxed, so Psyche-Imp thought of something else to torment me with so that I quickly began to feel unwell again. This was particularly aggravating as I'd been fairly free of symptoms for a few weeks. I took lots of Imodium that day, which soon settled my stomach.

I had actually discovered – Psyche-Imp notwithstanding – that I was still more than capable of doing light housework, washing, dish-washing and general tidying up along with short trips to the supermarket. Why I had felt unable to do any of these things before baffled me. I must have seriously believed myself to be dead or about to drop dead any minute. I began to wonder if other cancer patients think and feel this way. Has anyone else simply 'stopped' being alive and doing normal things because they think they are dead already? Maybe I'm just nuts.

I counted the days I had 'left'. It was stupid, I know that, but I truly felt that I had wasted the previous few weeks of living and that my life truly would end on the day that treatment started. At least, not end, but that life as I knew it, would stop; just like that. Even though

I planned to 'spend' those days well, I still actually didn't manage to go far, do much or achieve anything for myself or anyone else. Hence I felt disappointed in myself and life in general.

The day of the planning appointment arrived and I had diarrhoea. Of course I did. Typical! Undeterred, even though Psyche-Imp kept whispering into my ear that it would get worse, I ate Imodium until it stopped. I had absolutely no idea what to expect and so (as always) feared the worst. Uther, on the other hand, was bright, cheerful and seemed unfazed by any of it. I think he may even have told me to buck up and stop being so gloomy. It's the kind of thing he often says (whilst completely unaware that these remarks pull me even further down because they prove to me that I am weak, worthless, useless and pathetic just as Psyche-Imp wants me to be).

It was a fairly bright day when we left the house. Uther said he had checked on the computer and knew the way there and that besides, he had his Sat-Nav device if we got lost. He did have cause to sit and wait in his car because my bowel decided I wasn't going anywhere at all until it and Psyche-Imp between them said I could. Uther hates being late anywhere, whilst I am not so bothered. Even so, he was tapping the steering wheel with his fingers and looking rather agitated by the time I got into the car.

The road we had to travel is a very fast road indeed. Although the national speed limit in this country is seventy miles per hour, the average speed along that road is around ninety miles per hour. Even the lorries and trucks all seem to be travelling much in excess of the legal fifty-six miles per hour. Uther, of course, took it all in his stride. Psyche-Imp tried to scare me several times, but I do have confidence in my son's ability to drive, so the little blue blighter was wasting his time. The journey took just about an hour. We arrived at the enormous hospital, found the Cancer Centre and its adjacent car park with no trouble and in we went.

My heart began to thud as Uther and I sat in the large, airy waiting room. In the end, my stomach began to twist as well and I rushed to the toilet, finding these clean and pleasant to use too. When I was called, I left Uther sitting in an easy chair and followed the nurse past the Radiotherapy Reception desk and on towards a room which had thick, concrete walls.

I put my handbag down and began to take off my clothes, only to be told I need remove nothing at all, not even jewellery! With help from the nurse, I sat on the edge of a thick couch made, apparently, of glass and swung my legs up. The radiographer asked me to turn onto my front and slip my trousers and underwear down just a little.

A strange, rigid pillow with a hole in it was shoved under my head and I found myself staring into blackness. The radiographer lifted my arms so that I was hugging this rigid pillow. Both radiographers chatted and talked to me the whole time, which did help to keep me calm. One of them told me they had to make some tiny tattoos on my back. I laughed and told her to knock herself out as I am already pretty much covered in tattoos already.

In truth, I barely felt the tiny scratches made. I think there were four of them. One either side of my hips, one in the small of my back and one on my tail-bone – actually, that's the only one I really felt or was aware of.

The radiographers left the room, leaving me there prone on my tummy. I was aware of being slightly uncomfortable, not least because the couch I was laying upon was solid and made of glass. With my arms raised to hug the pillow-thing, this meant my rib-cage was pressing down onto the glass. It was uncomfortable, although not painful. The machine hummed and buzzed a bit and then the radiographers returned and helped me to get up. As I sat up, I asked one of the radiographers about the possible side-effects of the treatment, saying I had been told I might get diarrhoea. She nodded and smiled before telling me that I would be given drugs to control it and I shouldn't worry, it wouldn't be any worse than my symptoms had been before diagnosis. And that was it! I could go back to the waiting room. Apparently, I had to see the doctor and have some blood drawn, but apart from that, it was all done for the day.

In fact, I went straight to have the blood drawn after the planning scan. I barely had time to tell Uther what was going on. The nurse who took the blood was very pleasant; we talked about cats! I also mentioned to her my fear of vomiting and asked whether I would be given any strong anti-emetics when treatment began the following week. She made a note of my phobia and told me she would personally see to it that attention was drawn to it and its effects upon me. She told me I need not worry in the least and that I would be fine and very well looked after. Even despite Psyche-Imp being present, I believed her too.

When I emerged from that room, Uther had found himself a giant chair in the waiting room. He grinned at me when I sat next to him and told me he'd actually managed to find a chair which made him feel small! We laughed. Then Uther told me everything he had noticed and overheard whilst I was in both the planning scanner and having my blood drawn.

Apparently, there was a big, new machine 'down there' Uther pointed to a corridor nearby. He also told me that the department was running on time and several other small snippets of information. Now, as Uther was speaking to me, I noticed an elderly couple sitting quite close by. They were listening intently to everything he said. Whenever Uther paused for breath, they put their heads together and whispered, just loud enough to be heard by me. Their comments were along the lines of "That young man knows everything that's going on here." I tried to keep my face straight. Uther, completely unaware that he was the centre of the couple's attention, stood up and walked to a leaflet stand to pick out some of the folded papers which he then brought back to our seats. He handed them to me and proceeded to comment upon the contents of the first one he had looked at. The couple leaned closer and listened ever more intently. I'm quite sure if Psyche-Imp had been in that waiting room, he would have done something awful to the old couple. As it was, I'm fairly certain, the little blue bastard was still in the nurse's room I'd just left – probably poking his long nose into things which did not concern him in the least.

By the time I was called in to see the Oncologist, 'Mrs. Elderly Person' was hanging on every word Uther uttered and 'Mr. Elderly Person' was doubled up with suppressed mirth. This caused a wide grin to appear on my own face. Uther can be absorbingly entertaining without having the slightest idea that he is actually very funny. Of course, as soon as my name was called out, Psyche-Imp appeared from wherever he'd been and scrambled up my leg, snagging his claws in my new cardigan as he continued to my shoulder.

Dr. Gollins was as friendly as he'd been when I saw him at the Wrexham hospital. He reiterated a lot of what he'd said on that occasion along with a great many reassurances that my cancer was entirely treatable. Uther asked him several questions, all of which the doctor answered quite frankly and with a disarming honesty. Certainly, Uther seemed reassured; I however, felt the old panic rising and I'm pretty sure it was Psyche-Imp's doing.

I asked what would happen if I declined the surgery after the radio and chemotherapies. Dr. Gollins replied that it did happen. Apparently, some people declined the operation and went on to live full lives. However, he also added that this was extremely rare and an inadvisable choice for me to make. He further advised that I would be best to cross one bridge at a time and take the treatments first and then think about subsequent things like operations.

I felt a lot lighter as I left the hospital. Uther remarked on a pleasing garden with a most unusual sculpture visible and we stopped to look at it. I decided I had a week left to be 'normal' before the treatment began. Psyche-Imp muttered something in my ear about my never, ever having been 'normal' in my entire life and wondered, spitefully, why I thought I could suddenly begin normality now.

One of the facts I had learned that afternoon, through Dr. Gollins and the nurse who drew the blood was that it would be perfectly fine for me to take Imodium as and whenever I needed to in order to control the number of trips I made to the toilet. I kicked myself for having suffered for so long when it would have been safe to take quite a lot of Imodium all along. I resolved to take as much of the stuff as I needed and to spend the week I had left going out, shopping and doing anything else I felt I wanted to do.

Of course, the best laid plans of mice and men and all that rubbish meant that I actually managed to do very little during my 'last week of normality'. In fact, the way I felt, due no doubt, to Psyche-Imp's input, you'd have thought I was going to my death!

I felt depressed. I was always tired. I couldn't be bothered with anything at all. Oh, I ate Imodium all right, but then I did virtually nothing at all with my temporary freedom from the toilet. What a fool!

Peter managed to prise me off the settee one afternoon and we went down to the local garden centre (where I used to really enjoy going), but I immediately needed the toilet as soon as I got there and felt unsettled so I couldn't relax and have a good snoop around. Apart from that, I think I made one trip into town to the supermarket and a couple of trips to the local tip. It's so easy to get into bad, lazy habits and I was very much stuck into the rut of 'Oh, I've got cancer, my life is over'.

The day before the treatment began I had a visit from a social worker. It was clear this woman didn't like me and also did not understand the reasons why I appeared snappy and jittery. I resented her being there, to be honest, which was very foolish of me since she was there with the aim of getting me some help and support.

That last night, Psyche-Imp would not let me go to sleep. The little bastard jumped up and down on my stomach so I had heartburn and then felt sick too. Then he kept kicking me in the head so I got a headache and even taking both Paracetamol and Valium did nothing for it. Every time I did manage to doze off, I awoke suddenly after very bizarre and sometimes frightening dreams – none of which had anything whatsoever to do with either cancer or the treatment.

Of course, as is the way with the Law of Sod, I finally fell asleep at about seven in the morning, only to wake up again at ten thirty feeling like crap and needing the toilet most urgently – several times. I began taking Imodium almost as soon as I opened my eyes.

Both Uther and Zakh came with me on the first day of treatment. Uther had decided on a new route which would cut out about five miles and be more pleasant to drive. This went wrong because we were all so busy talking, Uther missed the turning we should have taken!

After a rummage in the glove-box and the application of the wonders of science (a Sat-Nav device) and a ten mile detour through a very pretty village or two, we finally got back onto the right road.

I'd forgotten to ask for my travelling expenses to be refunded for the planning appointment and so I asked about it when I arrived. It turned out that I hadn't brought the correct paperwork with me! I felt incredibly foolish, not to mention irritated, but Psyche-Imp wouldn't let me dwell upon that, oh no, he was determined that I should feel as frightened and shaky as possible without actually falling down in a faint.

It became hard to breathe, even though I'd got both the boys with me. I didn't dare tell either of them how I felt because there was clearly nothing at all to be afraid of. Also, I'd caught a cold from Uther and was coughing anyway. I knew if I said anything, both boys would tell me it was my smoking which was causing the sensation.

We walked into the radiotherapy suite reception and a fresh-faced, dark-haired young woman smiled and pointed us in the direction of the 'New Machine'. Apparently, all the machines had names and mine was called 'Ffynnon' and was the newest of all. Uther nodded his head and made a remark about me getting the poshest, newest machine so I would be fine. We went along the wide, brightly lit corridor into a small and comfortable waiting area.

There were only a couple of other people waiting. All smiled at us as we entered, although no-one spoke on that first day.

I had barely sat down when someone I took to be a nurse came along and called my name. She told me I was to have an interview first before treatment started and invited the boys to come along too. We followed her into a small room which had several easy chairs and a desk in it.

The 'nurse' turned out to be one of the radiographers. A colleague introduced herself, so there were two of them. Full of trepidation, I sat down and listened to what they had to say about the treatment and its possible effects.

Both Uther and Zakh asked a few pertinent and intelligent questions which were answered frankly and with smiles and reassurances. I asked nothing which made any sense. Psyche-Imp was very much in control of both my brain and my mouth at that moment in time and, had I not maintained a modicum of control, I would simply have curled up in the corner of the room and gibbered with fear.

We went back to the waiting room and sat for only about ten minutes. Uther watched the television and commented now and then. I believe it was a cookery programme – probably Masterchef or something. I couldn't concentrate on it and anyway, the sight of food was making my stomach churn. Then I was called in for treatment.

Actually, I was led out of the waiting room, round the corner into a very small area which contained just two chairs and a cold-water dispenser and told to wait there as I would be next. Now, this was exactly where Psyche-Imp wanted me; all alone and with no-one to distract or support me. As the radiographer walked away, I felt waves of nausea sweeping over me. I quickly snatched a cup and took a few sips of the ice-cold water. It did nothing to settle my nerves at all!

Looking back, I can't have sat there alone for any more than about eight minutes but it honestly felt like about a month! My stomach churned, my shoulders and neck tensed up so tight I could barely turn my head; I felt sick, thought I was about to lose control of my bowels altogether and possibly wet myself as well. Oh yes, and I began to shake – all over.

Although there was no door, just an open gap, through which I could see a long, high counter and a black box which lit up every now and then with 'X-Ray On' in yellow, I felt totally enclosed and ensnared. I now know this was Psyche-Imp's doing, but at the time I hadn't even realised the little sod existed. If I had, I think I would have strangled him there and then. At least I would then have been free of the fear he fills me with.

I noticed how very stout the walls were; at least a foot thick. The walls were probably lead-lined as well I thought. These thoughts were fleeting, you understand. I couldn't really think straight about anything. There were probably a lot more silly and inane things I thought whilst sitting there, but I cannot now recall them.

One of the radiographers came to fetch me; she smiled warmly and chatted about ordinary things as she led me past the high counter into a wide area where I could see to my left another high counter. There were two entrances ahead of me. One bore the legend 'Ffynnon' the other 'Gorwel'. I followed the radiographer along a short, aesthetically pleasing, curved corridor and entered a large room.

Centre stage stood 'my' machine. It was huge and shiny and in fact, very impressive. My fear began to trickle away as I stared around. In front of the machine, set about six feet away, a long, low platform stood. Beneath it I could see grey, shiny metal machinery. The platform was made of the same black and green glass as the one in the planning scanner. A second radiographer stood beside the platform. She had a file in her hand and smiled at me as she introduced herself. Her name was Claire. (I feel bad now because Claire is the only radiographer I really remember by name, but they were all equally pleasant and friendly).

I put my handbag down on a chair by the wall and slipped my boots off. "Will I need to take off my jewellery or clothes?" I asked.

Claire quickly reassured me that I need take nothing off at all, just clamber aboard and slip my trousers and underwear down a little.

The strange, hard pillow-with-a-hole-in-it appeared and both radiographers helped me up onto the platform and into a prone position. They ensured I was comfortable and then I felt the platform moving. Both women continued to chat to me as the machinery whirred. I was instructed to be 'a sack of potatoes' and not to try to assist them in any way. All I had to do was lie still and let them shove and prod and push my hips about until they had me in the correct position.

It felt very strange because I could hear them talking, hear the platform moving about and of course, feel it too, but, due to having my face in the hole, all I could see was blackness. I am nosey by nature and I wanted to lift my head and have a good look about. Clearly, finding me almost impossible to scare at that moment, Psyche-Imp had slunk off to do something naughty because I no longer felt remotely afraid.

Once they had me positioned correctly, I could hear them reeling off odd numbers behind me and checking. I was asked for my date of birth and warned that this question would be repeated every day, even though they knew full well who I was – a safety check which had to be performed.

Claire told me they were about to leave the room and reassured me that they would be able to see me at all times through the monitor. If anything at all was wrong, if I needed to move or anything else, all I need do was raise my hand and treatment would stop and they would come to see to me very quickly. I called out quite a cheery 'OK, thank you' which must have sounded quite muffled – my face being in the hole. I heard them chatting as they left the room.

I recall that first treatment very vividly, not least because I had the sensation of large, heavy stuff moving about over my back and head but could see nothing. I wondered how the machine moved. It looked as if it were bolted to the floor! Behind the sounds of the machine moving, I could hear a radio playing. That first day, I listened to Natalie Imbruglia singing 'Torn' as I had my treatment. I had to exercise extreme self-control so as not to tap my foot! Being completely still (apart from breathing normally) was important.

I counted the times the machine buzzed: six. Just as I was wondering what would happen next, I felt the platform beneath me moving backwards and down and heard Claire's cheerful voice telling me it was all done! I sat up.

"Is that it?" I asked, incredulous.

"Yes, all done for today," replied Claire as she helped me down. "It doesn't take long."

Good grief! All that panic and fear over – nothing at all as it turned out. I felt incredibly foolish but I chatted and smiled as I straightened my clothing and put my shoes back on.

Claire told me to go to the 'Cape Clinic' next and instructed me to make my way back to the main reception of the Cancer Centre and turn right where I would see another, small reception desk.

"Cape Clinic?" I asked.

"That's what we call it; it's short for Capecitabine – the drug you'll be on."

I smiled and said goodbye before wandering out of the room back to the waiting room where Uther and Zakh were sitting. They seemed surprised that I'd been so quick. I told them we had to go to the chemotherapy clinic next.

We found our way to the Cape Clinic waiting area without any problem. It was fairly crowded but we found seats. A harassed-looking nursing sister with her arms full of files and boxes came along and greeted us. She apologised and told us she was behind schedule but would get to me as soon as she could. Then she hurried away.

Now, I should have been absolutely terrified, but I wasn't. At least, not right then. Both Uther and Zakh were chatting and actually being quite silly very quietly which kept me well occupied for the first hour. The appointment was actually at four but the nurse had warned us she was behind schedule. By ten past five, I was beginning to get jittery again, despite the boys' foolery. Clearly, Psyche-Imp had got fed up prodding the radiotherapy machine, irritating the radiologists and making a mess and had come to find me.

It was actually getting along for half past five when we were finally admitted to the nurse's office. By this time, I felt utterly sick, terrified and tense. I'm sure both Uther and Zakh were aware of it because they chattered even more than they already had been, even joking with the nurse.

We sat in the small room and listened to the instructions for taking Capecitabine: they must be taken twice a day, within half an hour of food. If I found them difficult to swallow, I could dissolve them in a little warm water. The nurse went on to detail any side effects which may occur, of which, of course, nausea and vomiting figured – as they always do with almost any drug.

Psyche-Imp kicked me in the ear and I immediately starting spouting a load of old rubbish about my phobia and the fact that, were I to vomit, even once, nothing on earth would induce me to take any more of the tablets.

The nurse – Jill – smiled and did her best to reassure me. She asked me about anti-emetics and I explained that I already took an anti-emetic drug every eight hours and had done so for the past ten years. I told her I knew the action of this particular drug – Metoclopramide – is to empty the stomach quickly and asked if I could have an additional drug which would work in tandem with Metoclopramide to work on the 'vomit centre' of the brain. Simply to positively ensure I could not vomit. The nurse shook her head and advised against this course of action. She felt the Metoclopramide would work just fine on its own. She further thought that I would not have a problem with Capecitabine in that regard. Apparently by far the worst side effect was the sore and dry hands and feet – for which I would be given an emollient cream.

Both Uther and Zakh asked questions and made reassuring remarks to me, but Psyche-Imp was in full control by then. All I wanted to do was run away and forget about the whole thing, even if it did mean a horrible and painful death. I tried to chat and joke but I think both my boys knew my heart wasn't really in it.

The nurse went off to get the drugs for me and we were left alone in her consulting room. The boys changed seats – mainly because she had told them not to as she would get confused if they did! I laughed a little but Psyche-Imp kicked me repeatedly in the stomach and then began jumping up and down on my bladder and bowels. I wondered if I would have to run to the toilet.

Jill came back with a large pack, which she opened and showed us the contents. A lot of Capecitabine – I was to take three in the morning and three in the evening; a large box of Loperamide capsules (to counteract and diarrhoea) and a tube of emollient cream. Apparently, Jill had also spoken at some length to the Pharmacist who informed her I could take up to eight Metoclopramide in any twenty-four hour period. Since I already had these prescribed by my GP, there was no need to give me any more. She warned me not to use any other kind of soothing cream or hand cream as it could interfere with the radiotherapy. To my surprise, she informed the three of us that many hand creams and emollients contain, of all things, aluminium!

She asked if I would take my first dose of Capecitabine that evening or if I would wait until the next morning. I fervently assured her I would be taking nothing at all until the next day. With many smiles and plenty of friendly chatter, the interview ended, I picked up my pack of drugs and the boys and I left.

The hospital was virtually empty! By then it was well after six in the evening and I had been the last patient to be seen. We went back to the half-empty car park and both the boys commented on how pleasant the nurse had been and what a nice hospital it was.

I changed the subject quickly to that of traffic, which was plentiful at that time of the day on a major road. Every time the boys mentioned the chemotherapy on the way home, I quickly changed the subject again. Psyche-Imp was delighted. He'd got me utterly fazed and freaked out and intended to keep it that way.

When we got home, a little after seven in the evening, I dumped the pack of pills on the kitchen work-top and scurried to the toilet – where the world fell out of my arse and Psyche-Imp laughed himself sick. I just felt sick. Why wouldn't this bloody disease just go away and leave me alone? Why did I have to do this? Maybe I wouldn't do it at all. I went to make a cup of tea and sat through an hour or more of the boys talking about the chemo when all I really wanted to do was to run away and jump off somewhere high.

However, I had to concede, the radiotherapy had been nothing like as bad as I'd thought it would be and the radiologists had told me it may well be a couple of weeks before I felt any significant side effects at all.

When Peter turned up that evening, I had to tell him all about it, which meant I couldn't pretend it wasn't real any more. He also made reassuring comments but Psyche-Imp interpreted them as patronising comments and I felt intensely irritated. How the hell did Peter know these things? He'd never been through it himself and had not even worked on any cancer wards. Grumpiness overwhelmed me for a few minutes which gave Psyche-Imp a foothold. Very quickly I began to feel extremely nauseous again, which in turn, caused a panic attack. Peter sat and rubbed my lower back for well over an hour and tried to distract me.

That night, when I lay down, sleep refused to arrive. I tossed and turned and thrashed about; I was too hot, then I was too cold and then I had heartburn so had to sit up. As soon as that had settled and I lay down again,

I needed the toilet. This went on for several hours. By half past three in the morning, I was busy watching Pirates of the Caribbean for the second time and firmly believing I would never sleep again. I did doze fitfully for an hour, but then I was plagued by peculiar dreams and the need for the toilet so woke up. I re-set Pirates of the Caribbean back to the beginning and settled down to watch it ... and promptly fell asleep.

In the morning, when I woke, my first thought was the Capecitabine and the fact that I was going to have to willingly take this poisonous substance into my body. I immediately felt sick. I took the anti-emetic pill before I'd even sat up and then proceeded to rush to the toilet to experience my first bout of diarrhoea of the day.

The nurse in the Cape clinic had told me that one slice of toast – which is what I generally have for my breakfast – was not enough 'food' for the Capecitabine to work on. She'd advised me to have two slices at least. I made a cup of tea, glanced at the toaster and looked away quickly as my stomach began to roll. Not yet. I retreated to my safe little spot on the corner of the settee I'd just slept on, curled up and lit a cigarette. The cup of tea began to grow cold beside me.

Eventually, I uncurled myself and made a second cup of tea. I was half-way through drinking this when Uther appeared downstairs. He asked if I'd taken my chemo yet. I replied that I hadn't because I'd not yet eaten. He chivvied me and told me to get a move on and make my toast so I could take the drug.

I whined a bit. I told Uther I was scared it would make me sick. He visibly controlled his irritation with his cowardly mother and pointed out that he was there with me and would look after me if I was sick and added that the nurse had assured us I wouldn't be sick. Clearly, an oral chemotherapy treatment would be entirely useless if it was sicked up five minutes after having taken it. He also reminded me that the nurse had suggested I sip at the dissolved drug rather than gulp the half glass-full back in one or two mouthfuls.

With Uther there chatting, I made two slices of toast, another cup of tea and prepared the drug ready to take. I'd taken the trouble to purchase a special cup and spoon with which to take the stuff – which must not be used by anyone else or even washed up with the family's dishes because it was so toxic. (This did not help my feeling that I was taking poison, and Psyche-Imp was more than happy to point it out – several times).

I was to drink at least one glass of water immediately after taking the drug too. Now, ordinarily, I don't drink anything cold at all. Not ever – well, except for bottled spring water when I had a colonoscopy looming. So this water-drinking malarkey would be difficult for me. Psyche-Imp hastened to point out that I only had to drink the water so that I had a good lot to bring up when I vomited soon after taking the drug and the water. I contemplated two pieces of toast, a cup of tea, small amount of soluble poison followed by a glass of water: not pleasant on the way back out. Not pleasant at all. Still, I mused, it wouldn't matter what I brought up; if I was sick at all, I would die and that was the end of the matter.

I drank the tea; I ate the toast; I opened a bottle of water ready to drink (the water here where I live is so hard, it comes out of the tap wielding a baseball bat and a machine-gun) – then I lifted the cup with and its poison, which had turned a fetching shade of shrimp-pink and sniffed it.

There was no discernable smell, and I do have a very sensitive nose. It must have had some kind of smell because the dogs and Loki were extremely interested in it. I shoved them away, fearing they'd get the stuff on their noses or paws somehow and ingest it. I think I thought (with Psyche-Imp's help) that even a drop of it would cause the animals to glow in a range of psychedelic colours and grow an assortment of extra tails.

With Uther watching, I tentatively sipped at the contents of the cup. It was nasty, but certainly not nearly as nasty as some medicines I have taken – both pills, which I chew up, and liquid. I took another sip.

"Well done, Mum," Uther encouraged. "Come on, you can do it."

I took a couple more sips. Then I opened the bottle of water and took a couple of sips of that. There could not have been very much more than about fifty millilitres of medicine but it took me a full ten minutes to get it down with swigs of water in between each sip. I then continued to sip at the water bottle until the water level dropped below the label – which I judged to be about half a glass of water. And then I waited.

The world did not end. In fact, nothing happened at all. After fifteen minutes or so, I made another cup of tea and drank it down – and enjoyed it too. As the minutes ticked by it was obvious that I was certainly not going to sick up what I'd just taken. Psyche-Imp sulked; he sat on the arm of the settee with his hands under his bony bum, swinging his legs and shaking his head sadly.

As already mentioned, I'd caught a cold from Uther and so I sniffled and snuffled and, as the hours wore on, also began to cough – quite hard. Coughing always causes me to get anxious and to panic, just in case I cough hard enough to retch. Psyche-Imp watched with great anticipation as I had a coughing fit shortly after lighting a cigarette. Although my heart pounded and I also had need to rush to the toilet in order to avoid wetting and soiling myself, I didn't cough hard enough to retch. I glared at the cigarette in my hand. "Bloody fags," I muttered as the world fell out of my arse again. "I really should stop."

Psyche-Imp had been sitting on top of the toilet tissue, alternately picking his nose and scratching his back side. He stared at me. "You? Give up smoking? You can't possibly do that!" He then went off into gales of raucous laughter, fell off the toilet tissue and into the bin, the spiteful little bastard.

I found I needed to run to the toilet several times that morning – and for some unknown reason, I took no Loperamide at all. When I also began to feel faintly nauseous, I couldn't tell if it were the poisonous chemo-drug I'd taken, the diarrhoea or simply nerves which was causing the feeling. I'd been told I could take up to eight of my usual anti-emetics in any twenty-four hour period. I generally took only three – that is, one every eight hours. I told Uther I was beginning to feel sick and he encouraged me to have another 'pill'. I did.

As mentioned before, Uther really hates being late for anything, particularly appointments (which shows I brought him up well and properly with some nice stress-inducing hang-ups). When it was time for us to leave to go to the cancer hospital, Uther tapped his foot and kept looking at the clock whilst I continued to run to the toilet and back.

After no less than four trips in fifteen minutes, I took some Loperamide just before I rushed into the toilet again. Uther went out to sit in the car. "No pressure there then," observed Psyche-Imp as he watched me take yet more toilet tissue to my already sore nether regions.

I took some more Loperamide and left the house. My mind was referencing every public lavatory I knew of between my home and the hospital. The problem was, I mused, as I got into the car, I didn't actually know of any once we'd passed Wrexham.

I'd thought that the nausea would increase during the car journey but it didn't; it stayed at the gut-gnawing level it had been before I took the second anti-emetic. I coughed a few times and sipped from the water bottle which I'd had the forethought to bring with me. Several times, Uther asked me how I felt as the car sped onward.

We had a good journey that day. It only took forty-five minutes and we arrived just in time, which pleased Uther. This time, I had all the correct documentation and I spoke to the lady at the Reception desk about getting travel costs refunded.

The lady, named Eileen, was so helpful and friendly I almost forgot I felt sick at all. She filled in the forms and gave me another form with which to claim for the two trips I'd already made. She also handed over cash

– which I immediately gave to Uther for his fuel. We then made our way down to the radiotherapy suite.

I'd barely sat down on a chair in the waiting room when Claire came to call me through. This time, I didn't have to sit in the small waiting area. I followed the radiographer through to 'my' machine, Ffynnon – which, Claire informed me, should be pronounced 'Furnon'; apparently it meant 'well' as in water or wishing well.

I removed my boots and left them with my water bottle and handbag on the chair as before and then clambered (in a most undignified manner, I might add) up onto the table. Even though I'd already experienced this yesterday, I still felt nervous. It must have been Psyche-Imp's doing. My heart thudded in my chest as I positioned myself face-down.

Fortunately, I had a tissue in my hand. As soon as I placed my face in the 'hole' of the strange, hard pillow, my nose began to run. I commented upon it and tucked my hand under my face so I could 'catch the drips'. Claire and her colleague laughed at my muffled remarks about snot.

In any event, the new position of my arm seemed to have no effect upon the positioning of my hips and abdomen, so I lifted my other arm as well. This meant that my cheek was resting on one wrist and my forehead on the other. It actually felt more comfortable than the previous day, despite my back being a little more arched. I felt Claire or her colleague make pen marks on my lower back and listened to the numbers they were telling each other.

When the radiographers left the room, I listened to the radio but I cannot recall which song was playing – obviously something I didn't recognise. I began to wonder where the radiotherapy treatment came from and which bit of the machine actually moved.

Although I could not move or turn my head, I now had a little peripheral vision because my head was raised more than it had been the day before. I knew, for example, that something very large now obscured the dim lights of the room on my right. The machine hummed and buzzed and then it moved again. This time it had moved further to the right and downward.

For reasons best known to Psyche-Imp, I began to recite part of the script from Pirates of the Caribbean in the privacy of my head. The machine continued to move and hum and I shut my eyes and pictured Captain Jack Sparrow. My nose tickled; snot was about to drip from it. I dropped the tissue onto the glass beneath my face and continued with my mental recitation.

In no time at all, the lights came back on and I felt the glass table moving backwards and down. I sat up, snatching up my tissue to wipe my nose. When I stood up, I turned to Claire and asked her how many 'rads' my treatment would be.

She smiled and told me these days radiographers do not measure in 'rads' but in 'Grays'. I would have a total of fifty Grays throughout my treatment, given in small doses each day. I nodded, making a mental note to look up 'Grays' when I got home. I turned toward the machine which now stood like a giant sentinel in exactly the same position as it had been when I entered the room.

"Which bit of Ffynnon actually moves?" I asked.

"I'll show you," replied Claire. "It's actually the whole machine. Look."

She pressed some buttons and to my utter amazement, the whole machine began to twist around. I could see the large, circular disc, which must be the part over my body, now at a crazy angle to the right and the base of the machine balancing it to the left. Now, at a rough guess, I'd say the machine itself must have weighed the best part of a ton and a half – maybe more. This piece of engineering was most impressive.

"Where does the radiation actually come out?" I asked, stepping closer.

Claire actually looked pleased. She pointed up into the circular disc. "Do you see that strange shape in green up there? That's your tumour and the shape of the area being irradiated. Every time the machine moves, the shape changes. If you look closely, you will see the whole disc is made up of little tiny black shields about a couple of millimetres by one millimetre. They shield the rest of your body – that's so the radiation only goes into the tumour."

I stepped forward and peered up into the disc, fascinated. "Wow. That's really clever," I murmured. "So, only the part of my body actually affected gets the radiation?"

"Absolutely," Claire confirmed. "There are machines even more precise than this, but this really is a state-of-the-art machine and we're very pleased to have it here."

So am I," I agreed. "Thanks for showing me and sorry to be a pain; I'm very nosey, you see and also very interested in science."

Both Claire and her colleague assured me they didn't mind in the least and that it made a change to have a patient who was interested enough to ask how it worked and appreciate the precision involved. The ladies bade me farewell and escorted me out of Ffynnon's room.

I couldn't wait to tell Uther all about the machine and how it worked. I also told him I needed to find out what a 'Gray' was and how many rads it contained. I'd actually forgotten about feeling sick altogether.

We stopped at MacDonalds on the way back and Uther persuaded me to eat something, although I found I didn't really want it at all. The nausea came back big time as soon as the food appeared. I tried to eat, assuming that it was hunger causing the nausea and not the fact that I'd taken poison. I managed just a little; Uther finished off what I couldn't manage.

By the time we arrived home, I actually felt very sick indeed. I struggled with a cup of tea. Psyche-Imp jumped up and down on the arm of the settee urging me to put the tea down because I would vomit in a moment. I tried to ignore him; really I did, but the nausea grew in intensity until panic began to sweep over me. I had another anti-emetic pill and willed it to work.

Delighted with his efforts, Psyche-Imp took up station on my left shoulder and whispered, in his scratchy, spiteful little voice, a constant stream of promises ... that I would not only continue to feel sick, I would be sick too – and once I'd started, I'd never stop. In fact, as I shook and panicked, so Psyche-Imps' threats got worse.

The chemotherapy tablets had to be taken twice a day 'within half an hour of food'. I'd been to Marks and Spencer and purchased some ready meals I really like so that at least I could have something really nice to eat. I'd selected a chicken casserole with baby potatoes and broccoli shoots for my evening meal.

Both Lesley and Peter came round and there was a lot of laughter – mainly because Peter teased Lesley mercilessly about her short stature. Although I still felt very sick, between them, they did manage to distract me enough to stop me shaking. Since there had to be roughly twelve hours between doses, I put my meal on to heat so it would be ready at about nine in the evening.

Generally, when this particular meal is heating, the smell of it makes my mouth water in anticipation. This was definitely not the case that evening. As the aroma of chicken began to spread, so my stomach began to roil ever faster. My mouth did begin to water – but not in anticipation of receiving food, it was that sour water you get shortly before you vomit.

Shaking with trepidation, I took the food out of the oven and served it onto a plate. I took the meal through to the lounge and sat down with it. Even though Lesley and Peter kept talking and laughing as I tried to force the food down my throat, they were drowned out by Psyche-Imp's continual whispering into my left ear. "You can't force things down your throat when your throat wants to force it back up," the spiteful little sod advised. "You'll choke, you know. No-one will be able to save you. You're going to choke on that fancy, expensive casserole." He rolled off my shoulder onto the arm of the settee where he turned cartwheels of joy.

I only managed a very little of my meal. Try as I might and no matter how much I chewed, I simply could not swallow the food. After the first five or six mouthfuls, I became convinced I would vomit into my dinner. I gave up.

"It's no good," I moaned aloud. "I can't eat this."

Peter and Uther reassured me that at least I'd eaten a little and it would be sufficient. Someone made me a cup of tea and I gratefully accepted it, although I found that almost impossible to drink as well. The foul poison sat in its special cup of warm water, slowly dissolving and turning pink. I've always hated the colour pink at the best of times, now it seemed threatening.

With a bottle of water at the ready, I began to take the Capecitabine in small sips, each followed by an even smaller sip of water. It surprised me how quickly I managed to get the drug down. Due to continued conversation, I also managed to sip about a third of a bottle of water as well. This felt like an absolute novelty; I've never been able to drink much at a time, particularly water.

Lesley went home and Peter promised to stay with me through the night. Uther and Damon went to bed. The nausea increased and once again, I began to shake. I told Peter how ill I felt and he came to sit beside me on the settee.

We watched television, and more Stargate on the laptop. During the programmes, Peter rubbed the small of my back endlessly. For some reason, I couldn't have him touch the middle or the top of my back as it made me feel worse. We remained like this until about two or three in the morning.

Eventually, Peter told me he needed to lie down and told me I should try to sleep. I had another anti-emetic and half a Valium before settling down as best I could. Peter lay on the other settee and was asleep almost as soon as he put his head on the pillow. I watched the television – the recording of Pirates of the Caribbean ... again.

I could not sleep properly. Nausea still gnawed in my guts. I found a comfortable enough position, snuggled down and concentrated on Captain Jack, but this did not last long. The nausea increased and I sat up. Matters were not helped at all by a sudden hot flush. I picked up a book with which to fan myself. Gradually, the heat dissipated and I felt cooler and more comfortable. Once again, I snuggled down and tried to sleep.

The whole night passed in this pattern; get comfortable; concentrate on the film; begin to doze; get a hot flush; feel very sick; sit up; panic and shake until the nausea and heat subside a little. I watched the film twice through, although I kept missing the same parts when I dozed for a few minutes.

By the time Peter's alarm went off and he woke up, I'd had very little sleep and still felt very nauseous indeed. Concerned, Peter made me a cup of tea and advised me to take my anti-emetic pill. I told him I'd already had one. He suggested I take another. The conversation was interrupted because Psyche-Imp kicked me in the guts and I had to run for the toilet.

Between trips to the toilet I actually managed to drink two full cups of tea. The nausea subsided to a low level, although it did not disappear completely. Uther awoke and came downstairs to keep me company as Peter went off to work. I made two slices of toast and prepared the medicine, taking both back to the lounge with me.

It was not an easy task eating toast, but at least I felt a little less sick than I had done the evening before, so, despite Psyche-Imp and his chittering, I did actually eat it. I swirled the dissolved tablets around in the cup and stared at them.

"Come on, Mum," urged Uther. "Take the medicine. You need it to get better."

At that point, what I actually needed was to be able to run away; forget it all and run for ever. Of course, in reality, I can't actually run at all; it's all I can manage just to walk a little way. Psyche-Imp was delighted with my low mood, although the foolish little tyke had not considered what might happen to him should I decide to give up and kill myself. He would also cease to exist.

I did take the medicine. I also managed about half a bottle of water, taken in small sips. Shortly afterwards, I took another anti-emetic but although I did not vomit, in truth it did little to make me feel any better.

The next couple of hours were taken up with the usual trips to the toilet and before I knew it, the time had arrived for the journey to radiotherapy. I took Imodium that day and even though I didn't ask Uther to stop the car and find me a toilet, it was constantly on my mind. I rushed to the nearest hospital toilet as soon as we arrived. I took some more Imodium after I'd washed my hands too.

Once again, I had hardly any time to wait before being called in for treatment. The radiographers were as lovely as ever, asking me how I felt and if the weather continued pleasant outside. I explained I had diarrhoea again and they very kindly put an 'inco-sheet' on the table before I clambered on to it, assuring me that I should not worry, they were quite used to such things.

Actually, Psyche-Imp pounced on that remark and throughout the treatment, over and above the noise of Ffynnon, Psyche-Imp's scratchy little voice repeated again and again that I would shit myself and feel disgraced in front of these people. It was difficult to keep still. In addition to the constant feeling of needing the toilet, I had also developed a cough. For the last two of the six 'buzzes' I was holding my breath in order not to cough and move.

When the radiographers returned to the room to help me down from the treatment table, I felt a twinge of pain across my chest. I did not mention it, assuming I'd just moved awkwardly and pulled a muscle. As I put my boots back on and had a small coughing fit, the pain didn't get any worse.

Of course, as soon as I got outside, I lit a cigarette straight away. Strangely, the coughing fits seemed to occur between cigarettes rather than during them. I would not admit I had a smoker's cough; Psyche-Imp helped with that. He assured me I simply had a bad cold and had my sons to thank for that particular ailment. I stared at the cigarette in my hand and thought I really should stop smoking.

Psyche-Imp lay in my lap laughing fit to bust. He clutched at his round little tummy and waved his spindly legs in the air. Sparkling tears of mirth glittered beside his yellow eyes. "You?" he howled. "You can't!" I turned away and stared at the beautiful scenery whilst Uther's car sped homeward. I tried to drink it all in: the sky, the trees, the estuary we passed – almost as if I were saving it up for ... what? I couldn't take it with me and I knew I was going to die.

The nausea had actually gone for a while whilst I was being treated. At the thought I was shortly going to die it came back big time. I sipped at my water bottle and tried to concentrate on Uther's conversation, but the feeling did not go away. By the time we arrived home, I felt very sick indeed. I took another anti-emetic and on 'auto-pilot' made a cup of tea – which I struggled to drink. Finally, I curled up on the settee and tried to sleep.

Psyche-Imp had other ideas. Every time I almost dozed off, he kicked me in the ear and reminded me I felt sick and it would be foolish to go to sleep because then, not only would I vomit all over the furniture and the carpet, but also, I may choke to death too. Each time this happened, I startled awake. I tried to ignore the feeling of panic and concentrate instead on the television; that didn't work either. I did doze, perhaps for fifteen minutes altogether but not consecutive minutes. I felt exhausted, both emotionally and physically.

I began to wonder why I was such a pathetic wuss. How could I allow something so stupidly small to control me? Psyche-Imp roared with laughter again. He jumped up and down on my tummy until the nausea grew really strong and I became convinced I would vomit.

The evening passed in a haze of nausea and panic. Peter arrived and did his best to chat to me, rub the small of my back and keep me engaged, but I had travelled so far away from normality and sanity by then, everyone's efforts were in vain. I could think of nothing other than that I had to somehow force food down my throat later in the evening and take yet more of the foul poison.

In fact, I could manage no more than one and a half slices of toast and even that nearly choked me. Drinking tea or even water became virtually impossible too. I mixed up the tablets into the warm water and somehow got the solution down but I found it really difficult to drink enough water afterwards. I had yet another anti-emetic pill and half a Valium but the nausea did not recede.

Peter sat with me until it was time for him to go to music night. Then I had to rely upon Uther and Damon to keep me distracted. I could not bring myself to ask either of them to rub the small of my back, so I continued to fight the panic, the nausea and the fear just by listening to their conversation.

To be fair to the boys, they did stay with me until Peter came back from music night, and then they went to bed. Rather than feel relieved at Peter's presence, it was almost as if I'd saved up the worst of the panic for him exclusively. My body and legs shook uncontrollably. Even as he set up the laptop with Stargate I battled the urge to retch my heart up. Psyche-Imp was delighted; the little blue devil sat on my shoulder, whispering terrors into my head so that I could barely concentrate at all on the soothing action of the back-rubbing Peter was doing for me, never mind hear what the actors on the screen were saying!

Any behavioural therapist or psychologist will tell you it is almost impossible for the body to be able to sustain outright panic for very long. I kept repeating this fact over and over in my head as I watched Stargate and tried to concentrate on pleasant things – the fact that Peter's hand felt warm against the small of my back; that I was alive and not dead; the cats, the dogs – in fact anything at all. However, someone in authority has not informed my body that it cannot sustain panic for hour upon hour. At three forty in the morning, I still felt just as anxious, terrified and convinced I would vomit as I had done at eight o'clock in the evening.

The shaking now settled into a pattern of waves. For up to fifteen minutes at a time I shook from head to toe as if shivering with cold. Then it would die down a little and the nausea increased in intensity. Just as I truly believed I would actually vomit, so the shaking began again. Peter's arm must have been aching from the constant motion of rubbing; my back should have been sore by then rather than soothed – but it wasn't.

Somehow, Peter persuaded me into a semi reclined position on the settee and reminded me to take another anti-emetic. I'd not had one for some four hours. I complied, but somewhat jerkily. With further persuasion from Peter, I managed to keep an Extra Strong Mint in my mouth without spitting it out. As five o'clock approached, I began to feel so weary and hopeless I felt I really would perhaps be better off dead!

Peter reminded me that over the weekend, I would not have to take the chemotherapy drugs nor travel for the radiotherapy either. I felt intense relief about that. For some reason, I felt if I could simply get off to sleep, when I woke up, I would feel relatively well again, although I knew I would have diarrhoea to look forward to in the morning.

As it happened, I didn't need to wait any longer for the diarrhoea; the urge to 'go' swept over me all of a sudden a little after five thirty. I jumped up and ran to the toilet. Loki followed hot on my heels. He leaped into my lap just as the world fell out of my back-side and I hugged him close to me. Silent tears ran down my face and dripped off the end of my nose onto Loki's fur, darkening his beautiful orange to deep, rusty brown.

Now this is very strange indeed. Those few tears seemed to act as a kind of release valve because, as I sat there weeping whilst evil-smelling diarrhoea flowed from me, I began to feel slightly less sick. Loki may have helped, although I cannot be certain. I could hear Peter in the kitchen making a hot drink and suddenly, I wanted to drink a cup of tea.

When I emerged from the toilet with Loki running at my feet, Peter had made a hot cup of tea which I managed to drink most of. I also managed to smoke a cigarette – something I'd not been able to do for hours. Although nicotine is a stimulant, this did seem to calm me somewhat.

With Peter's help, I settled back into the semi-reclined position I'd been in before going to the toilet and actually began to watch Stargate with something close to attention. Peter moved over to the other settee but amazingly, he did not go to sleep. He spoke to me now and then, commenting on the storyline and asking how I felt. Although watching Stargate and enjoying it, I could feel myself drifting off to sleep. I mumbled replies which made little sense. Peter encouraged me to have some more Valium which I did, letting the pill dissolve under my tongue.

I only slept for an hour or so. I woke up because my chest hurt. Assuming it was the position I'd managed to get myself into, I snuggled further down onto the settee, pulled the cover over my shoulders and tried to go back to sleep. The chest pain got worse. I took a deep breath inwards – this made no difference to the pain at all. I sat up again. This made no difference either. Peter was fast asleep on the other settee. I couldn't bring myself to wake him up.

The birds were busy on the tree outside the lounge window which is a feeding station. There were dozens of sparrows and starlings, flapping and bickering as they pecked at the fat blocks, seeds and nuts hanging in the branches. I watched them intently, smiling now and again as their antics amused me. The pain in my chest remained at a constant level. In the back of my mind, I wondered where my GTN spray might be. I hadn't used it in a few weeks and had no idea where I'd put it. This must be some kind of angina attack.

After watching the birds for perhaps an hour, I lifted my handbag onto my lap and began to go through all the multitude of pockets. Sure enough, right at the bottom of the smallest section, there was the GTN. I lifted the small aerosol out and studied it for a while. I knew it would not make me feel sick but I already had a bit of a headache and I greatly feared it would make the headache worse which would cause me to feel sick again. I could hear my heart thundering in my ears; it was too fast. I gave in and sprayed the GTN under my tongue. I then looked for the Valium and took another half tablet. That was at around eight in the morning. I remember nothing after that.

When I awoke, just after noon, Peter was still fast asleep and Damon had just walked through the living room. He greeted me and asked me how I felt. I said I didn't feel too bad considering I'd had virtually no sleep. Damon asked why I'd not slept and I told him I was feeling sick and panicking all night. He remarked that it was a good thing I didn't have to take the chemo drugs over the weekend and hoped that I would feel better. I agreed fervently, even as the nausea began gnawing in my guts.

Now, either I had been thoroughly poisoned by just four doses of Capecitabine or Psyche-Imp was having a field day. I'll never know the answer to that. What I do know is, during the day, my nausea grew to immense proportions. I found drinking even a cup of tea or a sip of water almost impossible. In fact, throughout the day, Damon and Peter made cup after cup of tea and cup after cup was thrown away so that they could make the next one; I never took more than a couple of sips. The very thought of food made my guts churn painfully and nauseatingly. My mood was low, fear was higher than it had been for several days and I could not relax in the least.

With hindsight, I think I should have dosed myself up with Valium, but at the time, all I could focus on was the nausea ... and the constant running to the toilet. I didn't start off with diarrhoea, just several trips to the toilet. By mid afternoon, the panic had built to such immense proportions that I had constant diarrhoea to add to my feelings of sickness and misery and I still didn't or wouldn't take any Loperamide. I also began to ache from head to toe. Also with hindsight, this must have been due to the tension of panic (and still happens to me all the time), but then I didn't recognise it at all. And that, dear reader, was also Psyche-Imp's doing I am perfectly certain. The little blue bastard was having the time of his life!

When my chest began to hurt in the evening, I took a spray of GTN without saying anything to anybody. In fact, I was convinced I would die and I thought I was being heroic in not frightening anyone by articulating the thought – or should I say, fear. Now I look back, perhaps it would have been better if I had said something. At the very least, I may have gotten some reassurance from Peter or Uther or both of them!

Once again, Peter stayed with me over the night. We sat until very late watching all manner of rubbish on the television – none of which I could fully focus on because all I could think about was the fact that I felt sick and might vomit. Damn this phobia! And damn Psyche-Imp to hell too because it is his fault that the phobia has become so enormous.

By three in the morning, Peter was desperately trying to stay awake and failing miserably. In fact, he fell asleep whilst speaking to me – mid-sentence. For a few moments I waited for him to finish what he was saying, then I looked closely at him; he was fast asleep – sitting upright, his mouth hanging half open. As I bent over him, he gave an unexpected snort and turned toward the back of the settee. I jumped! Ever so briefly, the humour of the situation touched me and I grinned to myself. Then, Psyche-Imp kicked me in the guts and I had to run to the toilet – where I produced more foul-smelling diarrhoea and immediately, the nausea (which had sunk to a lowish level) returned big time. I actually retched.

I sat on the toilet, clutching Loki tightly and with my eyes watering with the effort of retching. I was about to vomit and it would go all over the floor because I couldn't get off the toilet. I knew I couldn't move anyway, so my fate was sealed. Loki purred and leaned even closer. I stroked his head absently as I concentrated all my efforts on not vomiting. Psyche-Imp leapt from the toilet tissue holder and kicked me in the throat; I swallowed hard. He did it again and then, having failed to make me puke, jumped onto my shoulder when he began pounding me on the back with his little blue fists.

I shut my eyes and began to hum the theme tune to Pirates of the Caribbean. Loki purred louder; the diarrhoea began to lessen and at the same time, the intense nausea eased slightly. I managed to get myself out of the toilet and back to the lounge, but I took a large plastic basin from the kitchen and placed it beside the settee – just in case.

Once back in the lounge, I scrolled through the television channels, found nothing which would engage me and so, once again resorted to Pirates of the Caribbean and Captain Jack. I recall thinking how strange it was that a children's film about pirates should so engage me, no matter that I watched it every single night. I popped an Extra Strong Mint into my mouth and tried to settle down.

Laying flat did not help at all; I got instant heartburn. It was then that I remembered I had forgotten to take my anti-heartburn medicine that day. Up I got again and went out to the kitchen to fix it. It is only about fifteen millilitres of water with a pill dissolved into it, but even that small amount was difficult to swallow, but I did manage it. I went back to the lounge and tried again to settle down.

The rest of the small hours of the night passed in various forms of torture. Every time the nausea subsided and I began to doze off to sleep, so a hot flush instantly woke me and I had to throw the covers off. As I cooled down, I became cold and either needed the toilet or began to feel sick again. I felt absolute despair; by seven thirty in the morning, I decided I would probably be better off not taking any treatment at all and allowing myself to simply die horribly. With that thought, Psyche-Imp grinned widely and curled up in a little ball on top of the cat. He instantly fell asleep; so did I.

When I awoke some four hours later, my first awareness was the fact that I felt sick – again. I reached for the anti-emetic pills, even before my eyes were properly open. On auto-pilot, I stuck one under my tongue and got up to go to the toilet. Peter was still sleeping.

Once my toilet activities were finished, I went into the kitchen, still working automatically, and made two cups of tea – one for Peter. When I entered the lounge carrying the cups, he was sitting up and yawning widely. He apologised as he thought he'd fallen asleep and hadn't meant to do so. I grinned, despite the nausea and told him how he'd passed out, mid-sentence and that it had made me smile.

I remembered to take the anti-heartburn medicine and I did drink the cup of tea I'd made. The anti-emetic appeared to be working. I even lit a cigarette as I regaled Peter with my fruitless efforts at getting off to sleep. I then went out to the kitchen and made myself a slice of toast which I ate as I also told Peter I had decided, during the night, to quit treatment and not to bother doing anything about this vile cancer. He shook his head sadly.

It is my belief that Psyche-Imp was still asleep at that point. Toast finished, I lit another cigarette and drained my tea cup. It must have been just then that the little swine woke up because Peter began to describe what would be likely to happen to me if I did indeed quit treatment: the cancer would spread; I'd not only feel sick, I'd be sick and more and more frequently as it progressed. It would move at the very least to my liver and lungs and I would die a horrible, painful and filthy death. Psyche-Imp kicked me in the stomach; I began to feel very sick indeed and bitterly regretted the toast and tea I'd just consumed.

Peter noticed how my demeanour had changed and he asked if I felt all right. I told him I thought I would vomit very shortly just as my body began its usual shaking and quivering. He moved to sit beside me, advised me to take another anti-emetic and rubbed at my back. This time, as he spoke, he didn't mention the cancer or the treatment at all. He asked me a lot of questions about what we'd watched the evening before on the television. Generally, I find it hard to talk when I feel so sick, but gradually, my one-word replies became two words and then three. Finally, Peter had managed to engage me so that my focus was no longer on feeling sick. I took another anti-emetic anyway and begged him to keep talking – which he did.

The cold I'd caught just a few days before had begun to make my nose run more than ever and to cause me to cough. Coughing is clearly not good if one is feeling nauseous. Although the panic had largely receded, even despite Psyche-Imp's efforts, every time I had a coughing fit, it came back with a vengeance. Peter was extremely hard pressed to keep me engaged at all, but he kept trying.

Damon and Uther put their two pennies worth in as well whenever they entered the room. Damon is very good at engaging me. Sometimes he talks absolute rubbish and is very funny with it; at other times, he speaks of particle physics or strange quantum ideas he's had (he's actually incredibly clever). Generally, one method or the other will work and I soon become fascinated or helpless with laughter. He used both techniques on that Sunday afternoon.

I managed to eat a few Extra Strong Mints during the morning and also drank at least half a cup of tea on about four occasions. I also tricked myself into swallowing a fair bit of water by sipping tiny amounts from a bottle every now and then. By early Sunday evening, I'd had three anti-emetics and was beginning to feel a bit better. I believe I managed some more toast in the early evening. Later, Uther prepared a chicken breast in garlic butter for me and I ate about half of it with a little boiled white rice. At last, the poison was wearing off I thought to myself.

"Yes, but in the morning, you'll have to take some more!" Psyche-Imp's scratchy little voice rattled around my head. I shuddered as a brief wave of nausea swept over me.

Peter had taken a whole week off work in order that he could drive me to the cancer hospital every day. I sent a few texts during the evening, sounding out a few friends, to see who was available and when. No way did I want to have to stay at the hospital, even though it was the nicest hospital I'd ever attended.

Purely because he did not have to get up early for work in the morning, Peter was able to sit up very late – or all night if it proved necessary. The boys went to bed and we sat together watching all manner of bizarre things on the Discovery and History channels. I did not feel at all sick by about two in the morning, although I was becoming increasingly aware of a heavy and pressing pain in the centre of my chest. This did not stop me smoking you understand. I noted the pain and lit yet another cigarette. I'm really good at being utterly stupid.

In fact, I felt quite relaxed – or at least, more relaxed than I'd been for several days. I put the cigarette out and told Peter I would try to sleep. He moved over to the other settee and settled himself down. I also went to lie down, but the pain in my chest increased. Alarmed, I sat up again; it did not subside. Peter noticed and asked if I felt all right.

When I described the pain, Peter himself sat bolt upright and I noticed the look of concern on his face. He bombarded me with questions which, as I answered, gave away the fact that I'd had chest pains during the night and once or twice during the day as well, but nothing like as bad as this pain had become. Peter got out of his makeshift bed and came over to me. He told me to take the GTN spray at once, which I did. The pain lessened but did not go away altogether. Peter advised me to take another shot of the spray. I already had a bit of a headache from the first shot, but I did as he advised – and the pain vanished within a few minutes.

I'm afraid to say that Psyche-Imp got the better of me once again at that point. I hadn't noticed the little sod as I was listening to Peter and taking the spray. Now, he head-butted me repeatedly in the temples and when that failed to make me panic, he resorted to jumping up and down on my stomach and punching me in the throat. Before many minutes had passed, I not only needed the toilet again most urgently, but had begun to feel nausea again. I rushed to the toilet and the world exploded from my rear end. I actually clutched at Loki and asked the fat, ginger tabby how one person, who ate virtually nothing, could have so much shit in them. He blinked his orange eyes at me and purred louder. I'm pretty sure I flushed Psyche-Imp down the toilet because the panic left as abruptly as it had arrived.

I went back to the lounge and sat down. With encouragement from Peter, I managed to lie down again. He sat at the foot of the settee rubbing my feet, which were on his lap. I must have dozed off almost straight away because I recall no more than that.

In the morning, Peter was already awake when I surfaced. He'd made tea and after I'd taken my first anti-emetic and been to the toilet, I managed to drink it all and ask for another. Peter obliged but asked numerous questions, mainly focusing on whether or not I had chest pain. I thought about it and admitted I felt a bit like there was something heavy sitting on my chest. I had several coughing fits – one triggered by lighting the first cigarette of the day. The feeling in my chest got no better and no worse, but neither did it go away.

"You know, I don't think you should take any more of those chemo pills," Peter remarked as I spat out something green with about sixteen legs and five arseholes. And I think you've got a chest infection at the very least."

"Nah," I spluttered, between bouts of choking, "It's just the fags. Anyway, I've got to take the damned poison or I'll die. You said so yesterday."

Peter agreed that he had said as much but that had been before he knew I was suffering chest pains. I drank another cup of tea and had some water too and listened to Peter telling me that he thought I should perhaps simply wait until I could see someone at the cancer hospital before I took any more.

It was only then that I became aware of the fact that I didn't feel at all sick. Not in the least. This was the first time the anti-emetic pill had worked as it had used to do before treatment began. My heart sank as I realised I was about to take poison again and that the feeling of wellbeing would not last much longer. I put some bread in the toaster and ran for the toilet.

As I ate the two pieces of toast – and enjoyed them too – Peter reiterated his feeling that I should take no more of the chemo medicine until I'd consulted with someone at the cancer hospital. I considered this as I munched through the toast. I really didn't want to take any more poison. In fact, I'd never *wanted* to take the damnable stuff in the first place! And yet, as I considered not taking the drug, despite all my ranting and railing of the previous night, I began to get anxious and worried that I would possibly drop dead during the radiotherapy treatment or whilst at home if I stopped taking the Capecitabine. I discussed my fears and anxieties with Peter and he advised that if the hospital said I should continue with the drug, I could resume taking it when I got home after treatment that day.

This seemed so reasonable I could find no objection which made any sense. Even so, probably due to

Psyche-Imp and his machinations, I decided to take just one Capecitabine that morning instead of the three I'd been told to take. I finished the tea and toast and went to mix the foul poison into some water.

Within about twenty minutes of taking the drug, once again, nausea grew rapidly. And once again, I was thrown into utter panic. I shook and quaked; I couldn't move from the settee for several minutes and I nearly had a very unpleasant and embarrassing toilet accident into the bargain.

I spent the rest of the morning until it was time to leave for the treatment centre, trotting backwards and forwards to and from the toilet and fighting with nausea and panic and completely failing to take the drug which would control the diarrhoea. I only managed to drink a little water in tiny sips from the bottle. I could not face a cup of tea and even smoked a lot less than usual. This was partly due to the coughing fits I kept having; every one of those caused a panic attack and one or two nearly made me retch, especially the ones which produced the vile, green lumps of phlegm.

Peter thought I should make an appointment to see the doctor and he said so on several occasions.

"Not a sniff," I replied. "They don't care about me. Anyway, they'll say it's just a cold and refuse to give me anything. Anyhow, by the time we get back from St. Asaph the surgery is closed and there is no chance of me getting over there any morning – I can't keep off the toilet for long enough!"

Peter shook his head and told me he still thought I should see the doctor if I possibly could. He even offered to telephone them for me and ask for a home visit or a prescription to be given over the phone. I refused. Why? I have no idea. Now, I look back and think how foolish I was; however at the time, I felt justified in my decisions.

We travelled to the cancer centre leaving just a little later than planned because of my need to rush to the toilet half a dozen times as soon as we should leave. I took some Imodium in the end but, as we travelled, I did not feel at all confident that it would work. In fact, as we sped along the busy A55, I looked at every possible place where we may be able to stop if necessary.

I did manage to keep my bowel under control for that journey, although I also had cause to rush to the toilet as soon as we arrived. I almost ran down to the radiotherapy suite, aware that I was late. No-one appeared to either notice or mind. We had barely sat down when I was called through to Ffynnon for treatment.

I explained to Claire and her colleague that I had diarrhoea and once again, she thoughtfully placed an inco-sheet on the glass table before I spread myself out on it. I had quite a coughing fit before lying down, but, once I'd spat out the lump of green 'alien matter' I was able to breathe fairly easily. Treatment was as quick as ever.

When it finished and as I got down and put my boots on, Claire asked if I'd enjoyed my weekend. I told her I had not been able to because it had been spent miserably between sitting on the toilet and panicking madly fearing I would vomit; further, that I'd been unable to eat anything much at all or even drink a cup of tea. She gave me a sympathetic look and advised me to go to find Jill from the Cape Clinic. I said I had every intention of doing so. I can't remember now whether or not I told her about the chest pains I'd been having.

Peter and I made our way to the reception desk in order that I could claim back my travelling expenses. As we approached Eileen on the desk, I noticed Jill standing talking to someone. I pointed her out to Peter and asked him to see if he could speak to her whilst I claimed the expenses. Eileen ushered me into her little side room and Peter moved toward Jill.

When I came out of the room, Peter and Jill were waiting for me. Jill asked me about the pains in my chest and had me describe them to her. She then asked Peter and me to wait whilst she went to find an oncologist. The hospital cafe was adjacent to where we were standing, so we went there. Peter brought a cup of tea each and we sat down on some very fetching emerald green chairs of unusual design. I remarked on them and how comfortable they were.

Trying to keep myself distracted from the nausea still gnawing in my guts, I told Peter the chairs would look nice in my lounge and we wondered, between us, where they had been purchased from – not to mention whether the hospital would notice if we slipped a couple into the car on our way out! I actually managed a chuckle at that prospect, even though I still felt very sick.

I managed to drink the tea and then, when Jill had not returned after a further ten minutes waiting, I told Peter I would step outside for a cigarette. He nodded and told me he would wait for Jill to come back. I hurried outside, completely missing the fact that my nausea had subsided to a great degree.

A lady who was clearly wearing a wig was standing outside smoking. With her was a large gentleman who made jokes as she smoked. I lit up and to my surprise, the man spoke to me. He asked me what car I was driving. I told him I wasn't driving myself but had come in a Vauxhall Vectra. He laughed heartily and told me, if I was quick, I could probably cram a couple of the cafe chairs into it without problem! The three of us laughed and that broke the ice so we began to converse.

I learned the lady was being treated for terminal lung cancer. Amazed that she would still be smoking even despite having such an awful disease, my first doubts began to creep in. "You're still smoking, you stupid woman," whispered Psyche-Imp. I tried to ignore him, but as the lady detailed her fits of coughing which lasted all night and explained this was the second set of treatments she'd had for the disease, I couldn't help but wonder if the rest of the human race was as mad as we clearly both were.

The lady went on to tell me that her sister had died from lung cancer just a few years before and added that she'd been blamed for causing it by smoking – even though her sister lived in Ireland and had never smoked! We laughed at the stupidity of the medics. Everything is blamed on smoking these days we agreed. I told her I had bowel cancer and this too was apparently caused by my cigarette habits. Both the lady and her companion thought it extremely unlikely. In fact, the man asked whether I usually ate the cigarettes or stuffed them up my arse rather than smoke them!

We were still chatting when Peter and Jill came out of the hospital and approached us. Jill quickly told me she had spoken with the oncologist and he had decided that

I should stop taking the Capecitabine immediately and bring the drugs back to the hospital with me the next day. I asked her (I think) if my radiotherapy would be less successful because I was no longer taking the chemotherapy. She backed away from the question and told me to speak to the oncologist tomorrow after I'd had my treatment.

"There. It's official now," whispered Psyche-Imp. "The hospital have told you that you don't have to take the poison after all. So it doesn't matter what Uther or anyone else says, you're in the clear." I repeated this to Peter as Jill hurried back inside. She hadn't reproached me for smoking anyway.

I felt much lighter and more well than I had done in many days as we walked back to the car after saying goodbye to the lady and her companion. In fact, I chatted animatedly all the way home, so relieved did I feel.

Later that day, I actually 'celebrated' by having something decent to eat and I enjoyed it too – although shortly afterwards I felt sick again, a matter easily resolved by taking an extra anti-emetic pill.

Uther was not at all happy to hear that I would no longer be taking the chemotherapy drugs. He shook his head whilst telling me I was being foolish and asking how on earth I expected to get better if I didn't take the drugs. I retorted that if I died of heart failure due to taking the damned drugs I would be even less likely to get better.

Peter rubbed the small of my back and my feet that evening and I think I fell asleep before about two in the morning – a lot earlier than I'd been asleep in the preceding days. This must have been quite a novelty for Peter, who had been awake with me as much as he could manage for so many weeks.

When I awoke in the morning, I actually felt quite well in myself. As always, I took the anti-emetic before I properly sat up or did anything else. Peter made a cup of tea whilst I went to the toilet. To my surprise, I did not have diarrhoea at all – the 'doings' were as close to normal as I'd seen in many weeks. I took the anti-heartburn medication and quickly followed it with one slice of toast. I cannot tell you, dear reader, how liberated I felt in my mind by not having to take the dreadful poison.

Unfortunately, things went downhill a bit after my toast. I had need to rush to the toilet some nine or ten times before it was time to leave for St. Asaph. I gave in to the need for medication and took some Imodium about half an hour before we left. Everything was under control by the time we set out and I passed the most comfortable journey yet.

Just after my treatment, Claire told me that I had to see one of the oncologists – a Doctor Raavi. Apparently, I should go down the corridor and wait in the radiotherapy reception area. She asked if I'd brought the chemotherapy drugs back with me. I said I had and also that I was mightily relieved to not have to take them.

I sat in the waiting area with Peter and watched other people; some were clearly patients and not at all well. Most everyone else though, looked perfectly normal and apparently healthy. Yet I knew that radiotherapy was almost always used for cancer and this was the cancer treatment centre. I think, whilst waiting for that meeting, another of my cancer misconceptions was shattered. I'd always thought of people with cancer as being deathly ill and unable to do anything for themselves – hence I couldn't possibly have the disease myself because I was so clearly not 'nearly dead'. In that waiting area I saw people laughing, joking together, walking and moving about with ease. In fact, I only saw one patient who was obviously on their last legs – an elderly lady wheeled through the waiting area in a bed. I tried not to stare but I got enough of a look to be able to see that the lady was clearly very old indeed, although her eyes were open and looked bright with interest and intelligence. It made me shudder, although I couldn't say why.

Doctor Raavi called us into a small consulting room. A young nurse came in with us and sat on a chair by the door. The doctor asked me what had happened when I took Capecitabine. I told him I'd been assured I would neither feel nor be sick but that I'd felt so incredibly nauseous I couldn't eat, drink or sleep. I added that I started getting chest pains after just two days of taking the tablets and in fact, during the break of treatment at the weekend.

The doctor was attentive and charming and to give him all the credit he deserves, he asked a great many questions; whether I'd had heart problems before; how I'd treated the problems over the weekend; had the GTN spray relieved the pain or not and others. I told him also that I have a life-controlling phobia of vomiting and so the feelings of nausea had caused me to panic almost constantly and that I'd thought at first this was the cause of the chest pains.

Doctor Raavi shook his head and explained that even sustained panic would be unlikely to cause such persistent chest pain that required two shots of GTN spray. He went on to say that generally, patients do not complain much about the side-effects of medications. Apparently I was an unusual case. In the doctor's experience, people doggedly continued to take the drugs purely and simply because 'the doctors have said they will make me better' and tried to get on with life, side-effects and all. In the case of chest pains, some of those would go on to have a heart attack – and a few of those would die!

Appalled, I fell silent. Peter asked a lot of questions but I was too busy suffering building panic to pay very much attention. Psyche-Imp jumped up and down on my tummy, making me feel the urgent need to go to the toilet; I crossed my legs and willed the sensation to go away – it didn't. For some reason, and most unusually, I thought (consciously thought) it would not matter if I had an accident. After all, I was wearing an incontinence pad and I was in a hospital. I began to relax a little and the sensation faded. Psyche-Imp was disgusted.

When I handed the box of chemotherapy drugs over to Doctor Raavi, the oncologist placed them on the back of his desk; Psyche-Imp sat on the packet and pulled faces at me, the nurse and the doctor. They didn't notice of course – why would they? The little blue bastard was a figment of my imagination.

I managed to rouse myself enough to ask the doctor if I now had no hope of a cure because I could not take the drug – to which he thought I must be 'super-sensitive'. I am over sensitive to a great many drugs (most of which tend to cause extreme nausea and vomiting) so I was not particularly surprised. A little part of me wondered if Psyche-Imp (or my subconscious mind) had anything to do with the oversensitivity.

Doctor Raavi considered me with his head tilted to one side before replying, very honestly, that he could not answer my question because, to put matters simply, he just didn't know. I listened as he went on to say that all the medics had were statistics which showed that people tended to survive for five years or more if they took both chemo and radiotherapy and then had an operation to cut the cancer out followed by more chemotherapy. Of course, the doctor added, there were other people who simply took radiotherapy alone, or had an operation or only had chemotherapy who also survived five years or more – just as there were some people who also had the whole lot and died anyway.

Psyche-Imp, who had been poking about on the doctor's desk whilst we talked, leaped across the room and handed on my shoulder. He took my ear in his clawed left hand and pulled it before whispering, in his scratchy little voice, "Five years is hardly worth any of it. You should walk away now and go home. Forget it all; you're going to die no matter what you do. By the way, you feel sick, don't you?"

I did get a sudden twinge of nausea but I rallied, recognising it as panic immediately. I swallowed hard. "So, I've still got a chance then, if I continue with the radiotherapy and have the operation?"

Doctor Raavi nodded. He patted the pack of drugs and told me to continue with the radiotherapy but to ensure I reported any further side-effects to the radiographers. I would no longer need to have weekly blood tests or attend at the Cape Clinic once a week.

I answered this with a coughing fit. Doctor Raavi waited until I'd caught my breath before advising me to see my own GP about my cough. I assured him it was only the cigarettes I smoked causing the problem, but he told me to see my GP anyway. Then he stood up and shook my hand and then Peter's. The consultation was over.

As Peter and I left, I became aware once again that I needed the toilet. I hurried to find one leaving Peter waiting in the radiotherapy reception area. What I had feared would be diarrhoea turned out to be nothing more than a very small amount of normal 'poo' and a great deal of wind. My step was much lighter as I rejoined Peter; I'm pretty sure I left Psyche-Imp back in the doctor's office – he certainly wasn't in much evidence as we travelled home.

Now, had I been a person with a normal amount of intelligence, I would have gone home and tried to get on with as normal a life as possible – except for the daily travelling for treatment. Looking back on things now, I can only think how badly I wasted that time. The fact is, I did nothing at all. No housework or chores, no dog walking, no exercise, hardly any shopping, no laughing or playing either. What a terrible waste! In fact, all I did was to sit or lie down on the settee, panic and feel sorry for myself. Just very rarely I managed to stir myself and take a brief trip up the road to the shop, but that's it.

I didn't even make an appointment to see the GP as Doctor Raavi had recommended. I ate very little, drank even less than my usual 'not enough', smoked far too much and mainly simply coughed my heart up, day and night – oh yeah, and I felt sorry for myself about it too. I did a lot of that.

Of course, due to Psyche-Imp (who, you must remember, I wasn't actually aware was there at the time) I panicked a great deal as well. I also listened to all the mindless, spiteful drivel Psyche-Imp spouted at me. He convinced me there was no point in trying to see the GP – after all, I would be dismissed as my cough being 'all in my mind' or 'anxiety' would I not? I was unable to sleep properly because the deep, hacking cough woke me whenever I did actually manage to get off to asleep. I still convinced myself – or Psyche-Imp convinced me – that I did not need to see the doctor at all and only had a bad smoker's cough even though I was regularly coughing up great, thick lumps of green and sometimes blood-streaked phlegm! Peter became increasingly concerned.

It was Peter who drove me to the cancer treatment centre every day that week. In fact, the poor man spent most of his waking hours in my miserable company trying to keep me from panicking wildly if the coughing caused me to retch; attempting to convince me to eat something more than one slice of toast a day; rubbing the small of my back for hour upon hour. The few hours the man spent sleeping were also in my company; often he slept the sleep of the utterly exhausted and I was still wakeful in varying states of panic and anxiety.

The cough continued relentlessly – and I continued, doggedly, to smoke cigarettes (which actually says a great deal about the utter stupidity of an apparently intelligent human being). By the weekend after Peter had spent the week playing nurse-maid to me and taking me to the cancer centre every day, I was bemoaning my fate with the awful cough which often caused me to retch and panic uncontrollably. To his credit, at no time did Peter suggest that I stop smoking;

I knew already that I should and would probably have bitten his well-meaning head off anyway, had he done so. What he did suggest was that I visit the GP – as did the radiographers at the cancer centre.

I'm afraid I cannot say why I did not visit the GP – other than it may have been that I thought I would end up seeing the patronising doctor or one of the others I was convinced did not like me. In all truth, I do not know why I held out and insisted I could not see the doctor. No doubt Psyche-Imp had a lot more to do with things than I like to admit. The little blue bastard sat on my head at night and laughed like a drain when I sat up coughing my heart up. It was probably him kicking me in the throat in the first place which caused the coughing fits anyway.

I took to drinking an awful lot of water, one sip at a time. I managed a couple of bottles a day. This may not seem like a lot to anyone reading this, but to me, it was a very great deal of water considering I only used to drink about eight cups of tea a day and nothing else.

When I wasn't travelling to or from the cancer centre or at the cancer centre itself, I was sitting on the settee with my legs and feet curled beneath me, usually holding my ribs tightly as I coughed and coughed and coughed. Psyche-Imp told me I had lung cancer – which I completely believed; maybe this way why I would not go to the doctor. I did nothing at all with my time between treatments. I barely read; I certainly didn't type or write; I hardly sat at the computer at all. I'd put my life well and truly on 'hold' and yet I was, in many ways, still in complete denial. Despite the radiotherapy and the possibility of my diarrhoea becoming much worse, my bowel symptoms had eased considerably – although admittedly, I used a lot of

Imodium to control symptoms I had previously simply put up with.

Weeks two, three, four and five saw me travelling with several different people. Peter's brother, Andrew – a driving instructor – drove me on two occasions. Lesley also drove me a couple of times as did another friend, Fiona and her mum, Lol came along for the ride. I even drove myself three or four times with Andrew, Lesley, Uther or Peter to sit in the car with me.

Toward the end of the third week, I felt like an old hand at radiotherapy and all traces of treatment anxiety had left me. I think this was more likely to be due to Psyche-Imp being distracted by all the lovely, shiny machinery and computers than anything else. The little git was not in evidence at all most days at the centre.

On the Wednesday of the third week of treatment, I had settled myself down on the glass couch and Ffynnon had done a couple of movements and the whirring and buzzing which showed the machine was busy working. I felt an unmistakeable tickle in my throat; I tried to take a slow breath in and hold it in order to remain still until the end of the treatment. This time though, Psyche-Imp must have crept into the room and kicked me hard in the throat. I coughed. I felt my stomach press into the glass and I knew my hips had moved. Worse than that, I couldn't get a breath in at all. I waved my hand above my head whilst I spluttered and choked in my prone position and sincerely hoping that Claire and her colleague could indeed see me as they had said.

I felt intense relief as the lights came up and I heard Claire's voice, reassuring me that they were there. I continued to splutter and choke, and then I retched loudly. Still prone, coughing was intensely painful in my ribs and stomach; I felt one of my lower abdominal muscles tug as I retched. Psyche-Imp was having a wonderful time. He danced about on my back and his crackly, spiteful little voice insisted I would vomit all over Ffynnon's couch. I began to panic; I really could not breathe at all.

Fortunately, as Claire laid a hand on the small of my back and told me they were going to move the couch so that I could sit up, Psyche-Imp fell off. I would hope the little swine got crushed in the gears of the couch as it moved. I managed to gasp out, "Water!"

My own water bottle was passed to me as I sat up and saw Claire and two of her colleagues anxiously gathered around me. Claire held out a tissue and I noted she had one of the horrible little grey bowls they use for vomit. Still I choked, even despite the water which I kept sipping at.

Just when I was giving in and certain I would vomit and disgrace myself by panicking and going crazy, I coughed up an enormous lump of blood-streaked phlegm. I tried to be discreet but I know Claire and her colleagues saw it. Claire held the bowl out for me to put the foul tissue in and handed me a fresh tissue. That should have ended the coughing fit but it didn't. I sat there, my legs dangling over the edge of the glass couch, spluttering and choking, my eyes watering and also, other areas I'd rather not mention, leaking under the pressure of the coughing. Fortunately, I'd been placed on an inco-sheet that day!

When I finally coughed up another great blood-streaked lump, had a long drink of water from my bottle and taken several deep breaths, Claire patted me on the shoulder and told me they would resume the treatment. The three women changed the inco-sheet I'd made wet and re-settled me into the prone position. Ffynnon began where it had left off and, in no time at all, it seemed, the treatment was finished.

When the lights came back on and Claire came back into the room, I apologised for the scene I'd made. Claire very kindly reassured me that coughing was always something which caused patients to move involuntarily and that they had dealt with far, far worse than my small coughing fit. She also added that I should not worry and that I really should go to see my doctor. Claire thought I had a chest infection and would need antibiotics to see the cough off. I assured her it was probably only due to my incessant smoking, but she insisted I see the doctor anyway.

When I got home that day, I went rummaging in the medicine cupboard to see what I could find. I had absolutely no intention of seeing the doctor if I could possibly avoid it. To my delighted relief, I found an old box of penicillin. I checked the date code on it; still good for a couple of months. These had not been my pills (I thought I was allergic to penicillin anyway) but had belonged to Peter when he and I were a couple and had lived together several years before. He is supposed to take penicillin daily because he has no spleen.

I rushed to the computer to check online what symptoms I should look for if I was allergic to penicillin and decided that, should I develop a rash, I would stop taking them. I am now completely certain that this was all Psyche-Imp's doing. After all, it was total madness! Rather than see the GP and ask for an antibiotic and mention that the cancer centre thought I needed one, I would take tablets not prescribed for me and something to which I thought I was allergic to boot!

Unable to swallow a pill the size of a paracetamol, I used my pill-crusher to reduce the tablets to powder which I then tipped onto a teaspoon and swallowed with a mouthful of water. Penicillin tastes like mould smells (for anyone who wanted to know)!

When Peter arrived that evening, I showed him the tablets, told him I was taking them and would continue to do so no matter what he said – since he clearly did not intend to use them himself. He did advise me not to take the tablets. He also told me to make a doctor appointment and get a 'proper' antibiotic. When I flatly refused and got rather verbally abusive into the bargain, Peter sighed and told me, "Very well. If you insist. Take two tablets at a time and three times a day – that's every eight hours."

I did just that; every eight hours I took the penicillin along with all the other tablets I took every day – anti-emetics, anti-diarrhoea medicine, anti-heartburn medicine, beta blockers, vitamins and Valium when panicking. Psyche-Imp sulked when I didn't come out in a blotchy rash; I was pleased because I could see an improvement within forty-eight hours. I told the radiographers at the cancer centre I was 'on antibiotics' but I neglected to tell them how that had occurred!

There really is little else to say about the radiotherapy treatment. I made it to the cancer centre every day without suffering the embarrassment and humiliation of shitting my pants and my cough began to improve – although it didn't go away entirely.

I purchased a 'Thank-you' card to give to Claire and her colleagues on the last day of treatment, which was a Tuesday. I felt like I should give them all a million pounds and a medal each – were I the millionaire that (I feel) I should be, I could have done that. As it was, a simple card had to be enough.

It felt very strange leaving the centre for the last time. I'd briefly seen Doctor Raavi, who had informed me that I would get several weeks of 'rest' and time for the side-effects to subside, and then I would be scheduled for surgery. Psyche-Imp jumped up and down on an empty chair, gesticulating and pulling faces; I ignored him. In my mind, this was just fine. I could run away home and forget all about having cancer for another few weeks. Actually, if I am totally truthful, I could forget all about having cancer at all. I'm very good at denial and hiding within my own head – despite Psyche-Imp and his antics.

Actually, another part of my mind was relentlessly counting down to D-Day – and as yet I had no date to put on that ambiguous count. What I should have done, of course, was to fill every waking moment with as much fun and activity as I possibly could. Did I do that? Absolutely not! I went back to my usual depressing 'sit-on-the-settee', 'sleep-on-the-settee', 'do-nothing-at-all'. This, with hindsight, was probably the biggest mistake ever. That's another thing I'm really good at – looking back and wishing I'd done things differently or better.

As a matter of fact, the first thing which happened after treatment ended – in fact, the very same day treatment ended – was that my cough got worse. I'd finished all the antibiotics I'd helped myself to and it hadn't gone away after all. Psyche-Imp convinced me (during one particularly nasty coughing and choking fit) that I'd at least got lung cancer, if not cancer all over. I had a massive panic attack and it was all Peter could do to reach past the little blue git and talk some sense into me. I ate some Valium and focused all my attention on Peter as he advised me to make an appointment to see the doctor.

Fortunately, the surgery opposite my home had a free appointment the very next afternoon. I had passed caring which doctor I saw, although I really dreaded that it may be the patronising doctor. I sat in the waiting room, coughing my heart into a handful of tissues and trying not to retch. Psyche-Imp slithered around on the counter, moving leaflets and peering with great interest at other people's prescriptions whilst I concentrated on not panicking and making a scene. I felt intense relief when one of the lady doctors opened the consulting room door and called me in.

As I entered the consulting room, I had an enormous coughing fit, which resulted in an evil looking, grey-green lump of phlegm being discharged into my handful of tissues. The doctor waited patiently until I'd cleared it and then smiled at me.

"Sorry about that," I began. "As you can see, I'm coughing my lungs up." I produced the empty pack of penicillin I'd taken and added, "Apparently, I'm not allergic to penicillin after all. I took these ... I ... er ... borrowed them from a friend (I'd removed the label) and although they helped at first, I'm still coughing my guts up."

The doctor inspected the packet whilst I began to cough again. She asked how long I'd been coughing and what colour the 'product' of the cough was. I told her – once

I'd caught my breath. She also asked what generally happened if I took penicillin. I had to reply that I'd no idea but that absolutely nothing untoward had happened to me whilst taking the ones I'd now finished. The doctor went on to explain that the ones I'd taken were not very strong and although they may have helped, would not be powerful enough to wipe out my cough. I nodded as I spluttered understanding. When she asked why I hadn't brought myself to the surgery sooner to ask for an antibiotic I felt rather embarrassed. It did seem incredibly stupid of me and I could think of no good answer. Instead, I shrugged and told her I thought it was only the fags causing the cough.

The doctor smiled. "But you don't usually cough your heart out day and night and you've always smoked, haven't you?" I went off into another paroxysm of spluttering and choking. When I'd finished that coughing fit, the doctor explained she'd give me some stronger penicillin but that I should let her know if it didn't work or if there was any kind of reaction. She then went on to speak about the cancer and the treatment I'd had so far. She told me she'd been appalled at the diagnosis and had feared I would not take the treatment because of my phobia. In my turn, I explained that I'd been unable to continue with the chemotherapy and had now convinced myself that any other treatment I had would be useless and that I wished I weren't such a big wuss.

The consultation took about twenty minutes, during which time the doctor was extremely supportive and very friendly and reassuring toward me. She thought I was incredibly brave, she said, in taking any of the treatment. I told her I was terrified of the proposed surgery, not least because of the general anaesthetic – in case it made me sick! In fact I also admitted utter denial and told the doctor I felt more well in myself than I had for many, many years so it seemed absurd to me that I'd got this awful thing inside me growing away and which would kill me if I didn't deal with it.

Psyche-Imp sat on my foot, miserably picking his nose and flicking the bogeys at the doctor. This, in his opinion, was not at all how things were supposed to go. I wasn't supposed to be aware of him for a start and neither was I supposed to be able to articulate my fears or admit being in denial of the disease. I certainly shouldn't even be considering the life-saving surgery.

I felt a lot better inside my head when I left the doctor. I collected the prescription and crossed the road back to my home – incidentally, leaving Psyche-Imp jumping up and down on the scales in the doctor's office.

This penicillin did not need to be crushed; it was in the form of capsules. I could empty the contents into a little water and swill it down my throat. I took one as soon as I got home. And then, I had something to eat.

The antibiotic had no detrimental side-effects at all. In fact, it began to work very quickly indeed because my cough lessened within the first twenty four hours. Fool that I am, I continued to smoke, although it had occurred to me that it would be a very good idea to stop before surgery at some point. Psyche-Imp sulked. Every time I had a positive thought or decided to do something, the little blue git kicked or punched me. If I didn't react, he wandered off to find something really annoying to do. With hindsight, I am sure he was responsible for blown light-bulbs, upset cat litter trays and a dozen other irritating little events.

Chapter Five: After Treatment and Pre-Surgery

The diarrhoea had almost completely disappeared. I had learned that it was most likely to occur in the mornings – but only if I woke up and found myself alone, also it happened within a few minutes of whoever may have been with me leaving. Lastly, whenever I began to give serious thought to the disease itself or to try and visualise the tumour, diarrhoea occurred. After several days of this, it suddenly dawned on me that most, if not all the diarrhoea *had* to be put down to anxiety. After all, generally, although I still went to the toilet a lot more than 'normal', I didn't have diarrhoea. One afternoon, when Lesley had come to chat and drink tea, I surreptitiously took half a Valium when Lesley mentioned she would have to be going shortly. It worked! Not only that, but I felt very calm in myself and was able to sit down at the computer and feel quite relaxed. Psyche-Imp was nowhere to be seen.

I had a visit from Isabel, the psychologist. I really like her very much and she is one of those very rare professionals who do not patronise in any way. She is also very good at listening. I told her how I was busy pretending it was all over but that, deep in my heart, I knew it had all yet to happen – and I was terrified. I also explained how I'd found a lot of the diarrhoea I suffered was clearly due to anxiety after all and how I managed to control it. In fact, after the first few days of taking half a Valium when these situations arose, I found all I needed to do was to place the packet close at hand; I didn't need to actually take any at all. Isabel thought this was a very good coping strategy and expressed admiration that I'd worked out all by myself how to control the anxiety attacks.

I found I could sleep a lot better too. I'd got into the habit of putting the recording of Pirates of the Caribbean on the television as soon as I thought I should like to go to sleep. I don't believe, once radiotherapy had ended, I ever saw or heard more than a few minutes-worth of the film. Certainly, I could recite the script up to about twenty minutes in! It began to worry me though. How would I cope in hospital if I could not go to sleep without Captain Jack Sparrow's dulcet tones soothing me?

Peter still stayed with me most nights. I have no idea how that man managed to sleep on a settee with the window wide open close by and get up early in the morning to go to work. Mostly, by the time Peter was getting up, I was dead to the world (and probably snoring).

I ended up having two courses of antibiotics and by the end of the second one, my cough had completely disappeared – except for the smoker's cough first thing in the morning where I had to shift a little clear mucus. It was such a relief not to be awake all night barking my lungs up and spitting out the foul green 'aliens'. Clearly, not only was I not allergic to penicillin after all, it had done the trick beautifully.

November arrived and I had set myself the task of writing this book during that month for the NaNoWriMo contest. It was ridiculously easy. I had no characters to control, no plot to invent or control – all I had to do was write. Since I type fast, I had fulfilled the required fifty thousand word count in the first five days! I felt inordinately pleased with myself, although I was mightily concerned that although the book is a factual account, some horrible little blue imp had appeared (Psyche-Imp). I continued to write and puzzled over this little mystery. Maybe there was a sane reason for my having inadvertently invented him.

I actually got my answer from Isabel on her second visit after radiotherapy finished. I chatted away, explained what the NaNoWriMo contest was all about and how I'd managed it twice before. When I told her I was writing about bowel cancer and its effects but I was very concerned because Psyche-Imp had simply appeared one day as I rattled my fingers across the keyboard, she actually laughed; and then she told me it was a classic case of 'externalising the problem'. Apparently, psychologists and psycho-analysts often use this technique and most particularly with fears, phobias or behavioural problems in children. I had, it seemed, externalised my own fears and phobias and made them into Psyche-Imp. I listened as Isabel explained how the technique worked and that I could do as many dreadful things as I could imagine to Psyche-Imp to make him go away and take all my fears and doubts along with him.

Just a few days later, when in Peter's car and aware of a panic attack sweeping in from nowhere, I brushed my left shoulder with my right hand and said aloud, "Sod off, you little bastard!" The window beside me was open and I had such a vivid mental picture of Psyche-Imp flying backwards out of the car window in a sitting position and landing on his bony back-side in Sainsbury's car park I roared with laughter. I think Peter must have thought I'd gone completely nuts, especially when I told him I could 'see' Psyche-Imp sitting on the tarmac, shaking his fist and that he was about to be run over by the car behind us!

Now, it seems to me that the main thing about any anthropomorphic personification is that you cannot actually 'kill' it. I mean, it's not actually 'alive' in the first place (even though Psyche-Imp felt very alive to me). However, I did enjoy myself immensely over a few days by torturing and taunting Psyche-Imp with ever more original ideas. I'm not generally a cruel person (I'm soppy about animals and anything too weak to defend itself), but I did some really terrible mental things to Psyche-Imp: I suspended him by his clawed toe over the gas ring so that his long, pointy nose shrivelled up and went black; I nailed his feet to the kitchen door whilst preparing myself an actual meal; I put him in the washing machine with the dark coloured clothes and imagined his little clawed hands scraping at the glass door as he turned round and round in the water – and many, many other small tortures.

Gradually, although I couldn't seem to get rid of him entirely or for longer than a day or two at most, he put in an appearance less and less. At the same time as this, I began to feel quite irritable and snappy. I now know this was due to the fact that I was actually facing my disease; it is normal to feel angry, sad, frightened, bereaved and a host of other things. At the time though, I could not explain to my sons or Peter – or even Lesley – why I would suddenly have dark moods and snap at people. It was very much like having Pre Menstrual Tension; I couldn't control it and if I tried, it got worse.

What I have not yet mentioned is that my sons and Peter do not see eye to eye most of the time. That's a colossal understatement. They resent each other immensely. Once I'd noticed how the boys disappeared to their rooms almost as soon as Peter arrived, I also began to notice other things. Peter made odd comments about things the boys should have done for me but clearly had not done. Sometimes, he added angry remarks to those observations – and I snapped right back in sudden defence of my boys. In their turn, the boys made snide remarks about Peter always being here and asked me what he actually did for me – nothing that they could see. I'm afraid I snapped back at them as well. Things were definitely not going well in the camp of Kat – and Psyche-Imp came back with a vengeance and expressed his delight by pissing in my tea, shitting on my dinner and jumping up and down on the TV remote so that the TV randomly changed channels usually just when I was watching something incredibly interesting.

About half-way through November, I had a telephone call one morning from Alison. She chatted pleasantly enough and she'd caught me in a good mood so I chatted back, telling her all my symptoms had subsided and that I felt very well in myself. And then, she told me the reason for her call was to book my operation. Psyche-Imp pricked up his pointy ears and turned from tormenting Loki to listen intently.

Alison explained that the ideal time for the operation was between six and eight weeks after radiotherapy had ceased, although, at a push, it could be as much as twelve weeks. She went on to mention Christmas and that my 'ideal' time would be in the week before Christmas itself. I swallowed hard. Psyche-Imp crept onto my lap, up my arm and onto my shoulder, in order that he could hear what Alison had to say as well. I barely noticed him; in fact, I'd forgotten all about him as I listened to the 'available' dates. I could have the twenty second of December if I wished. I would be in hospital for around five to seven days and so I could be home in time for the New Year. If I didn't wish to take this date, it could well be the end of January or even February before I could be fitted in to the schedule again – which in reality would be beyond the optimum time period.

My first thought (with added input from Psyche-Imp) was 'Bugger!' My second, third and fourth thoughts – which all followed rapidly one on top of the other were: I'm not having any operation; it's Uther's birthday on Christmas Eve; it's Damon's birthday on February the fifth – although not necessarily in that order.

I tried to stall Alison; I made objections to the operation in general for a start. And then, quite suddenly and unexpectedly, I became aware of Psyche-Imp whispering all this rubbish into my ear. I told Alison I would take the twenty second of December and that I detest Christmas anyway. I went on to say I was unhappy about having the planned operation and that I'd thought about it a lot. I felt I could not cope with an ileostomy due to the fact that the 'poo' leaks practically all the time and is in liquid form. Could I not have a permanent colostomy? I asked her.

Alison spent a good ten minutes telling me that the ileostomy was by far the better option and that it was only temporary. She reminded me that a colostomy was permanent and could never be reversed. I reminded her of my phobia of vomiting and the fact that post operative vomiting would be more than a little problem for me. If it happened, wild horses and a crowd of men bearing down on me with guns would not be able to get me back for a second surgery to reverse the 'temporary' ileostomy and so it would become permanent.

I must have been the bane of that poor woman's life. Everything she did to try to help me I balked at. I'd got an objection or some terrible fear or misconception about simply everything to do with hospitals. The telephone call lasted the best part of an hour. In the end, I agreed to visit with the surgeon, Mr. Billings again sometime before the operation to let him know that I wanted a permanent colostomy. Alison felt sure he would be appalled at the idea but be best placed to dissuade me.

When I put the phone down, my immediate reaction was diarrhoea – sudden and violent. I sat on toilet and cursed loudly. Loki, curled up on my lap as ever, turned his orange eyes on me and made a small, trilling sound in his throat. It sounded so much like a question that I stopped swearing and stroked his head. "Well, that's it, then, Loki. I've only got a few weeks left of any kind of normality. I can't believe I'm even thinking about having this surgery." Loki closed his eyes and purred.

Psyche-Imp grinned from one evil, pointy ear to the other. "You'll die, you know," he whispered. "Then they'll all be sorry they forced you to do it, won't they?" He actually said that and a lot worse. By the time I left the toilet, I had been utterly convinced that I would not only vomit, constantly and copiously but that I'd also, ultimately, die in horrible pain and filth.

I was once again, high maintenance over the next two to three days. I needed someone with me nearly all the time and I simply could not sleep at night at all. I'd spend hours, tossing and turning, trying to get off to sleep but being prevented by dreadful imaginings and images dancing round and round my brain. Even Captain Jack Sparrow could not over-ride these it seemed. Once I'd fallen asleep, I woke several times a night with no idea as to why I'd woken up. I would then start the whole business all over again; it was utterly exhausting.

Of course, now I realise it was all due to Psyche-Imp. I'd been caught off-guard again and the evil minded little swine was really making me pay. On the third morning after having had little or disturbed sleep, I actively spent some time visualising Psyche-Imp and pouring scorn and disgust at him. I then visualised him shrinking. This worked – a little. However, as soon as I stopped concentrating, back he came, as large as life and tormented me some more.

I realised I had about five to six weeks before I would need to go into hospital for the operation. I really wanted to spend that time well but, something else I realised was that I've actually forgotten how to spend time well. I've certainly forgotten how to be happy or how to enjoy myself. I wondered what I could do to remember such a basic thing. Surely, I hadn't always been flat and low?

For the first two to three weeks after treatment ended, Peter continued to stay here nearly every night, sleep poorly – or certainly not enough – and go off to work. He did go to his own home and sort out his own family matters and mostly, he also managed to continue with his music nights on a Friday. He also managed to persuade me to come out and watch him with his 'band' which was made up of the amateur musicians at music night.

The gig was local – in fact in the same place where the band played every Friday evening, just in the larger room. They call themselves Monterey Jack and the

Malcontents. Considering Monterey Jack is a type of cheese, even I, with my depleted sense of humour, saw the funny side of the name. They printed off tickets to be sold at five pounds each and declared all the proceeds would go toward the spinal unit at the Orthopaedic hospital in Gobowen.

I persuaded Lesley and her friend Vicky to come along too. Also Lesley's ex-partner, Steve decided to come along as well. I stuffed myself full of Imodium and determined that I would not only go out with my friends but would also enjoy myself.

I did enjoy myself too. I even got up at one stage to dance although I couldn't manage more than three minutes due to instantly getting chest pains and losing my breath. I chided myself for having been so inactive for such a long time. I hadn't even been walking the dogs so had got very badly out of condition.

I took the dogs out a couple of times in those first couple of weeks after treatment and even though I had to use my GTN spray each time, I thought perhaps I could increase my fitness level if I resumed daily dog-walking.

Although well intentioned, my days have always been governed by a time-line very different from the rest of society. Although I wanted to take the dogs, by the time I found myself ready to do so, it was almost dark or raining or both. It was late in the year after all. So that didn't happen. My fitness levels didn't increase at all.

I did begin to do a little more around the house, even though I had to keep constantly stopping to recover my breath. Even so, I still didn't do enough to increase my level of fitness. Every bit of activity caused my heart to pound too fast and I felt breathless and light headed.

On 13th October I answered the phone at around eleven in the morning and spoke to Rosemary, who was doing her very best to be brave as she described how her husband, Tom had become seriously unwell and the paramedics who attended thought it was a stroke and had admitted him to hospital. She phoned me to tell me before following in her own car. Shocked and appalled, I felt dreadful. More than anything, I thought I should be there to support Rose and hold her hand as she'd always done for me but instead, all I could do was worry about both her and Tom. I willed him to recover and called Rosemary frequently for updates.

At first, the news was quite good. After the initial two days, Tom had begun to recover but was struggling to sit, eat, drink or stand. His balance had gone. I largely forgot my own troubles whilst worrying about Tom and how Rosemary might be feeling.

I had developed yet another horrible cough at around this time and took myself off to the doctor to complain about it. Dr. Fox immediately prescribed an antibiotic because, she said, the radiotherapy treatment would have weakened my system and left me open to 'all kinds of nasties'. I collected the medicine and took some immediately.

Later that day (which was 26th October 2011), I took another call from Rosemary and she was weeping uncontrollably. This was so absolutely unlike my stoic friend I was appalled. At first I could barely understand what she was saying. Over and over she kept saying 'Tom' and I began to fear that perhaps he might have worsened or be close to death. I asked her if she wanted me to come. Suddenly calmed, in a small, childlike voice, she replied, "Yes, please!"

My sons and Peter were amazed that I would even consider going such a long way. Woking is around two hundred miles away from St. Martins and they all knew I only felt 'safe' sitting on the settee in my usual place. From not going anywhere at all, I was suddenly intending to drive myself to Woking.

Of course, I had only the vaguest idea of the route and I had never driven on a motorway before. Although she sounded really grateful, even Rosemary expressed her concerns on the telephone. I, in a complete departure from my normal, terrified self, shrugged my shoulders and insisted I would find my way there and it didn't have to be a big problem. Psyche-Imp clambered up my back and began frantically whispering objections into my ear. I brushed him away and got on with looking for stuff to take with me to Woking.

In the end, after much discussion and a very quick packing of a few essentials into a small rucksack, Peter drove me more than half way to Woking and we met Rosemary at a Service Area. After a quick coffee each, Peter left to drive to Coventry, where he would be teaching the next day and Rosemary drove us the rest of the way back to her home. She looked terrible. I listened as she told me that Tom had been expected to be discharged from the hospital that day but they had found he had unacceptably high blood pressure and something wrong with his heart. Rosemary was, understandably, terrified.

In all the thirty-five years I've known Rosemary, I've never seen a spot on her face. On that evening I noticed several spots on her chin. I commented about them as we travelled through the darkness. She nodded and complained she also had a mouth full of ulcers as well. She thought it was stress. By the time we got back to her home, I'd put two and two together and realised she probably had Shingles. I said as much and that she should see her doctor.

Rosemary being her usual 'oh, I'll manage' self, dismissed my thoughts with a wave of her hand. She assured me it was nothing more than a few spots and mouth ulcers. We chatted for a while, although nothing like as late into the night as we normally did. Rosemary went to bed and I curled up on the settee. The house was absolutely freezing as always because Rosemary has no central heating and, to add to that discomfort, there was something wrong with Rosemary's 'Sky Box' so there was no television for me to listen to as I fell asleep.

Knowing I was almost as entirely safe at Rosemary's house as at my own, I read a book I'd brought with me about giving up smoking, still smoking as I did so (those were the instructions in the book). Rosemary had already stopped her habit and Tom – who, up until his stroke, had smoked more than forty a day – had been forced to stop too since he was in hospital.

The next day, I became even more convinced that Rosemary herself was unwell – very unwell. However, she insisted we go to Ashford hospital to visit Tom. With Rosemary driving along packed and busy roads, we made the trek. I felt surprisingly well, even though I'd forgotten to bring both my beta-blockers and GTN spray with me and had experienced a few pangs of chest pain during the previous night and in the morning.

Rosemary, on the other hand, began to look worse by the minute. I tried to keep my concerns to myself, but when we were sitting at Tom's bedside, I noticed she had several more spots along her jaw-line and going up into her hair on the left of her face. She also looked incredibly flushed.

Tom was actually much better than I had expected him to be. He was speaking well and only occasionally forgot the word he wanted. I had to tell Rosemary not to say the word for him, but rather, prompt him with the first letter of the missing word, or simply wait. Tom was walking with the aid of a stick – which was also much more than I had thought he'd be able to do. He seemed very much his old self in fact.

Before we left the hospital, both Rosemary and I needed the toilet. It was then that I pointed out the new spots forming in front of my eyes on her face. She peered into the mirror and only then admitted she felt like crap and had an awful headache.

When we finally got back to Rosemary's house, I told her she must telephone the doctor in the morning and get an emergency appointment. I also said I had no idea as to how contagious Shingles was, but I was convinced that was what was wrong. She looked doubtful. Only when I told her she did not want to put Tom or any other patient at risk did she agree to go to the doctor.

Once again, Rosemary retired to bed not long after ten o'clock. Before she went upstairs, she'd presented me with her laptop and invited me to use the wi-fi network to find something to watch.

I set it up on a chair close to the settee and struggled to recall how to get television series up online. Eventually, I managed to get an episode of Stargate SG1 to play and I snuggled under the thick duvet with just my eyes and nose peeping out so I could watch.

Psyche-Imp had clearly taken longer than me to find and get to Woking. He arrived a little after midnight, kicked me in the guts and sent me into a full-blown panic attack. Very quickly, I felt sick and needed the toilet – both at once.

Shaking with both cold and panic, I managed to stuff an extra anti-emetic into my mouth before darting up Rosemary's incredibly steep staircase to the one toilet. One of the cats came to sit in front of me as the world fell out of my arse. I focused on the tortoiseshell cat (although I could not recall if I was looking at Foxy or Wolfie) and willed the panic to depart. It did not; Psyche-Imp was clearly extremely pissed off that I'd escaped him for more than twenty four hours and fully intended to make me suffer.

When I'd finally finished, I crept down the stairs and into the kitchen where I made myself a cup of tea. I took this back to the settee with me, trying not to allow my shaking to slop the tea on the carpet.

Somehow, I managed to concentrate enough to re-set the laptop so I could focus on Stargate. I also took half a Valium and then shortly thereafter, lit a cigarette.

I slept little. Every time I dozed off, Psyche-Imp kicked me awake or punched me in the head. All night long I dozed fitfully and panicked intermittently – even though there was absolutely nothing to panic about.

Rosemary got up and went straight out to the doctor in the morning. She'd managed to get an emergency appointment. I got up, made tea and sat thinking. The previous day, when we'd been at the hospital, a nurse had indicated that Tom would be released on Saturday.

The Sky repair man was also coming to Rosemary's house on Saturday. It began to occur to me that I would have to go home that evening because, once Tom arrived home, I knew I could not expect Rosemary to leave him unattended to drive me home or even half-way home. I sent Peter a text to this effect and asked if he would be available to collect me where he had dropped me off.

As always, Peter rang me rather than texting a reply. I explained that Rosemary herself was unwell and that Tom should be coming home the next day. Thankfully, Peter agreed to collect me. He invited me to send him a text to let him know what time Rosemary and I would be at the Services and then he rang off.

Rosemary came home at that point. She looked miserable. "You're right. I have got Shingles," she grumbled as she entered the room. "I've got to ring the hospital to see if I am allowed to visit today or not."

I went to make tea, leaving Rosemary on the telephone. I was intensely worried. How on earth would she manage to look after Tom if she was unwell herself? More importantly, was it safe for her to be around Tom at all in his weakened state? Should I stay and do what I could for the pair of them or stick with my plans to return home later that evening so as not to be in the way?

When I came back into the room, Rosemary was crying. I put the tea down and hugged her as she told me the hospital had told her to stay away.

Eventually, her tears subsided and we began to talk of practical matters. I explained that I intended to go home that evening and why and asked if she felt well enough to drive me to the Services on the motorway. Rosemary said she would, even though she agreed she felt ill. She refused my offer of staying a couple of weeks to help out and I expressed regret because I felt as if I'd been about as useful to her as a chocolate fireguard. However, Rosemary insisted just knowing I was there had helped her a lot and that she'd really only crumbled because she'd expected Tom home, they'd found another problem *and* the television was on the blink.

Once she was more cheerful, Rosemary devised a plan for seeing Tom. She would drive to the hospital with me. She instructed me to go to the ward, plonk Tom in a wheelchair and bring him down to the main foyer where they could spend an hour together.

About halfway to the hospital, Rosemary admitted the spots were very sore and painful and that she had a pain, much like toothache, all along her jaw and behind her ear. Once again, she looked flushed and unwell. Her eyes had kind of sunk and her skin looked papery.

When we arrived, I left Rosemary sitting in the foyer and hurried to the ward to see Tom. He looked up as I came through the door. "You've got a scabby wife," I joked. "She's not allowed onto the ward and she wants me to put you in a wheelchair and take you down to the foyer to see her."

Tom actually laughed. He stood up and told me he would put his trousers on and that I could think again if I thought he was going anywhere in a wheelchair. He insisted he would walk.

I felt like a gooseberry, sitting there next to Tom and Rosemary in the hospital foyer, but at least I didn't panic. I expect Psyche-Imp had been left behind at Rosemary's house and was probably tormenting the dog and cats.

All too quickly, the visit was over and I escorted Tom back to his ward. I waited whilst a nurse cheerfully packed most of his belongings into carrier bags and explained that Tom would actually be sent home by hospital transport. I said goodbye and lugged the bags back to Rosemary.

When we were back in the car, Rosemary complained about the pain she was suffering. I asked if the doctor had given her anything for pain; I knew he'd given her some anti-viral pills. I managed to persuade Rosemary to stop at the pharmacy near her home (where she'd collected the anti-viral medication earlier that day). I left her sitting in the car and went inside. I asked to speak to the Pharmacist.

I purchased some calamine cream to be applied to Rosemary's spots and some strong pain-killers which would be safe to take with all her other medications. Just as I was leaving, I asked the Pharmacist how contagious Shingles actually was.

"It's poorly understood," he replied. "I should think it is really only a risk to anyone undergoing chemo or radiotherapy, to be honest."

Psyche-Imp appeared immediately and kicked me in the ear. I took a sharp breath inwards.

"Is anything the matter?" the Pharmacist enquired.

I told him I'd just finished a course of radiation therapy for cancer but that I hadn't completed the chemotherapy course.

The man looked faintly alarmed. "Oh, I see," he said, at length. "Well, my advice would be not to get too close and certainly not to touch the lady at all."

Too late! Psyche-Imp hopped up and down on my shoulder, fell off and rolled onto the floor laughing fit to bust. I mentally stamped on him hard and simply murmured, "Too late!" to the Pharmacist and left.

I felt terribly guilty needing Rosemary to drive me to meet Peter. She looked so ill and said she felt very weary and in pain. I suggested I should walk to the station instead and get a train to somewhere that Peter could collect me from. Rosemary insisted there was no need for that and she could drive.

I told Rosemary I felt as if I'd been utterly useless and needing her to drive me just made that feeling worse. She reassured me and said that, without me, she would never have gone to the doctor at all, simply put the spots, pain and ulcers down to stress and got on with her life. She also said that having somebody with her with whom she could talk things through had put everything back into perspective and she felt as if she could now cope – even though she was unwell. She felt intensely worried that I'd catch the Shingles and told me she herself felt guilty for having even needed me to be with her. I laughed off her concerns and told her it was about time I supported her rather than the usual other way about. I told her I was certain I would not catch Shingles at all. Of course, Psyche-Imp had plenty to say to me on that score; he tried to convince me that I'd already caught Shingles. Completely un-panicked, I knocked him onto the floor and kicked his bony backside out of my way before getting into Rosemary's car.

It was dark and drizzling when we finally met Peter at the Services. None of us stopped for coffee. I got out of one car and into another. I couldn't even give Rosemary a hug goodbye because she wouldn't let me touch her in case I caught the Shingles.

By half past nine in the evening, I was once again at home. I took a beta-blocker immediately and settled back down onto the settee. At least my house felt a lot warmer than Rosemary's had done. I also found I really appreciated my television and the ability to watch Pirates of the Caribbean even more as I went off to sleep.

Hallow'een came and went and although I made a token effort, and encouraged Damon to put up decorations and paid for sweets, hot-dogs and burgers, my heart really wasn't in it at all. Somehow, it seemed intrinsically wrong to be celebrating my favourite festival of the year not knowing if I would even be alive for it the following year. This is, of course, all Psyche-Imp's doing. Most people would've had a really big bash so as to leave a fantastic memory should they pass away.

Peter had continued to come to sleep on the other settee most evenings and being a selfish and dreadful person, I was no longer grateful. Psyche-Imp was not much in evidence for some reason and Peter and I had begun to irritate one another (as we had used to do years before when we were a couple). There were one or two blazing arguments, something I would ordinarily avoid like the plague because I hate confrontation of all kinds. I felt uncomfortable; I wanted to tell Peter to sod off and never come back but somehow, I managed to bite my tongue.

The boys had no such compunction. They all queried why I put up with being shouted at or criticised by Peter and why I allowed myself to be drawn into arguments when I was so clearly upset and fragile already. Uther in particular, insisted that Peter's presence was damaging to me and to the family as a whole. He told me I should 'get rid of' Peter for a while before everything fell apart completely

I tried to think of a reason to do just that, I was feeling pretty miserable at the time and Peter often seemed to (quite inadvertently) make me feel worse. He had been wonderful for weeks but he no longer rubbed my back or feet for me and seemed to spend most of his time sitting here in bitter silence with a grim expression on his face.

On 2nd November, when I sat down at the computer to check my emails, I found one from 'Create Space' – Amazon's on-demand publisher – with whom I had published both the first parts of my autobiography and my first attempt at NaNoWriMo, a fictional story called 'Hero's Tale'. Intrigued, I opened it and read:

"Hannah Livingston, of BBC, called in to our Member Services Department with aims of contacting you with regard to your title 'Hero's Tale' (3450948). She "would like to have a chat or conversation" with regard to the content of Hero's Tale for a program she is working on for BBC. Her contact info is listed below."

The message ended with both an email address and a couple of telephone numbers.

My heart began to thud painfully inside my chest. I felt dizzy and somewhat faint. The BBC? The BBC wanted to do something with my crappy little NaNoWriMo story? I sat there, opened mouthed, staring at the computer. Basically, the book was utter rubbish because I'd never edited it at all or really done anything with it. The story might one day make a good story but I'd bashed it out in just twenty-seven days and published it as it was – typos and all. Maybe the BBC thought I was a child prodigy or something? I took some Valium, sent texts to Uther, Zakh, Peter and Rosemary about it and had a cup of coffee.

Before I'd even finished the coffee, I'd called the telephone number. It was answered by a woman who agreed that she was Hannah Livingston and that she did work for the BBC and had been trying to contact me. My heart thumped erratically. I took a quick spray of GTN spray – it wouldn't do to have a heart attack or anything, just when things were looking up. This might end up being my way to leave something for my sons after a lifetime of achieving nothing. I listened as Hannah explained that, having now contacted her, she would get her 'Producer' to call me. She didn't go into any details at all, even though I questioned her about Hero's Tale, wanting to know what she thought of the book. She admitted she hadn't read it herself and I felt acute disappointment. Still, this 'Producer' would ring me later and I'd learn just exactly what the BBC had planned for the book and how much they were willing to pay to use my story and ideas.

Psyche-Imp had been well and truly banished from the house. For a couple of hours, I felt as if I were walking on air and as if nothing in the world could ever harm me again. Finally, my writing had been 'discovered' and I would be able to come off benefits and earn myself a living doing something I loved. I grinned from ear to ear as I waited for the call from this 'Producer' person.

When the phone rang, I had to stop myself from snatching it up too eagerly; I didn't want to appear too desperate. I counted to five and then answered in a calm voice. The man at the other end introduced himself as 'Meirion Jones' (which I thought was a most peculiar name). The first thing he said, after 'Good afternoon, was some compliment or other about my writing; I've never really been able to cope with compliments but, since I was alone, I blushed and mentally 'preened my feathers' because someone from the BBC thought I was a good writer.

I still did not suspect anything was amiss even when this Mr. Jones told me he was a journalist and had been following my work on the 'FanStory dot com' site online. I listened as he explained that he was really actually interested in my biography and most particularly the second part of it (which I had yet to finish or publish). The reason for this turned out to be that his Aunt, Margaret Jones had been the headmistress of Duncroft, the Approved School I had been incarcerated in. He said he knew the place well and had visited there frequently. He thought my descriptions of both the building and the staff members was incredibly accurate and had 'transported him back in time' so that he felt he could actually hear their voices again. Psyche-Imp appeared and began jumping up and down in front of my face, his yellow eyes wide with warning and for once, a very serious expression on his ugly, blue face. I turned my back on him and continued to listen to what Mr. Jones was saying about my wonderful writing.

When he mentioned the 'Special Visitor' that we used to see frequently at Duncroft who I had stated had sexually abused both me and other girls at the school on numerous occasions, Psyche-Imp clambered up my back and began swinging on my hair and scratching at my scalp with his clawed hands, shrieking wordlessly that I should panic and throw the phone down. I ignored him, although my heart was now beating extremely fast and my chest had begun to hurt again. Mr. Jones asked me bluntly, "Was this 'JS' you mentioned by any chance Jimmy Savile?" I agreed that it was indeed Jimmy Savile and then listened as Mr. Jones went on, at some length, about how both he and his parents had been incredibly suspicious about those visits at the time and had even fallen out with his aunt over it.

Now, this is a bizarre thing to have to try to describe. On the one hand, my heart was thudding most painfully; on the other hand, my spirits had sunk deep into my boots and probably beyond as I realised that the BBC were not in the least interested in me as a writer after all. Psyche-Imp was indicating frantically that I should not only hang up but that I should also go out into the garden and bury the phone at least six feet deep. I swatted the little bastard away and cursed because the BBC now had both my landline number and my mobile phone number. I told Mr. Jones I was ill with cancer and really didn't want to talk about the past at all. I'd only written the biography to 'offload' painful memories, on the advice of a psychologist, and uploaded it to the FanStory site for help with punctuation, grammar and writing style. He told me he wanted to make a programme for 'Newsnight' about the fact that Savile was a paedophile. I told him he'd have to do it without me and repeated that I had cancer. And then, I hung up.

Depression settled around me like a cloak. It was probably deeper depression than usual because my hopes of success as a writer had been lifted so incredibly high, albeit briefly. Even Psyche-Imp seemed to have lost some of his vigour; the little blue imp sat beside me on the settee with his large head resting in his bony hands and his long, pointy ears drooping almost to his shoulders. Damn and blast the bloody BBC! I sent texts expressing my disappointment and fury at the BBC's dirty tricks to get me to contact them to Uther, Zakh and Peter and rang Rosemary – even though she had more than enough problems of her own to cope with.

Over the following ten days I had call after call from Meirion Jones of the BBC. He understood I wasn't very well; he knew it was difficult for me; he could understand why I wouldn't want to speak on camera, but there were also others from Duncroft and elsewhere who had made the same claims. Every time he called I told him no and also every time he called, my resolve weakened a little more. In fact, I'd come to the point where I felt I would do anything just to get the BBC to leave me alone! Eventually, and I suppose this is quite predictable, particularly for someone as weak-willed as me and in such a fragile state both mentally and physically, I agreed to do the damnable interview – on camera and in my own home.

Zakh had come home three days before the interview to stay for a few days to include his birthday on 12th November. I suggested Zakh sleep in the single bed installed in the living room. I was still sleeping on the settee and it seemed madness for me to go upstairs, try to sort out Zakh's old bedroom and make up a bed when there was already a perfectly good bed made up in the lounge. Zakh agreed.

Peter seemed extremely miffed by the fact that Zakh would be sleeping in the bed. I supposed, at the time, this must be because he himself had spent weeks on a very uncomfortable settee. Peter remarked that he did not need to be here at night if Zakh was here and so intended to stay away for a few days.

Intensely relieved, I agreed. I think Peter was surprised by that, but also, in his own way, also relieved. He certainly really needed to get some decent sleep and in all truth, we needed a break from one another as well.

Much to Psyche-Imp's utter disgust, since I couldn't afford a decent birthday present this year for Zakh, I bought him a book he wanted and decided I would give up smoking, which Zakh had been begging me to do for years. I finished reading the book about stopping smoking, put my last cigarette out and after saying 'goodnight' to Zakh on the night of 11th November 2011, I laid down to go to sleep.

No-one was more surprised than me when I got up the next morning and didn't immediately light a cigarette. Psyche-Imp tried his best; he rattled the ash-tray – so I emptied it and put it away. He sat on my shoulder as I did things and whispered "You want a cigarette, Kat!" Every time this thought occurred to me, I resolutely told myself – either aloud or silently – I was very glad I no longer smoked and I certainly did not want a cigarette at all.

Despite Psyche-Imp's efforts, I had no panics all day and, it seemed, fewer trips to the toilet as well. In actual fact, I found not smoking to be ridiculously easy. I wondered why I'd never tried to stop before.

This happy state continued over the next few days; I hardly thought about cigarettes at all. In fact, I began to become aware that the house and everything in it stank of stale smoke and I worried because I had the BBC coming. With Lesley's help, I washed walls and curtains, shelves and everything else in order to try to freshen the place up a bit.

The people came from Newsnight on 14th November 2011. It was Meirion Jones, Liz MacKean – who was to interview me – and a cameraman. Peter hurried from the work he'd been doing so that he could be in the room to support me as I was, by that time, a complete nervous wreck, unable to eat, sleep or function in any way at all. In fact, I did nothing but sit on the settee with Psyche-Imp in my lap and shake violently in the few days before the Newsnight crew arrived.

It seemed like about a year as the interview went on. I recounted everything I had put in my biography and I also told Meirion Jones and Liz MacKean over and over again that they would not be allowed to air the programme. I predicted they would be stopped somehow – which was the only reason I had agreed in the end to do it. Basically, to get them off my back secure in the knowledge that I could then continue to fall apart with cancer and panic without having to worry about appearing on television; I just *knew* the programme would not be permitted to be shown. They both insisted I was wrong and that Savile would be exposed finally for the pervert he had been all his life. When it was all finally done, I was so glad when those people finally packed up their stuff and left. Meirion Jones told me the programme would be on air during the first week of December and thanked me most profusely for my input. He added that he really did think me an exceptional writer. I sarcastically replied that I clearly wasn't a good enough writer to earn myself a living from it but I somehow kept my mouth shut about the dirty tricks which had been used to persuade me to contact him in the first place. I had managed the whole thing and still not succumbed to having a cigarette! Not only that, I hadn't even wanted a cigarette. I felt incredibly pleased with myself for not smoking.

Zakh went back to uni and I still continued not to smoke. Lesley was amazed. In fact, whenever she came to visit between after 11th November, if she wanted to smoke, she went outside.

On 18th November, Zakh sent me a text to ask if I could put a few quid into his bank account in order that he and his mates could go hire the university facilities to play a game of six a side football. I agreed and although I had very limited money myself, transferred the funds immediately.

I sat at the computer, having put some washing in the machine, done the dishes and remembered to eat. I actually felt very well indeed – certainly more well and healthy than I'd felt during the past seventeen odd years.

The text alert went off on my phone. I opened the message; it was from Zakh. Quite simply, it read: "I have broken my leg. Waiting for an ambulance." I stared at it for a few seconds before sending a frantic text back asking how badly it was broken and asking for details on what had happened.

For a long time, I got no reply. I began to feel intensely anxious at that point. My feet were tapping as I searched on Facebook for any news. I found a comment from one of Zakh's friends and added my own to it by way of a question as to what happened and whether Zakh was badly broken.

During the next two hours I received sporadic reports from both the friend and from Zakh himself. He'd been taken to hospital; he was using gas and air for the pain; he'd gone to X-Ray and so on.

Finally, when I learned he had broken both bones in his leg, dislocated his ankle and torn off most of his ligaments, I snapped. I craved a cigarette; in fact, I couldn't think of anything else at all save cigarettes.

Now, when I stopped, I threw away my lighter and the remaining cigarettes. That rubbish had long gone. I wasn't about to go digging through rubbish anyway. I thought I may be able to resist if I had to put my shoes on, get into the car and go to the shop. I sat back down at the computer and tried to write to take my mind off the craving.

To the right of the screen, Psyche-Imp popped his head around the monitor and beckoned me, his evil little yellow eyes twinkling and a broad grin on his ugly mouth. I glanced that way.

An old, half used pack of cigarettes sat on top of a pile of junk in the little basket there. Before I quite knew what I was doing, I'd snatched the pack up, crammed a cigarette into my mouth and rushed to the kitchen to light the foul thing on the gas cooker.

I inhaled a huge lungful of smoke; it was vile! Even so, I didn't put it out. Why I was doing something so incredibly stupid, I have no idea. I smoked most of it and then, as the taste got worse (they were cheap cigarettes anyway, which was why I'd never smoked the pack in the first place), I put it out. I then spent about an hour beating myself up for weakness and feeling incredibly stupid.

Using Zakh's accident as an excuse, I smoked another a little later and then another. Finally, I gave in and took myself up to the shop and purchased a decent pack of cigarettes. Psyche-Imp was thrilled to bits and laughed all the way to the shop and all the way back.

Later that evening, when I was feeling sick, panicky and not a little sorry for myself – utterly unable to eat anything – Psyche-Imp did cartwheels across the lounge and landed on my lap, where he kicked me hard in the stomach. The diarrhoea began almost immediately. Damn and blast that little beast and my own weakness!

I wish I could say that I stopped smoking again in a couple of days, but I didn't, so I cannot. Within a day or two I was smoking more than ever – and coughing my lungs up again. I hated myself; I hated Psyche-Imp too – with a passion!

Uther and I travelled to Leeds a few days later to visit Zakh in the hospital. He'd had one operation and was waiting for another. We couldn't afford the trip but we went anyway. All I could think of was my 'little boy' being in hospital, in pain and broken. The fact that he was twenty didn't make any difference at all.

For the second time since the radiotherapy stopped, I made a long journey. And, for the second time, I made it without incident. In fact, even without taking Imodium, my bowels behaved perfectly all the way there, during the four hours we stayed with Zakh and all the way back – even despite the fact that there were signs and plaques all over the hospital saying what a wonderful man Jimmy Savile had been!

I certainly felt less stressed, having seen my boy, even though I counted the cost in having no money left with which to either live on or buy more cigarettes; he was worth it.

Zakh was able to have both his mobile phone and his laptop in the hospital with him, so we were able to keep in touch. He was due another operation once the swelling had gone down on his leg.

Although I was a lot more active than I had been before the radiotherapy treatment, I still didn't really do much each day. When I look back now, I think I wasted those weeks of waiting as well. There is so very much I could have done but didn't.

I managed to stir my stumps and put the dogs in the car and take them up the hill once – but only once and then I had to use a walking stick and needed my GTN spray as well. Apart from the trip to Leeds, one dog-walk and a few loads of washing, I did nothing. Well, I did write a little, but that hardly counts as activity.

The thought of my own operation began to loom large in my mind. I found I was far more terrified of the possibility that I might vomit due to the anaesthetic than I was of the actual operation itself – which is foolish in the extreme, but the vomit phobia has controlled me this way all my life, so for me, although foolish, I guess it was normal.

At around the same time, I began to fall out with Peter more and more. Every time he came to the house, we seemed to bicker and argue, misunderstand and annoy one another. Things were so similar to how they'd been when we were a couple and before we'd split up that I began to dread him coming round at all.

In fact, if Peter telephoned me, everything he said to me appeared (to me – no doubt courtesy to Psyche-Imp) to be said to deliberately terrify or upset me, annoy or offend me. Peter made a lot of complaints about the boys too and I was offended and saddened.

That the boys had all noticed how argumentative Peter and I had become and that it was not helping my state of mind in the least, they too began to complain to me about Peter! This is *exactly* what the situation had been like before Peter and I split up as a couple; I felt like piggy-in-the-middle. Neither the boys nor Peter addressed their issues with each other – they all loaded them directly on to me.

Psyche-Imp thought this was just fine because it left me vulnerable to him and his attacks. Once again, I became panicked – for no apparent reason; I also became extremely irritable and snappy toward everyone. Psyche-Imp clapped his hands every time I bit someone's head off or made a sarcastic comment.

Only Lesley was brave enough to tackle me about it. She bluntly pointed out to me that I was being angry, rude and unpleasant in general – much like I had been when Peter and I had been splitting up years ago.

Appalled, I turned inward to take a look at myself. I had no credible explanation for my behaviour, which even I had to admit, was less than acceptable. I assumed it was due to the cancer and possibly the stress of the upcoming television programme about Savile and I told Lesley that. She nodded and agreed it probably was – and this was the reason she'd never risen to my baiting. At least *one* of my friends had the wit and intelligence to work out what I couldn't even work out for myself!

At about the same time as I was struggling with myself and bickering with everyone, Peter began to appear less and less at night. He made excuse after excuse not to stay with me – well, they were excuses as far as I was concerned.

Peter complained that he couldn't breathe properly when sleeping on the settee; I retorted (sarcastically) that it was probably soaked in cat wee – since several of my cats have a distressing tendency to spray on anything and everything. He told me he was suffering from Seasonal Adjusted Depression or 'SAD' syndrome. There were other reasons too, but I simply took it as what Peter meant to say: that he no longer wanted to support me. I got snappier and more and more sarcastic by the day.

The strange thing was, Peter clearly did not want to be here and, at the time, I would have rather he hadn't been here as well. But neither of us actually told the other the truth.

In the end, when Peter wasn't here one evening and I found both Uther and Damon sitting up late with me, laughing and chatting, I realised I had to tell Peter to take a break.

Peter had already realised what it took me two weeks or more to work out (I can be incredibly dense sometimes). He stepped back with good grace and I was left to the company of my sons.

I suddenly received a text a day or so before the Newsnight programme had been due to air. It was from Meirion Jones. In it he expressed great regret and said I had been absolutely correct about the programme being stopped. It would not air after all.

My first reaction was intense relief. It washed over me like a soothing balm and even Psyche-Imp fell off my shoulder and into a deep slumber on the floor. I trod on the offending little swine as I moved to the settee to sit down and digest this piece of information. I sent out texts of my own, to the usual suspects, stating that the programme had been cancelled after all. Several people replied, mostly everyone was relieved, although Uther was particularly indignant that his mother, who was so sick, had been pressured and stressed for what turned out to be nothing whatsoever at all.

It was the text from Uther that got me thinking, and thinking, in its own turn got me angry (with some help from Psyche-Imp). By the time an hour had passed I was furious and shaking, alternately feeling intensely sorry for myself and mightily aggrieved at what I'd been put through whilst possibly dying of cancer. Could I not even bloody die in peace? I thought. I grumbled and gruntled my way through the rest of the day. Gradually, as the night-time approached, I began to feel scared and inexplicably panicky again. Psyche-Imp had not only woken up, he was getting his own back, Big Time. Somehow, I got through that night, but I cannot now remember how.

With the possibility of being seen on national television having been removed, I coped reasonably well with the approaching operation. Yet, after a while, Psyche-Imp took to appearing late at night or in the wee small hours of the morning after the boys had gone to bed. Once more, I was obsessing about the possibility that I might vomit after the anaesthetic. I could not sleep for awful thoughts and images dancing across my brain.

Matters were not helped when I learned that Zakh had been very sick indeed after his second operation. I began to obsess about the whole thing, and actually thought I may have to call it all off.

I had two more trips to the hospital. The first was to the 'pre-operative check-up'. Uther drove me and came in to the consultation with me.

Firstly, we saw a Pharmacist who wanted to know about all the medications I take regularly. It seemed I was supposed to take the medicines with me for her to see, but I forgot to do that. Instead, I reeled them all off and the doses. To my surprise, the Pharmacist told me to take them all as usual, even when 'nil-by-mouth'.

Uther and I went back to the waiting room to wait for the check up with a nurse. It was then my bowel decided to play up. Of course, it could just as well have been Psyche-Imp, even though I was unaware of feeling anxious or worried. I had to dash to the toilet, which was just off the waiting room. I was absolutely appalled when I farted, really loudly! Surely, since I could hear conversations in the waiting room quite clearly, people in the waiting room must also have heard my arse trumpeting? I felt almost too embarrassed to exit the toilet at all afterward. Psyche-Imp sat on the wash hand-basin and picked his nose, turning his head this way and that as if inspecting the contents of his large ears.

We didn't have long to wait before being seen by a nurse called Janette. She took my blood pressure, listened to my chest and then took a sample of blood. I told her I thought I had caught a cold from one of the boys and she advised me to see my GP to get a prophylactic antibiotic – just to make sure I had no infection when I arrived for the operation.

She told me what would happen when I arrived – which was to be at eleven in the morning for surgery in the afternoon. I was given some 'Pre-Op' drinks to take home with me. I had to drink four of these cartons the evening before and the other two in the morning before eleven. I peered at the cartons; apparently a lemon flavoured drink. I'm not much of a fan of cold drinks and have only recently learned to drink water. I thought I wouldn't look forward to taking them.

I would only be 'nil by mouth' after I arrived at the hospital. Janette told me I could have toast and tea for breakfast as long as it was before half past seven and then only clear fluids until eleven. Since I do not generally get up until eleven, I shuddered at the prospect of eating so early in the morning.

However, on the way out, Uther pointed out that, as he knew me well enough to know I would probably not sleep the night before the operation – out of sheer panic, having tea and toast before seven thirty probably would not be a problem. I had to agree with him. Just talking to Janette had made my stomach churn and I felt more than a little sick as I left the hospital. No doubt this was Psyche-Imp playing his games again.

I went home, dumped the bag containing the drinks on the cupboard – and promptly put the operation out of my mind altogether.

I was to see Mr. Billings again because I'd told the colorectal nurse I wanted a permanent colostomy rather than the planned temporary ileostomy. Peter came with me to that appointment. I'd prepared a list of questions for the surgeon.

Once again, I whined on about vomiting and the fact that I could not deliberately do anything which may make me vomit. Once again – although he had a wearied expression on his face – the surgeon reassured me that everything possible would be done to avoid this.

I asked if I would have IV antibiotics; yes, as standard, the surgeon replied. I asked whether I might get peritonitis or some other kind of infection because there is no bowel preparation pre-operatively. The surgeon assured me that he dealt with this all the time and that I would be extremely unlikely to get any infection at all.

In fact, I asked a host of rather pointless questions, all of which the surgeon answered patiently. When I stood up to leave, I told Mr. Billings I have trouble trusting medics and that I had been badly let down more than once. He replied he often had trouble trusting patients!

Only when I got outside the hospital, did I think to myself that I would be putting my body and my life into his hands – he would not be doing the same with me.

I should like to be able to say that I spent my last week or so well and that no time was wasted at all. If I said that, I would be lying. I wasted my remaining time; all of it.

Zakh came home, staggering about on crutches with his leg in a fetching blue cast. I found myself making him sandwiches and toast and fetching or carrying stuff for him. Apart from those few small things, I did nothing of any value at all. In fact, more than ever, I seemed to simply sit on the settee and let the time just slip away.

And the time did slip away; very fast. Although I'd learned, in Peter's absence, to sleep in a room on my own again, I still put Pirates of the Caribbean on every night to go to sleep to. I worried as to how I would cope in the hospital without it. I also worried and stressed every night about the operation itself, although somehow, despite Psyche-Imp and his incessant whispering, I got through the nights without taking any Valium – I don't know how.

And then, all of a sudden: The operation is tomorrow. I write in the present tense now because I am sitting at the computer, trying to keep myself calm and not shake too much. I'm frightened; very frightened indeed.

I know, in my heart, that the operation has to be done. Over the last day or two the tumour has been bleeding a little once more. Obviously, it has to come out and the sooner the better.

I've been the usual drama queen, of course I have. I've discussed with the three boys what they need to do in the event that I die – although I don't think I'm really considering dying. Certainly, I'm far more worried about how they'll all deal with it if I do. Despite anything Psyche-Imp can say, it won't matter to me if I'm dead.

I'm still trying hard not to focus entirely on the fact that I might vomit. I'm not always successful. Psyche-Imp is still about. He tends to skulk around and creep up on me when I least expect him. I've had a few bouts of diarrhoea over the last few days. I'm sure they're down to him.

I intended to stop smoking on Tuesday the twentieth of December – the operation is on Thursday the twenty second. I failed miserably. I am aware that my lungs are clogged up with nicotine, tar and all sorts of other poisons. I'm cross with myself for not trying hard enough. I'm more than a little worried that smoking in itself may cause me to die – either under the anaesthetic or later on.

I am going to stop writing now. If I go through it all and come out the other side, I will add the final chapter to this book. If I don't, I've asked Uther to do it for me.

Chapter Six: The Operation

Here I am now, some fourteen and a half weeks after the event and this is the first time I have been well enough to actually sit at the computer. It is also the first time my mind has been clear enough to write.

That is a very long time and you must be wondering why it took me so long and why I am still not feeling well. I will try to start at the beginning and relate things honestly but in truth, a lot of what I have to set down has a vague, dream-like quality. Some little things I can remember very clearly; other things, which are probably most significant or important, I have little or no memory of.

Did I sleep the night before the operation? I cannot remember. I think I may have slept a few hours. I also think Uther stayed up with me and that he slept on the other settee.

I also cannot recall if I had the prescribed tea and toast before seven thirty in the morning – I expect I did. I know I did manage to consume all but one of the Pre-Op drinks. Strangely, they were quite refreshing, if too sweet for my taste.

Peter phoned in the morning to say he could not make it for eleven. He said he would join us at the hospital certainly before I went down for the operation. I'm not sure what I felt about that. Probably not a lot as both Uther and Lesley were keeping me chatting as much as possible.

I do recall that I made several trips to the toilet and that all of them were fruitless ... nothing happened. Very odd indeed! Perhaps it was something in the Pre-Op drinks which stopped me from 'going'?

Eventually, we set off to the hospital with me in Lesley's car and Uther alone in his. This decision had been made because Lesley intended to go somewhere else after I'd gone down to surgery and Uther would need to get home. With hindsight, I should probably have travelled with Uther, but at the time I was so self absorbed with fear, Uther's feelings never occurred to me.

We got to the hospital too quickly for my liking. Part of me wanted the journey to take hours. Another part of me wanted to run away and leave both Lesley and Uther perplexed and angry. Of course, I didn't run away; I smoked. I had two cigarettes in Lesley's car (and so did she) and another when we arrived at the hospital. Psyche-Imp watched me out of slitted yellow eyes as I ground the last dog-end to pulp underfoot and stated that it would be my 'last' cigarette. And then, the little beast snorted with laughter and began to turn cartwheels round the car park.

We asked at the reception desk for the 'Arrivals Lounge' we'd been told to report to and got instructions as to how to find it – on the first floor.

There was hardly any confusion – well, we walked the length of the wrong corridor but were soon set straight by a friendly nurse. Another, very friendly, smiling nurse greeted us at the right place and directed us into a lounge full of chairs and tables at which were sat several groups of people; none of them looked particularly nervous or worried.

As we sat down around a small table I wondered if I were the only person to be terrified out of my wits; as I wondered this I suddenly realised that I was, in fact, remarkably calm – much calmer than I had been for many, many months. I did chat to both Uther and Lesley but inside, I was analysing myself and wondering where the calm had come from.

Peter arrived and joined our group. We all chatted some more. And then a nurse came and led me away to a small room, leaving Uther, Lesley and Peter seated at the table.

In this small room was a bed, a couple of chairs and a peculiar looking piece of machinery which I decided was some kind of hoist. The window, open a little, showed only the brick wall of the building a few feet away. It closely resembled a prison cell and I should have been panicked but I wasn't.

The nurse sat on a chair and invited me to sit on another at the other side of the room beside the bed. She had a large file on her lap and a pen in her hand. Thus began the pre-operative questions. There were dozens of them. So many things I was asked about were already in my notes. I began to wonder if, in fact, anyone had read my notes and knew what they were doing at all!

When the questions were complete, I was required to undress and get into a very fetching (not) hospital gown and a pair of dreadful bandage-net knickers with a small pad inside them. Apparently, these would be cut off and disposed of whilst I was under anaesthetic. Another nurse came into the room bearing with her a delightful pair of compression stockings which (with help from a gadget) she rammed onto my lower legs up to my knees. My toes poked out of the ends; clearly, hospital supplies were not used to women with such enormous feet!

I sat there, on that chair, feeling somewhat bemused but not at all afraid whilst the nurses chatted to one another. The door opened and another lady poked her head around the door; she smiled at me. I listened vaguely to her conversation with the other two without the slightest idea of what they were talking about.

Someone else, who looked rather familiar to me, entered the room. She introduced herself as Claire but I'm afraid I cannot now recall where I'd seen her before; that she was some kind of Colorectal or stoma nurse was a relief. She told me I had to help her decide where exactly, on my abdomen, I wanted the stoma located.

I pointed to an area about halfway between my hip bone and my belly button; the stoma nurse said it was a good choice but would need to be a little higher or the bottom of the bag would catch in my knicker leg. I didn't object; after all, she knew about these things more than me. She made a mark with a big, black felt tipped pen. It was about the size of a ten pence piece. I wondered if it would rub off but before I could vocalise this thought, the stoma nurse stuck a piece of clear film over it. This job complete, she chatted a little with the other two nurses and left, all smiles and encouragement in her brief farewell to me.

At that point, Uther, Lesley and Peter were ushered into the room. One of the nurses hurried off to fetch another chair, the other stayed for a short time to finish some writing in my folder and then she left too.

Uther moved to the machine by the bed and began to inspect it. I still sat on the chair on the other side of the bed. Peter moved to the window and looked out of it. Lesley sat on the chair lately vacated by the form-filling nurse. Uther actually jumped guiltily when the nurse came back with another chair. I tried not to snigger.

I have no idea how long, exactly, (or even approximately) we waited in that room. Looking back, it seems like an age but I suppose it cannot have been much more than an hour or so. It was certainly long enough for Uther to fiddle with the machine, the window and the machine again, altering the height of the arm and the brace and anything else he could find that moved. Peter teased Lesley (as always) and Lesley made her usual replies, although somewhat subdued. In any event, the three of them kept me fairly well entertained during the waiting period so I did not have any opportunity to dwell on the upcoming surgery and thus panic.

When a nurse came in and said it was 'time' my heart felt like it did a somersault inside my chest. She asked who would be walking down to theatre with me. In an instant, I replied, "Uther". This had actually been discussed by me and Peter at some length a few days previously and he had told me it would be him that would accompany me to theatre, even though I felt unsure about it.

I noticed Peter glare at me with an expression like thunder on his face and I also did not miss the gentle smile Lesley tried to hide. At that point, as Peter made to walk off, I knew I'd upset him by not choosing him to accompany me after all. However, it suddenly came to me that I had instinctively chosen Uther; in the absence of Psyche-Imp, instinct could be the only valid reason.

Of course, Uther (I believe) was blissfully unaware of the bad feelings my choice had fostered. He walked beside me the length of a corridor and into a kind of cubby hole where we were invited to sit down.

Yet another nurse came and she held a large folder. Several more questions were asked; I cannot now recall any of them. In fact, from here on in, the whole experience has a weird, dream-like quality. I answered the questions.

We were led a little way down another corridor and then I was told to say farewell to Uther. I hugged him tight; he looked scared although he was trying his very best to appear calm and unflustered.

I walked away, with the nurse, leaving Uther alone in the corridor. I wondered if he would manage the house and the animals, Damon and Zakh, the bills, everything if I didn't wake up. I think that was the only time not waking up from the anaesthetic occurred to me and then it was only a brief thought. I was far more worried about actually waking up and vomiting than of dying!

The nurse chatted as we walked into a small room which I immediately recognised as a place where the anaesthetics would be applied. I did chat to her in reply but I also stared around myself with open curiosity.

The male Anaesthetist greeted me in a friendly manner and invited me to be seated on the trolley-bed. I was required to answer yet more questions before being turned around with my feet on a stool and a pile of pillows on my lap. This was the position I had to adopt for the spinal anaesthetic.

I'd had several epidural anaesthetics in my life before and so I knew the procedure well enough. It didn't hurt, although the antiseptic spray was freezing cold and made me wince!

Once the epidural was in place and everything taped down, I turned around, lay down and watched as the Anaesthetist inserted a Venflon-thing in my left hand. I already felt extremely detached and not at all panicky.

Almost as soon as the Venflon had been fixed, the Anaesthetist turned to his table and picked up a syringe. He clipped it into the socket on the Venflon.

"What's that for?" I asked.

"Anti-emetic," he replied.

I nodded, satisfied. I watched the stuff go in and wondered how strange it was that I could feel nothing in my veins.

He turned back with another syringe.

"And that one?" I asked.

"Another anti-emetic," the man replied.

Good, I thought to myself. They are obviously taking my phobia seriously and doing everything they can to prevent vomiting.

I asked the question a third time as another small syringe was clipped onto the Venflon. This also was an anti-emetic. Three different ones!

Finally, with the nurse holding my right hand (she'd been there all along) the Anaesthetist turned around with a very large syringe full of something white. I briefly thought of the Amateur Transplants Anaesthetists Song as I asked, "And that's the stuff that's going to knock me out, yes?"

I don't recall his reply as I'd 'gone'. Out like a light. Now I think about it, there must have then been a flurry of activity to breathe for me, with tubes and all sorts. Best not thought about or I'll panic, even now.

And that was that. I recall nothing else until much later in the day. It must have been evening visiting time. I kind of opened my eyes and saw Uther's face leaning down to me. He looked concerned.

I was laying curled on my right side facing bars. I felt dizzy and strange, certainly very tired and kind of sick. I remember saying something like "Dizzy, sick, tired."

I turned my head and saw Damon standing at the foot of the bed and Peter sitting at my left side. I think I fell asleep again, although I have a vague recall of the curtains being tugged closed around my bed and a flurry of activity with nurses who insisted I roll onto my back. They were doing something to my abdomen but I just went to sleep again.

I now know that when I had turned onto my right side and curled up I'd managed to dislodge the stoma bag and it had leaked all over the bed, into the wound and on to me. What a good thing I can't actually recall it! The result of this leakage was to plague me for the next several months and further.

Most of my time in the hospital is remembered in snatches only. I slept a lot; I felt sick quite a bit, although I did not actually vomit, for which I was grateful. There are a few lucid memories but not many.

There were several 'leakages' from my new stoma bag. The nurses came along from time to time and emptied the bag into a small paper kidney dish. The contents were liquid and smelled absolutely foul – something I remarked upon frequently. Now and again they discovered that the bag had come adrift from my abdomen or needed changing for another reason and did this for me. I was not particularly interested in what they were doing to be honest; I felt very panicked, being so far out of my comfort zone and, as the effects of the anaesthetic wore off, so my neurotic state of mind worsened. In fact, it would be true to say that Psyche-Imp had not only found his way back to me but had taken up permanent residence in my bed with me!

The little blue swine sat on the foot of my bed picking his long nose and flicking the product at passing health-care staff. Nobody appeared to notice him. I tried hard to ignore him and the mounting panic but it was often impossible. Fortunately, I only had to ask the staff who came with the medication and they cheerfully gave me Valium (which made Psyche-Imp curl up on the end of the bed and go to sleep for a few hours at a time).

Looking back now, it seems hard to believe I spent the whole of the Christmas period in hospital. I had visitors every day, although I cannot for the life of me remember it more than as a vague recollection of certain faces being there. I think Caroline came most days and Lesley once or twice. Peter, Zakh, Uther and Damon came every day but I was hardly good company, even though they tried their best to cheer me up.

I am ashamed that I never even remembered to wish Uther a happy birthday when he visited on Christmas Eve because I was far too preoccupied with feeling nauseous and wallowing in the self-pity and panic that went with it. My wound hurt too despite the spinal anaesthetic still being in place.

The urinary catheter (which had become mysteriously blocked several times over the few days since the operation, probably due to Psyche-Imp standing on it or something) and spinal anaesthesia were actually removed on the same day – although I can't now recall which day that was.

There were several more 'accidents' with the ileostomy bag either coming away from the skin or leaking. I hated the mess and the smell but the nurses simply cleaned it all up uncomplaining; I tried not to complain too much. In fact, I remember feeling very dirty and guilty about other people having to mop up my shit – ridiculous as I had no idea how to deal with it myself and in any case, I was not mobile enough to scuttle off to a toilet.

One evening, a student doctor came along to my bedside. She informed me she had to take blood from me. I willingly stuck my arm out for her. It was my left arm because there was still a drip running into my right arm with yet more antibiotics to counteract the 'possible' infection I may have due to the bag leaking onto the wound site so often.

She messed about with her needle and 'missed' the vein in my left arm no less than five times. It was getting sore. Despite the drip, I suggested she try on the other arm as the vein was much more prominent. Never before had I ever experienced anyone having a problem with drawing blood from me. During the iron infusions, a nurse had 'missed' the vein in my hand once but never in my arms where the veins stuck up like a junkie's paradise.

The young student obligingly moved to the other side, murmuring apologies for her failure. I gritted my teeth. She did not inspire confidence at all. I felt like a bit of a guinea pig to be honest – as if she were just practising on me.

For some insane reason, after six failed attempts at the huge vein in my right inner elbow failed, the young woman attempted, three times, to access the vein in my right hand. These punctures too failed miserably.

She moved back to the left hand side and tried four different locations on my left hand and arm. When these all also failed she looked at my feet – huge veins have always stuck out across the top of my bony feet.

"I'm afraid I'll have to try there," she indicated my feet.

I felt thoroughly irritated and frustrated that she had been so unsuccessful, almost as if I and my veins were at work to thwart her; no doubt Psyche-Imp had something to do with it. "Knock yourself out," I grumbled, trying to keep the sarcasm out of my tone.

The drawing of blood from a foot is extremely uncomfortable. I squeaked; who knew that a needle going into a vein in a bony foot could sting so badly?

The blood drawn, the young student murmured another apology and hurried away. I stared down at the several punctures in arms and hands. Eighteen in all! Good grief!

I don't recall the surgeon coming to do his ward round on most days although I'm certain he must have done so. The day I do recall is the one when all the problems (as I recall it) starting. It must have been about the 28th December, although it may equally well have been the 27th.

The surgeon, Mr. Billings, came along and smirked at me. I was sitting up in bed clinging on to a sick bowl and fighting off panic. Psyche-Imp was sitting on my shoulder telling me that nobody would come to help me and that I was all alone; according to him I would vomit and panic and show myself up entirely. The surgeon had no idea of course that Psyche-Imp was present; he made some remark about my holding a sick-bowl and smirked again at his own wit. He asked how I felt – apart from nauseous.

I complained that the wound hurt quite a bit, itched and felt extremely sore and tender, so much so that even my clothing laying lightly across the wound was causing distress; the spinal anaesthetic had been taken out the previous day as had the urinary catheter but the painkillers the staff had been giving me were doing nothing to relieve the burning sensation in the long wound.

Mr. Billings came to the bedside and asked me to lift my gown. When I did so, he ripped off the sticky, poo-stained dressing and peered at the wound beneath.

I peered at it too. It was the first time I'd seen it. It looked red and angry and ran from just beneath my breast bone, all the way down my tummy to my pubic bone. I didn't like it one bit.

"Your gall bladder was full of stones when I opened you up, so I whipped it out for you," Mr. Billings told me as he peered down at the angry red scar. It also looked slightly 'wet'.

"Did you? I asked. "So does that mean I'll no longer get such awful heartburn then?"

"Yes, that'll sort it out I'm sure," Mr. Billings agreed. He leaned down and sniffed at the wound before turning to one of his student doctors (two of them followed him like shadows), the young woman who, the previous day had done her very best to turn me into a pin-cushion. I didn't hear what he said to her.

"It's infected, isn't it?" I asked, my nausea temporarily forgotten.

Mr. Billings replied "It certainly looks that way; it's a dirty old operation, it was bound to happen, especially since you've had a spillage or two from the bag."

I nodded vaguely, completely forgetting that, just a few weeks beforehand, that same surgeon had told me there was 'little or no chance' of any infection occurring at all. The surgeon moved away to see another patient. The young student however, pulled the curtains around my bed and disappeared from my view leaving me isolated and confused. What was going to happen now?

"Hah! Now you're really on your own!" Psyche-Imp jumped off my shoulder and did a little jig on my knees. "You can puke to your heart's content now and they'll all be able to hear you but nobody will help you!" He fell off my knees and rolled on the bedcovers laughing and holding his fat little belly. I kicked him and he fell onto the floor.

The student doctor chose that moment to re-enter the cubicle. She must have trodden on Psyche-Imp but she didn't seem to notice him. She had with her one of those grey paper kidney dishes and inside it was a thing which closely resembled a crochet hook – once she'd taken it out of its sterile wrapper.

Intrigued but not afraid (why would I be afraid?) I watched as she bent over the wound and poked the hook-thing into it just adjacent to my belly-button. It didn't hurt at all. I watched as a little yellowish fluid escaped and then the wound split open a bit. I felt faintly alarmed but dismissed the fear. I was in a hospital; obviously the wound would be re-stitched once this young woman had done whatever it was she had to do.

I watched as she repeated the manoeuvre a little lower down. This time, the wound gaped open a couple of inches; I could see bright red 'meaty' flesh flecked with small lumps of yellowish ooze. The student murmured "Oh dear. I'd better go and tell Sister." Without another word, she put the hook back into the kidney dish, slipped between the edges of the curtain and vanished from my sight.

I peered down at my abdomen which now had an angry red scar from the sternum running downwards about three inches to a gaping hole about an inch or so wide and about two inches long. As I watched and breathed, it appeared to be lengthening; the interior of the upper hole was bright red and looked very much like plastic. The gap narrowed to almost closed at my navel and then opened out wide beneath it all the way to my pubic bone. There was no actual blood but everything inside looked 'wet' and there was a faint sickly-sweet smell which reminded me of rotting meat.

The curtain swished apart and Sister came along with another nurse and the student doctor. She made some reassuring noises at me, not that I took much notice – I was too busy being nauseous again and it had nothing to do with the wound. I tried to concentrate on what the nurses were doing so that the nausea would subside.

In fact, the nurses didn't really do that much that I could see. Some kind of bag was fixed inside the gaping wound and then a great big wad of padding was taped over it. A few minutes later, someone came along and added a small pack of something to my drip. I believe I asked what they were doing and the answer was "IV antibiotics for your infection, love."

So; the chance of infection was 'negligible' but it had happened to me. Surprise, surprise! I think I had known, even when I went to see Mr. Billings to question him about the operation that all and any complications would happen to me no matter what precautions were taken. Psyche-Imp was so overcome with mirth he laughed himself into a ball and rolled off the bed. To my immediate satisfaction, the woman coming with the meal-trolley ran him over.

I felt mildly hungry once Psyche-Imp had been squished for a while. The food produced soon changed my hunger back to nausea. I cannot recall now what it was – as I mentioned earlier, a lot of the hospital stay is a total blur. I do recall that, even on Christmas Day, the food was totally vile and inedible.

It is reasonable to assume that a great deal of my nausea was in fact, hunger because I could not bring myself to eat the food produced by the hospital. How anyone was supposed to recover and get stronger on the badly prepared, poorly stored and transported, foul fare I have no clue.

Nurses and a dietician tried to tell me that I needed to take supplementary drinks if I would not eat. I quickly told them I did not want the drinks and could not have them anyway as they contain iron – to which I am allergic. Fortunately, this rather lame (but true) excuse was accepted and they did not press me further.

Another patient, across the room from me, was not so lucky. She had to take the drinks regularly and absolutely hated them. I sympathised with her as she ground her teeth and grumbled about the vile food and what had been done to her body.

A small group of physiotherapists were attached to the ward – or at least, appeared regularly on the ward. For the first day or two, whilst I still had both epidural and catheter in place, they ignored me. The day I had the catheter removed though they made a beeline for me and told me I needed to get up out of bed and move about.

It felt very strange actually moving. I hadn't realised quite how numb and strange I'd been feeling. First of all I sat on the edge of the bed. The physiotherapist only gave me a minute or two before telling me to stand up and move across to the armchair beside the bed.

I achieved this, although I felt decidedly wobbly and a little dizzy. Apparently this was to be expected. I sat in the chair for a short time and a nursing assistant came along with a basin of water for me to have a wash. She closed the curtains around my bed, put the basin on the table, gave me my sponge bag and left me to get on with it. Psyche-Imp appeared. I knew he was going to make things difficult for me.

I didn't do much of a job of making myself clean. In all truth, I didn't actually care. I still felt most peculiar, nauseous and dizzy and being clean was the last thing on my mind. More than anything, I wanted to turn the clock backwards and not be in hospital at all.

Psyche-Imp sat on his hands on the edge of the table swinging his legs over the edge. Every now and then he spoke, in his scratchy little voice which only I could hear. He said spiteful, nasty things – none of which I can now recall. All I do remember is that I began to panic sitting in that chair behind the curtain. I didn't feel steady enough to stand up and make my way round the bed but there was no other way I could reach the bell to ring for a nurse.

In the end, I stood up and moved, clinging on to the edge of the bed, until I reached the end where I could pull the curtain aside a little.

One of the nursing assistants immediately saw me and came to help. She pulled the curtains back completely, took the basin of wash-water away and asked if I needed help to get back into bed. I told her I would sit in the chair for a while. Just that little movement seemed to be enough to send Psyche-Imp packing for a while and the panic receded.

There is no coherence to thinking back to my days in hospital; it is merely a jumble of fractured memories and weird feelings and sensations. I cannot think in any logical order of events either. For example, I know that the wound was opened up just a day or two before I got sent home and yet I recall that experience most vividly of all.

At some point I was introduced to Jaime, the Colorectal nurse who would be the person responsible for teaching me how to manage my stoma. The lovely young nurse, with a soft voice and caring attitude did a great deal to give me more confidence in myself and my ability to cope with what had happened to me. I tried hard to pay close attention to what she told me as she showed me how to remove the bag, clean around the stoma and replace the bag. Even that seems fractured now I look back upon it. I can only think that the infection had made me even more ill than I knew.

The day before I left the hospital a nurse came long to change the dressing on my gaping wound. She used a thing that looked very much like a giant cotton bud to wipe around inside the wound after she'd removed the bag-thing. The smell of rotting meat was even stronger than before.

In my semi-self state and not at all aware of what one's insides should smell like when exposed to the air, I thought nothing of it. I think I was probably fixated on Psyche-Imp again; I do know I felt sick at least some of the time on most days.

Nobody seemed to think I was peculiar or strange – or even incredibly stupid, which is how I now view my behaviour and actions whilst I was hospitalised. Although the memories are fractured and weird, I still cannot believe I didn't notice the obvious signs of bad infection or question anything anyone said or did! I even meekly took every bit of medication offered to me although half the time I had no idea what I was taking or why I was taking it. Madness!

It was Peter who came to take me home on 29th December. I think it was about half past two in the afternoon, but it could have been later (or earlier). He borrowed a hospital wheelchair and fussed around me as I shuffled into it.

I sat in the wheelchair and stared at the ward as Peter accepted a plastic bag containing medication for me and spoke to the nurse who handed it over. I said a vague farewell to one or two of the other patients and we were off.

I don't recall the journey through the hospital at all. We must have gone in a lift but I don't remember doing so; we must have gone through the main corridors but we may as well have been on the moon for all I noticed or remembered.

Peter helped me into his car and I sat there like a cabbage whilst he returned the wheelchair to the hospital. I thought nothing much and could not even rouse myself to 'people-watch'.

The only enduring piece of recollection I have of the journey home is when we were travelling past the winter trees and shrubs before the first bridge, which runs over the river. It is most of the way home, well, nearly at MacDonalds so I consider it nearly home. I looked at the bare trees with their lonely, naked branches waving at the overcast sky and asked Peter if he thought I'd be better 'by the time the trees are fuzzy'. Strangely, I cannot recall what his answer was! Spring, with its fuzzy trees is my favourite time of year; I wanted something to really look forward to I think. I know I felt nausea during that journey but also I was so weary that even Psyche-Imp's attempts to panic me failed miserably.

When I got home the boys had clearly made an effort to tidy up some. I had very much left the house in the few days before surgery – not that I have ever been a particularly good housekeeper anyway. My new bed was made up in the corner of the room and someone had thoughtfully purchased some extra feet for the bed to make it about eight inches higher. This would be easier to get up and down from than before.

I tottered inside and made my way to the settee, which also seemed higher; it turned out it had been raised up on bricks. I believe I had a cup of tea, which Peter made for me and then I felt so weary I simply wanted to sleep.

With Peter's help I managed to get undressed and get into the bed. Peter had managed to raise the head of the mattress and had piled pillows into a 'bunny nest'. I slipped under the duvet and sighed. It was good to be home ... even if I couldn't see the television!

I recall very little else of that first day at home. I must have eaten and drunk something, although I cannot recall what. Peter was there all the time with medicines for pain and medicines for nausea and anything and everything else I wanted. That night Peter slept on the settee.

I woke every hour or two. I felt very sore and uncomfortable during the night and it was this sensation which kept waking me. Peter awoke quickly and came to me to give me pain relief and once to help me to sit and stand so that I could go to the toilet.

I found I could not manage as the Colorectal nurse Jaime had advised me, to kneel or squat in front of the toilet to empty the bag; my legs simply would not hold me and if I tried to squat I fell over; the same with kneeling. I recalled that one of the other patients on the ward had spent Christmas at home and also found the same problem. She'd told me she used a jug at the sink and just washed it clean afterwards.

Peter brought me a plastic jug from the kitchen and I placed it in the small sink. Being quite a small jug, the contents of the bag practically filled it, but it didn't overflow. I was able to tip the liquid away and rinse out the jug. I became aware that the smell from the bag contents was very much stronger than 'normal' poo and the air freshener on the toilet wall was empty. I had to ask Peter to bring in a spray air freshener.

Just this little activity exhausted me. Peter had to help me back to bed; I think I fell asleep again almost immediately.

Chapter Seven: Aftermath

The day after I returned home, there was a knock at the front door quite early in the day. Peter went to open it and found a cheerful District Nurse waiting there. He let her in and led her over to me and my 'corner' of the room – which (along with help from Psyche-Imp) I became aware was extremely untidy, dirty and cluttered. The table was so filled with cups, books, papers, other general rubbish and oddments that the nurse had nowhere to set down her things or to sit and write. Instantly, I felt ashamed and worthless.

The nurse introduced herself as Andrea and she smiled constantly as she asked me and Peter questions. One of these questions was directed at me and along the lines of "Do you know why I am here?"

I replied "To see to the gaping holes left in my tummy."

Another nurse arrived whilst Andrea was still taking down notes and filling in her forms. Once the paperwork had been done, Andrea asked permission to look at the wound. I agreed and she lifted my nightdress and, with extreme care, peeled back the taped on wadding. I looked down.

The two wounds had almost become one large wound. Just a fraction of skin above my tummy button remained attached to the other side but, above this and below it, the bright red, stinking meat of my insides was visible.

I asked Andrea if she'd seen this kind of wound before and she said she had and worse than mine too. She even warned me that the wound might, over the next few days, 'de-hiss' further and turn into one large wound.

I took all this information in but for some reason, at that time, I did not understand the seriousness of the matter in the least. I simply wanted to know when I would be able to get up and about and be more myself. Andrea informed me that I would probably spend most of my time in bed over 'the next few weeks'.

Together, the nurses changed both the dressing and the stoma bag, made sure the area was clean and that I was not suffering too much pain and then, packing up their equipment, turned to leave. Peter asked if they would return later the same day or the next day and Andrea told him they could always be reached by telephone and, so long as they were not needed urgently, would return daily to tend to the wound.

After they'd gone I managed half a cup of tea and immediately fell asleep.

When I awoke, I was shivering and felt both incredibly cold and very nauseous. Peter took my temperature and found it to be raised. He telephoned the District Nurses and left a message on their machine. They'd gone home for the day and so nobody would collect the message until the morning.

Miserable and frightened, not to mention fighting off Psyche-Imp and his gift of panic, I asked Peter to bring me Loki to cuddle. Peter returned in no time with the fat, ginger cat and plonked him onto the bed. I'd really missed Loki whilst in hospital as he'd been such a support to me, particularly in the toilet. I thought he'd love to curl up and keep me company but instead, he gave me a thorough sniffing before widening his eyes, flattening his ears and leaping away. I fought back silly tears and turned my face to the wall.

The worst things about being stuck in bed were that I had to remain flat on my back – not comfortable for me as I'd always slept curled on my side, which now was not at all possible – and that although I could hear the television, I could not see it.

Had I been more myself and not so ill, I would have read avidly but, due to excessive tiredness, extreme nausea and the accompanying dreadful shaking due to Psyche-Imp induced panic, I could not read at all. In fact, my head ached far too much to be able to read.

When Andrea arrived the next day bringing yet another colleague with her, Peter explained that I had a temperature, felt very sick and was unable to eat or even drink much. He further told her that he knew a swab had been taken when I was still on the ward in the hospital but that a telephone call had proved fruitless because the ward staff felt unable to disclose to him the nature of the swab results. Even so, as a trained nurse, he felt sure I had some kind of infection.

Andrea took down the dressing on the wound. The last little piece of scar had now parted where it had been hanging together. Now I had one large, gaping wound rather than two smaller gaping wounds. The sweet but sickly smell of rotting meat filled the room and I knew the infection must be bad. I already felt very sick and the smell from the wound did nothing to lessen it. Straight away, Andrea telephoned the hospital and had the call transferred through to the ward I'd been on.

I listened as she introduced herself as the District Nurse caring for me. She reeled off my name, date of birth, hospital number and all manner of other things and then began to protest. She sounded intensely irritated and I roused myself from my misery to attend to what was going on.

It seemed the hospital ward admitted that they had the results of the swab they'd taken from my wound but refused to tell them to the District Nurse! Andrea frowned, took a deep, calming breath and politely suggested that the ward staff call my GP and inform them of the swab results, but for some reason they refused to explain, it seemed it was impossible to do this either. The only suggestion from the ward staff nurse was that Andrea contact the Colorectal nurses and ask them to deal with the problem. Furious, she rang off, stared at her colleague for a moment in utter perplexity and then called the hospital again to speak to the Colorectal Nurses.

Apparently, the Colorectal nurse said she would call out on the Monday to see me and meet with the District Nurse. A time was set and then Andrea and her colleague saw to re-dressing my wound. They were using some kind of bag fixed inside the wound which was supposed to catch most of the 'exudates'. Even so, quite a lot of blood and pus had leaked onto the outer wadding of the dressing they'd taken off. The ileostomy bag needed replacing again as well because there wasn't quite enough intact skin for the flange to adhere to and it quickly became detached every time it was applied. I think Andrea advised Peter to treat my fever as best he could with Paracetamol and cool cloths until they had the results of the swab.

Disgusted by the whole business, I turned my face away and tried hard not to retch. Psyche-Imp for once was silent. I'm pretty sure the little blue git was probably prodding the wound with his long, bony fingers. I kept feeling little stabby pains inside the wound.

I hardly slept that night at all. I shivered with the temperature and shook from head to toe with panic associated with the feeling that I was about to vomit even though I'd eaten nothing at all for at least two days. My head pounded and I felt dizzy, disorientated and weak. Peter or Uther had to help me, first into a sitting position and then out of bed and support me along the hallway to the toilet on the few occasions when I needed to go. I ate nothing at all and I barely drank anything either. Peter gave me pain killers and other medications at regular intervals and the time passed so incredibly slowly I thought the night would never end.

The next day, Sunday, passed in much the same way. Peter managed to persuade me to drink about half a cup of tea in the morning, but, because I instantly felt sick afterwards, he was unable to persuade me to eat or drink anything else at all. In the middle of the afternoon, the telephone rang. The handset had been placed beside my bed on the assumption that various friends and relatives may wish to call me. I answered the call, "Hello?"

A voice I didn't recognise said "Good afternoon, Karin. You don't know me, but I am a journalist with The Sun Newspaper and I understand you have some very revealing allegations to make about Jimmy Savile. Is it safe for you to talk to me now?"

My heart felt as if it had turned over in my chest. Instantly, I felt more awake than I had done. "Who the hell are you and where did you get my private telephone number?" I croaked by way of reply.

"Er ... I've told you who I am. I ... er ... I don't recall who gave me your number but ..."

"Leave me alone!" I yelled. I hung up and, shaking, handed the phone to a very perplexed and anxious Peter. Of course, he wanted to know what it was about and I told him. The thing is, my house phone is not registered in my own name *and* the number is ex-directory. The only way for anyone to get my number and relate it to me personally is to have been given it. I felt very upset indeed and not a little shaken. I really did not need this kind of thing whilst so ill.

When Andrea came that day she was alone. Dimly aware that she was extremely worried about me, I agreed to try to drink a cup of tea and perhaps put my dentures in and attempt a piece of toast to eat. I'm sure I heard Peter explaining about emetophobia but whether Andrea understood it or not, I have no idea.

The wound was equally as smelly as it had been the day before and the exudates had increased; the wadding was soaked through. Instead of placing another bag inside the wound, Andrea padded it out with something called Sorbisan AG before placing the dressing over the top. She was so kind to me I could have wept. She told me not to worry and to try to both eat and drink, even though I felt rough as I needed to build up my strength in order to get better. Reassuring me that she would see me the next morning along with the Colorectal nurse, she left, taking all the soiled dressings with her in a bag.

I did manage to drink two or three half cups of tea over the rest of the day and in between those, I slept. I could not bring myself to put my dentures in my mouth and so I ate nothing at all that day, even though I was heartily encouraged by everyone. I simply felt too unwell.

I slept during the night, only waking up twice; both times, I called out in panic and Peter immediately came to me. He'd been asleep on the settee. The first time I woke, Peter gave me more medications and persuaded me to drink a little water. The second time, he helped me to the toilet and I did my best to empty the foul bag which, despite my not eating, was still filling up with evil smelling brown water. Psyche-Imp was nowhere to be seen. In all truthfulness, I think I was so ill at the time I wouldn't have noticed him if he'd stuck pins in my eyeballs.

Somehow, I managed to make it through to Monday morning. I felt absolutely terrible and, on top of it all, another two journalists had phoned me; one on the house phone and the other on my mobile. I was rude and unpleasant to both of them. In fact, Peter took the mobile from my unresisting hands and spoke to the reporter, telling him I was trying to recover from an operation for cancer and was far too ill to be bothered. I lost interest after a while; extreme depression had set in. I did not dare vocalise how I felt for fear of being shouted at by my lads and maybe even Peter. In truth, I was bitterly regretting ever having consented to the television interview or the operation in the first place. I should have known, with my luck in life, any and all possible complications would apply or happen to me, with or without the presence of Psyche-Imp. It seemed my prediction that Newsnight would not after all, go ahead had resulted in the people at the BBC handing out my personal details willy-nilly to all and sundry. As always, I did not weep; in fact, if anything, I felt disgruntled and angry and just ... well, low. Once again, in the privacy of my own head, I began to ponder ways of killing myself which were so absolute that, even if caught, nobody could interfere or do anything to stop me.

Jaime, the Colorectal nurse turned up first. She inspected the bag and decided that, when the wound had been satisfactorily dealt with, she would change the ileostomy pouch and inspect the stoma itself. I liked Jaime, but I could not summon much enthusiasm and I think she largely guessed at my mood. Just as Peter asked her if she had found out whether or not I had an infection, Andrea arrived.

It turned out I did have an infection. It was e.Coli inside the open wound, no doubt as a result of the wound having filled with shit several times. No wonder I felt so incredibly ill and it was so raw and sore. Andrea telephoned the doctor immediately to ask for a long course of antibiotics to be prescribed. She turned and told Peter he could go across to the surgery in about an hour to collect them and that he would need to ensure I took one every six hours.

Between Jaime, Andrea and Peter, the wound was stripped down and cleaned thoroughly and the ileostomy bag (which had leaked a little and so caused the skin surrounding the stoma to become raw and inflamed) was changed. Jaime said she would have a think about the possibility of trying a different style of bag for my stoma and told Peter and me to ensure that, as soon as I became aware of any 'stinging or burning' sensation, we should get the bag off and replace it because that sensation always meant some kind of leakage was happening. Peter paid far more attention to her instructions than I did. Once again I felt tired and depressed merely wanting to be left alone to sleep once the wound had been photographed, re-packed and dressed.

One day followed another as days generally do. I existed in a haze of Psyche-Imp induced nausea and panic, generalised malaise, unwanted telephone calls from reporters and a few unsolicited visits at the door from other reporters, exhaustion, depression and utter despair and hopelessness. I could not envisage ever being able to get up and move about ever again. With the gaping great wound in my abdomen, which appeared to me to be getting wider and deeper by the day, I couldn't even have a bath or shower, never mind kill myself! I had not taken a bath or washed my hair since the day of my operation – the 22nd December 2011 and it was by then mid January. I hadn't actually even had a wash, once I got to thinking about it. Nobody had brought me a bowl of water or my wash-bag or thought to see to my hair or anything. Even the District nurses hadn't even asked if I was managing personal hygiene. Surely, I thought, as Psyche-Imp pointed out that I smelled like a sewer, they must've been able to smell me? Why hadn't they commented or even asked?

When a different District Nurse came the next day, around 9th January, I asked why nobody had thought to help me to wash or bathe or wash my hair. For a moment or two she looked perplexed and then rallied wonderfully. She told me I should have asked about it before hand. I could be given a 'shower proof' dressing which would permit me to be cleaner at least. This would need to be ordered and so it would not be possible for her to manage it that day. She promised to attend to it the next day. I already knew that someone would be coming the next day from 'Tissue Viability' to see if I would be a good candidate or not for something called 'VAC Therapy' which actually sounded pretty terrifying!

Later that afternoon I was visited by Fiona and Lol. Fiona works as a Health Care Assistant at the local hospital and was appalled when she saw me and how my unwashed and filthy hair hung down in sticky rat-tails, never mind the ground in dirt on my face, neck and arms. Together my two friends shooed all the men out of the room and proceeded to fetch a bowl of deliciously warm water, several flannels and towels and then, they gave me a bed-bath! It was wonderful to actually feel clean! I held the flannel over my face for several minutes inhaling the scent of my Yardley Lavender soap – which I'd purchased for myself as a reward for being brave enough to have the operation in the first place.

Although I'd used clean incontinence pads every time I went to the toilet ever since leaving hospital, no-one had offered me any clean underwear (and in all fairness, I hadn't thought to ask for any, probably because I was just so weak, low and miserable and in such pain every time I tried to move). Fiona and Lol saw to that problem as well. They gave me lovely clean knickers and a fresh pad, a clean nightie and then helped me to get out of bed and sit on the settee whilst they stripped off the bedcovers to change them all.

Uther was summoned to bring fresh bedding and Peter put the dirty bed linens in the washing machine. Once the bed had been remade, along with a great deal of laughter, Lol and Fiona took me into the kitchen and, between them, managed to lean me over the sink (which was very painful and made the wound gape wider beneath its wadded dressing) and wash my hair for me.

I cannot tell you how wonderful it felt to be thoroughly clean. A great deal of my depression lifted almost instantly. I no longer picked up the scent of stale sweat every time I even twitched under the covers. Now I could smell my Lavender body spray mixed with the fabric softener I regularly use for my laundry. My hair soon dried and I could lie back on my freshly plumped pillows and enjoy Fiona and Lol's company. Thoughts of suicide left along with the dirt which had been washed off me. They didn't stay as long as I would've wished them to but I so enjoyed seeing them and the help they gave me. They promised to come back again soon and Lol wagged a warning finger at me before she left, "You just make sure you start eating again, Kat. You're skeletally thin you know. You'll never get better if you don't eat."

I promised I would do my very best and in fact, just after they'd gone, asked Peter if he wouldn't mind making me some scrambled eggs on toast. He helped me to get up and sit on the settee and then produced the meal in short order and sat beside me as I ate with a pillow and a tray on my lap. I actually enjoyed the food and managed to consume most of it. Peter kept apologising for not having thought about washing me or getting my hair washed, but I dismissed his concerns with a wave of my hand.

"It's my own fault," I said, "I didn't ask for any water to wash with or any help to wash either."

I wish I could say that I got used to being stuck flat on my back in bed, but I never did. More than anything, I wanted to be able to turn over onto my right side and curl up in order that I could sleep properly. Of course, this was impossible. Not only was there the gaping wound to think about, but the ileostomy bag was on the right and I knew that laying on it whilst semi-conscious in the hospital had already caused it to come away, leak and cause the infection. I didn't want to risk that again, although the damnable bag came away all on its own often enough even with me laying flat on my back.

It became a frequent event for me to wake up in the middle of the night and find that the wound dressing was soaked in liquid shit, not to mention that which had got onto the bedclothes. I hated every second of it and I swung rapidly between dejected depression and furious outrage at what had been done to me. I really would have been better off dead, surely? How could this be called any kind of life? As far as I was concerned, this was far worse than being confined to the house because of constant, almost uncontrollable diarrhoea. At least I could curl up and sleep comfortably back then, even if I did have to keep getting up to go to the toilet!

A couple of days before the people were to visit me from 'Tissue Viability', someone called Julie came along with Andrea. Jaime came on that day too. Julie took some blood and spoke kindly to me, although, when she heard me complaining to Jaime that I still continually felt as if I needed to 'poo normally' even though I wasn't connected, she said (in what I thought was a very patronising tone) "You have to treat your stoma as your bottom now and forget about the other part."

"I can't bloody forget it," I retorted, irritate beyond measure. "It feels like I need to keep running to the toilet just like I used to do. When I give and go to the toilet I just sit there for ages and nothing happens – of course, nothing can happen because all the poo is going straight into the bag without going through my large colon at all!"

Jaime told me the sensation of feeling that I needed the toilet all the time was called 'Tenesmus' and was actually quite common in people who'd had the same operation as me. She insisted it would pass eventually and advised me to continue taking all the pain killers, which may help to relieve it somewhat.

On that day, Jaime also brought me the excellent news that the histology lab had tested the parts of me which had been cut out and found no evidence that the cancer had spread into the lymph nodes which were removed along with the section of rectum and colon. I don't believe I really took on board how significant that was when the news was delivered. Certainly, several hours later, when talking to Peter, I suddenly recalled it and had a look at the piece of paper Jaime had left for me. It certainly was good news. It meant, in essence, that the cancer had been caught before it had spread right through the bowel wall and onward.

By the time the Tissue Viability people came to visit me on 10th January, the wound had grown to its largest point. It measured 182mm long by 88mm wide by 45mm deep. The deep, tension stitches holding the remains of my guts inside me were clearly visible amongst the 'meat' and 'slough'. The sickly smell was always present, even when the infection had apparently gone. All in all, it was quite disgusting. I marvelled that so many people could come along and peer at the filth which was me and not be retching with shocked disgust.

Tissue Viability enthusiastically stated that I was an ideal candidate for the VAC machine. The District Nurses (three of them on that day) explained to me that this was a marvellous new invention. I would have a special dressing on the wound and then a small, portable machine would be attached. This apparently would behave like a miniature vacuum cleaner and 'hoover' exudates from the wound whilst bringing the edges closer together. It promoted much faster healing they told me. Of course, I had my doubts, but since I am not a medic and had never heard of this proposed therapy I just agreed to give it a try. The nurses told me they would order the machine and dressings immediately and then would bring it to be attached the following Monday. In the meantime, my daily dressings had to be continued. I only half listened as the group of people talked about how to 'manage' the stoma which was so close to the wound and presented difficulties. I may even have dozed off to sleep.

Having had two weeks off work immediately after Christmas in order to be available to help to care for me, Uther had to return to work. I missed him, even though there were nearly always people about.

The Social Worker, Steve had visited and managed to increase my care hours from eighteen a week to thirty. I was able to employ both Lesley and Peter on these hours, which made me feel a whole lot better about my two friends doing so much for me. At least they would now be paid for their efforts.

And yet, at around that same time, Lesley came less and less often. She frequently did not reply to texts I sent her or calls I made to her phone. Whenever she did reply, she assured me there was nothing wrong and that she would be round to see me 'later' or 'tomorrow'. And then, more often than not, she just failed to turn up. I began to suffer paranoia immediately. What had I said or done to upset or offend Lesley? Despite several text messages with that direct question, she didn't reply.

The reporters continued to call sporadically. It was rarely the same people. Nearly every call was someone from a different newspaper or television station. Just one person called several times. Mark Williams-Thomas. I spoke to him at least twice and was extremely rude on both occasions. By the day the nurses came to fit the VAC therapy machine on 16th January, I was afraid to answer the telephone at all in case it was more journalists and reporters.

Several people turned up all together on the 16th January for the inaugural application of the VAC machine. I felt relieved to see Jaime amongst the sea of faces, some familiar, others not so, but all friendly and speaking words of sympathy and encouragement.

The VAC machine itself turned out to be about eight inches long by an inch or so thick by four inches wide. It was grey and shaped like a flattened pear and had both a power cord and a long lanyard so I could be mobile and get about. Apparently, one lady told me I'd even be able to drive with the machine in situ! I thought that highly unlikely, mainly on account of hardly being able to walk, never mind get into the car to drive anywhere, but I kept quiet. Another person told me that I really should be getting up by now and moving about; apparently, I was doing myself no favours at all by 'lazing around in bed all day'. Andrea didn't say anything of the sort; when I took in a sharp breath to defend myself, she pointed out to her colleague that in addition to the wound, I also suffered from Fibromyalgia and Unstable Angina and was doing my best to get mobile. She squeezed my hand and told me not to worry before handing me the machine so I could look at it properly before she began to attach it. She advised me to leave the machine plugged in overnight when I was moving about least and then, during the day, to unplug it. Apparently, it would run for around twelve to fifteen hours on a single charge.

Interested in spite of myself, I watched as she clipped on a small, clear 'tank' to the front of it. Inside the tank, a couple of strips of strange, papery stuff were visible. Next came the dressing itself which had to be done in a certain way before the machine could be attached.

First, Jaime removed the stoma bag and completely cleaned the stoma and the surrounding skin. I expressed my worries that the stoma would leak and squirt everywhere and Jaime said it didn't matter if it did, everything would quickly be mopped up and cleaned again. She smiled and stood ready at the foot of the bed with a handful of large dry wipes in order to be able to do just that should it become necessary.

I watched, interested for once, as the wound was stripped down and cleaned thoroughly. A single sheet of something which closely resembled thin, wet and rubbery plastic was spread inside the wound; the edges overlapped onto my skin and Andrea carefully trimmed them, making sure they went nowhere near the stoma itself and adjusted the sheet so that it was only covering my innards which were exposed. As she worked, she joked about having been good at Arts and Crafts at school which, she felt, was standing her in good stead now. Psyche-Imp sat on my shoulder watching intently. Now and again he poked me in the ear but he didn't say anything and so I remained quite calm, despite my worries of shit squirting everywhere uncontrollably.

Next, Andrea took out a coil of what looked, to me, very much like grey-black packaging foam! It was around half an inch square and about a yard and a half long coiled up into a disc. I had to hold one end in place at the top of the wound as Andrea, unwound the coil and unrolled the coil, working the foam back and forth on top of the rubbery film she'd already put inside me until the wound was thoroughly filled up with the stuff. And then, with me holding one end of the foam in place and Jaime holding the other with her fingers spread wide, Andrea carefully cut a round hole about three inches in diameter just off centre of a sheet of something about the size of a piece of A4 paper. I kept my fingers where I'd been told to 'hold' the foam in place and watched as she carefully peeled the backing paper off this sheet with a hole in it. It now looked remarkably like a sheet of laminate film! Psyche-Imp sniggered at the thought of how much heat would have to be applied to laminate. I pulled his evil, long nose and told him to shut up.

Carefully, Andrea stuck the film over the foam placing the three inch hole over the stoma – which left the raspberry coloured stoma in the middle of the hole with around an inch and a half of bare skin around it. Andrea realised one sheet of sticky film was enough to completely cover the whole wound and its foam contents so she added another piece which she cut into strips and squares to make a patchwork of the sticky film which would be 'watertight' and also 'airtight'. Jaime then applied the stoma bag – and just in time because, no sooner had the bag been stuck down, the stoma began to work in earnest. Jaime expressed concern that the 'output' from the stoma appeared to be nothing but brown water.

"It's always like that," I replied.

"Well, it's supposed to be about the consistency of toothpaste," Jaime advised me, "this tells me you're not eating nearly enough. You'll have to eat a lot more to get it working properly."

I didn't argue. My food intake had increased quite a bit and I felt that I was eating at least as much as I had used to eat before the operation. Yet, although I had put on a little weight, I was still as skinny and bony as I'd always been. I wondered how much more I'd have to eat, but I didn't permit myself to dwell on it because there was a lot more to be seen.

It felt odd and kind of 'tight' to have so much sticky stuff on my skin. The black foam bulged out and I sub-consciously thought about the dreadful scenes in the film 'Alien' which made me shudder. Psyche-Imp sat on the top of my head and laughed fit to bust. I felt intensely relieved that only I could mentally 'see' the little blue imp. I couldn't mention him to anyone but Isabel the Psychologist of course; they'd have all thought me stark raving bonkers!

Once everything had been stuck down and prepared, the machine itself had to be applied. Andrea cut a small hole in the sticky stuff about the size of a five pence piece right in the middle of the foam and placed a thing which looked like a sucker over the hole. A tube came off this and led to the machine. She stuck more sticky film over the sucker and then asked if I felt ready for her to turn the machine on. She assured me she'd been told it didn't hurt a bit but I still felt intense trepidation as I nodded that I was ready. Psyche-Imp rubbed his hands together in anticipation of pain. Everyone else leaned forward slightly as Andrea flicked the switch and, with a very soft hum, the machine began to work.

Quite slowly, the black foam shrank back toward my abdomen. It didn't hurt in the least. I watched, entirely fascinated as the foam flattened and then the edges of the wound itself began to draw closer together. I noticed a few little bits of bloody exudates slide up the thin tube from the sucker and queried this.

"Yes, that's what it does." replied one of the other women present. "It'll suck all the gunk out and store it in the tank. It doesn't hurt, does it?"

I shook my head. "No, not at all. It feels a bit tight and weird I suppose but it doesn't actually hurt. At least, not right now. Is that it then?"

Andrea told me I could get up and move about as much as I wished with the machine in situ. The dressing would be 'shower-proof' she told me, although it wouldn't cope with being immersed in a bath of water. There were various lights on the machine. One indicated that everything was working as it should, another was an alarm. If anything went wrong, an audible alarm would sound and the light would flash red; then there were various steps to take to try to remedy the problem. If the power was low a light would flash amber and then red. If the power remained good, the light would stay green. Peter paid close attention to all this. I'd already got fed up with the technicalities and was busy rubbing my hand over an abdomen which, although having a thick black strip down it, was more intact that it had been for nearly a month. I tapped at the foam; it was actually rock hard!

Everyone packed up their stuff and with a lot a friendly goodbyes and good luck wishes, they left. Peter sat beside me and we inspected the machine and the strange dressing as we chatted about what a clever invention it was. Peter told me he had seen something similar on a hospital ward but that it had been huge and cumbersome and certainly did not leave the patient mobile as this machine would do.

To test the theory of mobility, I got up and walked across the lounge and then to the toilet. The machine hung on its long lanyard at my side like a small handbag although it weighed very little – certainly an awful lot less than any handbag I've ever used. Psyche-Imp sat in the toilet and sulked; he was certainly becoming aware that I noticed him less and less as the days passed by.

Had I not had a stoma bag which needed to be changed at least every other day, the machine dressing would have been able to remain in place for a week at a time. As it was, the stoma bag could not be changed without also disturbing the wound dressing and seal, so close were the two together. The first change of dressing is when I learned that although the machine and the way it worked was not at all painful, the removal of the dressing gave pain and discomfort a whole new meaning – unfortunately, this also meant that Psyche-Imp also got a new lease of life too!

The first time Andrea had to change the dressing Peter was here and this was just as well because it turned out to be something Andrea could not manage all on her own. For a start, she simply did not have enough hands (even borrowing mine too). First, she switched the machine off and turned away to get all the things she would need ready and to hand, expecting that the vacuum would have released within a minute or two. This was not the case at all. Although the black strip felt a little softer, it was by no means slack.

Andrea began to pull back the sticky film and the ileostomy bag came with it. Just to be awkward (and I am absolutely certain that Psyche-Imp had something to do with this), the stoma immediately began to leak and I needed both hands to catch the vile output in a handful or two of cotton swabs. Peter had a scented ostomy disposal bag ready and Andrea had intended to drop the half-full bag into it. However, the ileostomy bag was still fastened to the sticky dressing film. It seemed the whole dressing, foam and all, would need to be peeled back and dropped into the waste bag as one unit.

Andrea stuffed the open hole of the bag with swabs so that the contents could not leak out as the stoma was already leaking. Between her and Peter, they began to peel back the film ... which hurt as, since I am a mammal I have lots of soft, downy, tiny little hairs on my tummy just like everybody else and the sticky film was tearing them all out at once! Holding the swabs over the now spurting stoma, I gritted my teeth and tried to stop my eyes watering. Psyche-Imp jumped up and down on my chest. Every time his sharp little feet landed, so the stoma squirted out more filth which I had to catch.

When it came to pulling away the actual black foam, this was of course encased on the top side with sticky film and on the underside – which was next to the open wound – with the soft, rubbery film ... which had stuck to the wound bed in places. As Andrea pulled it back, I yelped before I could control myself and then ground my teeth in agony as she continued to pull the film away.

Finally, the whole came free and Andrea stuffed it all into the bag and Peter tied it up. Tears were trickling down the sides of my face and falling into my ears.

Psyche-Imp was leaning over me and peering into the hole. Every now and then, he poked a finger inside and I felt a stabbing pain and jumped violently.

Andrea sluiced the wound with saline and then carefully wiped all around the edges with Cavilon (which is a soothing solution and does not sting raw flesh). I continued to mop up what seemed like gallons of liquid shit and had almost made my way through a whole packet of swabs.

"If the output is that liquid, you're still not eating enough, Kat," Andrea advised as she opened a new pack of swabs and handed them to me.

Peter insisted that for the two days since the machine had been in place, I'd eaten very well and had at least four meals a day as well as snacks and lots and lots of jelly babies (which were supposed to thicken the output). Andrea said she'd contact Jaime to ask what could be done about the problem. In the meantime, we had to deal with what we'd got – namely an ileostomy spurting liquid shit and a now open wound.

I kept the swabs mopping up and Peter kept cleaning round the area with wet wipes as Andrea applied first the bottom layer of film inside the wound and then the foam. Since I could not help to hold the foam in place because I was holding back the torrent of poo, Peter had to assist with the placement of the stuff.

At last there was a gap in the ileostomy activity and Andrea was able to get the sticky film over the foam and round the stoma. She applied the stoma bag and then was able to take her time to finish off the dressing and fasten the VAC machine with its fresh tank to it. As soon as she switched the machine back on, the foam shrank back into a neat strip and the edges of the wound pulled together again. Immediately I felt more secure and certainly, a lot less stressed. I glanced at the pair of bags we'd filled up with soiled swabs and other dressings and breathed a huge sigh of relief.

After that day my appetite began to improve somewhat although I still often felt nauseous and shaky and the feeling of needing the toilet if anything became stronger. In any event, I began to eat a fruit yogurt and two slices of toast every morning, followed by cola and crisps for elevenses, either a couple of sandwiches or bowl of soup and bread for lunch, further snacks mid afternoon and a decent meal in the evening which usually consisted of something like chicken casserole or some kind of pie with potatoes and vegetables.

I also began to make more of an effort to get up and get dressed for at least part of the day, although I still tired incredibly easily and needed to sleep often. This was when I discovered that my clothes no longer fitted me. Everything I owned, bar one pair of ancient, pull-on trousers, was far too small. I asked Uther to buy me some leggings from Sainsbury's in a size fourteen. I'd always been a size ten to twelve but nothing in those sizes would go anywhere near me now. Uther managed to get me some and they fitted me ... but only just. I knew if I continued to put on weight, I would soon need a size sixteen.

The output from the stoma continued to be completely liquid and, when Jaime next came to visit with the nurses, she advised me to start taking Imodium (Loperamide) again. I wondered if this was actually a good idea because I was still taking the anti-emetic drugs I'd been taking for ten years or more and I felt that Imodium worked in exactly the opposite way to

Metoclopramide. Surely, I reasoned to Jaime, the two drugs cancelled one another out did they not?

She thought they probably did but reminded me that I had used both before when I was quite ill before diagnosis and after diagnosis during radiation therapy. I agreed to try taking the drug to see if it made any difference. Jaime did not fail to notice that I had put on some weight and complimented me on having managed to achieve it. She asked how much I got out and about.

At that point, which was around 28th January 2012, I had to admit that I truly felt like I was going completely crazy because I had not been out of the house and had in fact, barely moved from my bed since coming home on 29th December. Jaime said I really needed to try to get moving more and build my strength up so that I could go outside, even if it was only for a brief walk around the house. She thought I would feel loads better and a lot less depressed and isolated if I could only get out once in a while. Whilst I agreed with her idea on principle, I also thought I would need some clothes to wear which actually fitted me and which I did not, at that time, have.

It was at around that time that Emily came along. I'd known her since she was a schoolgirl as she had been very friendly with Uther and they'd attended the same school. She'd found herself in the uncomfortable position of being unemployed, despite having gained a degree in Graphic Art at university.

She just happened to call in to visit with Uther and it was during their conversation, when Emily said that although she'd had a job for a while, she'd been made redundant and been unable to find any other work. It was making life very difficult for her. Uther suggested that, since Lesley appeared to have turned her back on me entirely and I had both Council funding and need, perhaps Emily could work for me.

We both agreed immediately. Emily's details were given to Sally, the lady who does the wages on my behalf and Emily began work.

I felt comfortable in Emily's company and thought this a far better arrangement than employing a carer recommended by the Council who would have been a stranger to me. I've always had trust issues with people and a lot of the help I needed might involve quite personal and intimate things like washing, dressing and changing the stoma bag or wound dressing.

For those first couple of weeks, Emily was there ever such a lot and helped me to sit up, get out of bed, get to the toilet and gradually, over time, encouraged me to walk around the kitchen and hallway to get used to being up on my feet. She ran errands for me, fetching stuff from the shop and, once I'd found something sack-like to wear over the leggings Uther had acquired, she came outside with me. At first we just hobbled up and down the lane a bit. And then, I got into the car and drove to the shop with Emily as a passenger.

The trip around the shop absolutely exhausted me, but I felt good that I'd done it. Since the VAC dressing was so much more secure and actually prevented any leakage from the bag, I began to get more and more confident.

One day, just after the nurses had been and changed the dressing and the bag, Peter took me over to Wrexham to Sainsburys. I found some nice clothes which weren't too expensive – although, since I still wasn't smoking, I did have more money than I had used to have at my disposal. I bought more leggings and about four loose, baggy tops.

A few days later, I found some more baggy tops which were quite pretty on eBay. I bought those too. I was beginning to feel a lot more hopeful and upbeat, although I did still get some dreadful periods of depression when, once again, I felt suicidal. I have to say that these periods began to grow less and less frequent, but they were still shockingly powerful. Psyche-Imp grinned his evil grin every time my spirits began to sink and he leaped onto my shoulder to whisper sickening thoughts into my head.

One day, before I could control my mouth, I let forth such a torrent of depressed, suicidal, hateful thoughts, that Uther was appalled. Caroline happened to have called in for the first time since my operation (she'd been unwell herself); she was listening as I ranted about much I hated life, the universe, everybody in it, what had been done to my body, the fact that nobody ever hugged me ... and Uther leaped up to come and shout at me. Sadly, Uther is very large. He was clearly upset and angry and shouted at me that I had clearly forgotten how he'd taken two weeks off work and had slept on the settee, waited on me hand, foot and finger and most certainly did hug me when lifting me up to go to the toilet! Caroline was terrified. I was gutted and screamed back at him that he didn't understand and had no idea what it was like. Caroline hurried away as soon as she was able to. I felt bitterly ashamed and also extremely disappointed that Uther clearly couldn't understand how hard it had been to stay in bed, unable to have any freedom whatever or privacy, for over six weeks, never mind how my body had been ruined, deformed and scarred. It was particularly hard for me to cope with because I had only gone ahead as a 'trial', not because of me or because I had any desire to live or fight cancer but for the boys. I suddenly remembered the promise I'd forced from the nameless person – and decided to call it in.

Psyche-Imp jumped up and down with glee. He ran around my shoulders, screaming encouragement into my ear, tugging at my once-again greasy, straggly hair which hadn't been washed for over a fortnight. I knew he was there but I made no move to swat him or get rid of him.

The more Psyche-Imp talked to me, whispered to me, told me I'd had enough, the more determined I became to go somewhere and kill myself. Why should I continue living this miserable life with this disgusting, stinking body which was now so deformed? I thought. I went back to bed and lay, pretending to be asleep, thinking of a fail-safe method with which to commit suicide. I actually did fall asleep after a little while.

When I awoke, Psyche-Imp was waiting for me. I had a massive panic attack – apparently without trigger or cause. I shook from head to foot; I felt sick; I felt as if the world was going to fall out my arse (even though my arse was not connected). Emily had gone home, Damon was nowhere in sight and Peter was at work. I thought I was alone.

Somehow, I battled the panic (I can't remember how) for over two hours. If not for that panic attack, I would have got into the car, driven away somewhere remote and committed suicide. The panic attack saved me – clearly Psyche-Imp does have some sense of self-preservation after all.

Andrea turned up to do the dressing and, during the course of changing the bag and dressing, I haltingly told her how I felt. She was very reassuring and suggested that she ask someone to visit me who could help me with 'body-image' at the very least. She recommended that I get out of the house even for a little while and no matter how tired it might make me.

I felt better for talking to Andrea. Psyche-Imp slunk away and I could think, reasonably clearly again. It felt stupid to have to wait for the little blue bastard to go away for a while before I was able to think properly, but that the time that really was what it was like. Psyche-Imp had become all too real.

Rational thought took over and despite my still low mood, I decided that suicide was a foolish thing to do, having already gone through so much. I mean, I'd had the radiotherapy and the operation – done the difficult bits – so why top myself now? I looked down at my stomach with its thick, grey stripe through it and noticed how I now had rolls of fat I'd never had before as well. That's when I went out into the kitchen and stood on the scales (we keep our bathroom scales in the kitchen for some insane reason). I found I weighed very nearly eleven stones!

Shocked, I stepped off the scales and stood in the middle of the kitchen, looking down at the belly and thighs I'd suddenly grown (it seemed) overnight. When did that happen? I'd been five feet nine inches tall and nine stones and two pounds ever since I was fourteen years old. After the operation, when I'd been weighed just before leaving the ward, I was just a little over eight stones, so I knew I should put on some weight ... but not this much! My spirits sank again. Now, in addition to being deformed and scarred and having a leaking bag of shit hanging off me – I was also fat. Never had I felt so ugly in my life before. I've never been vain but have always more or less eaten what I liked and ignored my slender frame – or now I realised, I'd actually taken it for granted. I shuffled into the lounge in search of my tape measure. I think it was probably a good thing I couldn't find the thing that day. I sat down at the computer and idly opened the email folder to find over a thousand emails in my inbox! Well, it had been the best part of eight weeks since I'd checked them. I couldn't face sifting through them all, so I left them there and sat down on the edge of the bed. Perhaps I should start trying to run up and down the stairs? I'd not been able to even walk up the stairs properly long before I got cancer due to Fibromyalgia and Angina. What a ridiculous thought. I leaned back and snuggled into the pillows. Before I knew it, I was asleep.

Over the next week or so, with Emily as an almost constant companion and Peter coming to help regularly as well, I managed to force myself somehow to get up and move about a bit more. I made sure I had my GTN spray with me at all times and regularly took all the painkillers that the doctors had so thoughtfully prescribed (and which I'd hitherto often forgotten to take). Even so, I found I wearied extremely quickly and often had need of the spray.

The next time I went to buy clothing, I realised I would need an even bigger size ... a sixteen! The few people I saw whilst out all remarked at how much better they thought I looked with a little weight on my bones, but I still felt incredibly fat, ugly and self-conscious. I wouldn't even attempt to wear jeans or trousers because the stoma had been positioned exactly on my waistline so the waistbands of jeans and trousers crossed it and the bag leaving a bulge above and below the band. Very ugly indeed. I felt sure everyone could see it.

The nurses continued to visit every other day to change the VAC therapy dressing and bag. Andrea always asked how I was feeling in myself but none of the others ever did. I think they either hadn't read the notes or hadn't realised just how bad I really felt.

I was delighted when Isabel turned up one day. Apparently, we'd had an appointment and she'd spoken to the nurses and they'd told her it would be very much better if she could visit me at home. When she arrived, Andrea and a colleague were still here changing the dressing and Isabel asked if she could see the wound. She winced when she saw it. Although it had shrunk somewhat, there was still a gaping hole in my tummy and the deep tension stitches were now in loose loops and very visible. The nurses always had to ensure they didn't get caught in the sticky dressing as they were not sure if they were safe to take out or not.

When the nurses had gone, Emily tactfully made herself busy elsewhere and I began to talk to Isabel. I told her, with complete candour, that I often felt like 'offing myself' and that I now felt fat, ugly and deformed. I could not come to terms with what had happened to me and what little confidence I had managed to build up over the years had vanished overnight with my cancerous growth and flat, unscarred tummy. I felt I wanted to sue the hospital for disfiguring me and in particular, Mr. Billings, the surgeon, who had told me that the chances of infection were 'negligible' but that, once I'd got an awful infection, just commented "Well, it's a dirty old operation." I felt I had been dismissed out of hand and that nobody realised quite how much it all mattered to me.

Isabel seemed to understand completely. It felt really good to have another adult with whom to speak who was not either directly concerned with my care or as a member of family. I could say the dreadful things I was feeling and thinking without fear of causing upset or disgrace and without seeming ungrateful – which I undoubtedly was.

I explained to Isabel how Psyche-Imp was still very much present and now and again, simply took over and caught me completely unawares. I even told her I'd thought about how to kill myself. She said I should speak to the doctors and ask for some anti-depressants and that, if they needed to speak with her, she would back me up. I felt that was very useful and made a mental note to try to see Doctor Fox as soon as possible.

Before I ever managed to remember to get a doctor's appointment, I had an appointment to keep with the Oncologist in the Shooting Star Unit of the Maelor Hospital. I didn't want to go. I was certain he was going to put me on chemotherapy again and that I'd have to take the wretched tablets for six months at least.

Jaime counselled me well and told me I should attend anyway and that I always had the option to refuse to take the tablets. She thought they may not even be necessary in view of the histology results I'd had, which were excellent.

Eventually, I was persuaded to attend and Peter took the day off work and came along with me for that appointment. I had to go have an armful of blood taken again, and for some insane reason, I was weighed and measured again as well. I was appalled when the scales showed me to be eleven and a half stones! In fact, I could think of very little else in all the time I was waiting.

Eventually, Linda, another Colorectal nurse, called me and Peter through and we sat in a small examination room waiting for the Oncologist to come through from the room next door. I'd only ever met Dr. Simon Gollins once before, so I didn't recognise him when he entered the room, holding my file under his arm.

He offered me his hand in greeting and sat down opposite me. Psyche-Imp clambered up my back and sat on my shoulder, picking his ear. My stomach clenched into a knot of trepidation.

"Ah. Right, ah ... Ms. Ward. Um ..." Mr. Gollins opened the file and peered down at a page. "I've, ah ... had your results from the pathology laboratory and ..." he flicked a page or two over, "I can see that there was no evidence of ... ah ... cancer ... ah in any of the lymph nodes which were removed and therefore," he closed the file and leaned forward slightly. "In view of the reaction you had to Capecitabine prior to surgery, I do not think it would be wise to put you back on it. Anyway, it does not appear to be necessary since the lymph nodes were clear."

I looked at Peter. Psyche-Imp whispered in my ear in his scratchy-scratchy voice, "He's lying! You're riddled with cancer. You're going to die!" Mentally, I knocked Psyche-Imp off my shoulder and stamped on him until he howled in frustration and pain.

"Does that mean the cancer has gone?" I asked.

Dr. Gollins nodded. "It does indeed. Of course, you will need to have a colonoscopy about once a year through your stoma ..."

"What?" I squeaked. Psyche-Imp picked himself up off the floor and leaped into my lap where he repeatedly kicked me in the guts. "But ... but ... how will they do that? I've got an ileostomy and it's tiny!"

"Really?" Mr. Gollins glanced at Linda, who nodded. "Oh. Well. My mistake. I thought you had a permanent stoma. It'll be via the usual route then."

I had begun to feel sick, no thanks to Psyche-Imp and his efforts. I tried to breathe deeply and still my rapidly thumping heart. "Is that it, then?"

Mr. Gollins smiled. "Yes. This is where you and I part company. Of course, the Colorectal nurses will continue to support you as long as you have the ileostomy and I am sure they will always be willing to advise. Your GP will be your first port of call for any other problems."

Suspicious, I glanced at Peter, who had, so far, said nothing at all. "What about the cancer coming back?" I demanded.

Mr. Gollins shook his head. "Unlikely. Very unlikely. The lab seems sure that we got it all. Mind you," he opened the file again, "There were a number of polyps as well as I recall. You might be called for genetic testing ..."

"Does that mean there is a risk of the cancer recurring?" asked Peter.

"Not generally, no. We make sure we monitor ex cancer patients for at least five years. As I said, there will be regular colonoscopies and any further polyp growths will be removed."

"What about other cancers?" I asked. "Am I more likely now to get other cancers?"

Mr. Gollins smiled again and shook his head, negative. "Generally we find that is not the case. You'd have to be very, very unlucky to get any other type of cancer as well as bowel cancer ..."

Peter and I looked at each other. I stood up. "Oh. Well, that's a given, then. It just remains to be seen where the next cancer will appear." Peter stood as well.

"Thank you," I said to Dr. Gollins. "Sorry I was such a difficult patient."

"I ... er ... I intended to examine you," Dr. Gollins said.

"No, thank you." I replied.

"I see. Very well. I am very glad you are now clear of cancer, Ms. Ward. Goodbye." He stood up and left the room.

Linda shook her head slightly.

"Is that it?" I asked. "Can I go home now?"

"Yes. Jaime or I will be in touch. Take care, Kat." She replied.

As we left the room, Psyche-Imp leaped from the floor onto my shoulder and clung to my hair. He began to whisper into my ear but I wasn't listening. On the way back to Peter's car, all I could talk about was the possibility of getting another cancer. For some strange reason, even though I knew that it would be Psyche-Imp who would start and promote the cancer and the fear which went with it, I didn't feel scared at all at that time, in spite of the little blue bastard's best efforts.

Peter shook his head as we got into the car. "Seems mad that the best they can say is that you'd be 'really unlucky' to get another cancer, doesn't it?"

"All the time you've known me and you're surprised?" I snapped. I shoved Psyche-Imp off my shoulder and watched as a car ran him over. For several minutes the little blue sod lay as flat as a piece of paper in the car park. I turned away. I couldn't even snigger as I felt inexplicably angry and also somewhat bereft, although I couldn't have explained why I felt either.

The routine of District Nurses coming along to change both the bag and the VAC dressing continued every other day for another couple of weeks without any problem. I had become used to the dressing and bag being so secure and there not being any leaks and due to that, I had gained confidence.

Emily had come along with me as I drove the car up to the local shop, although I sat in the car and waited as Emily went in for the shopping. I really felt self-conscious about the VAC machine looped over my body with its little tank full of bloody exudates.

I sat at the computer a few times, although I could never manage very long. I did manage to sort through most of my emails over a period of about a week or so.

I'm not sure when it was that I suddenly decided I wanted to 'do' the Sport Relief Mile. I'd never done anything like it before and, prior to the cancer, even then was probably not capable of even walking a mile, never mind running it. Everyone thought I was mad.

I chivvied and bullied the rest of my family and Peter and Emily too into doing the mile with me. I booked us all in online and told Emily that it would give me something to aim for.

I also told the District Nurses what I intended to do. None of them said anything to discourage me, but I could see from their faces that they thought I was completely daft, if well meaning.

I began to try to walk every day, just a little way. I drove up to Ifton Meadows with Emily and the dogs. Using a walking stick and letting the dogs run loose, I walked a little way along the path, took a puff of GTN when the pain began in my chest and then walked a little way further.

Emily was infinitely patient with me. Not only did she see to the dogs and everything else which needed attending to, she both encouraged me and sympathised with me when I became irritated at my own weakness, exhausted or just plain tired. I was often very grumpy indeed.

The deep tension stitches were beginning to really get in the way of the VAC dressing and none of the District Nurses were keen to cut them away or get rid of them. I found myself getting really worried. I often felt griping pains across my abdomen and worried that my guts might fall out because the stitches were no longer tight enough to hold them in. One of the District Nurses – I think it was Sarah – arranged, via one of the Colorectal Nurses, for me to see Mr. Billings the surgeon to get his advice.

It was well into February at that time and the District Nurses were telling me that they intended to discontinue the VAC Therapy soon. This worried me no end. I couldn't bear the thought of being without the security of the sticky film dressing.

One night, about a week before the VAC was taken away for good, Peter had come over and was lying down on the settee. He'd intended to stay the night anyway and was almost asleep. I was dozing; I hadn't moved for some time because I was reading. All of a sudden, the alarm on the VAC machine sounded.

At first, I could not identify what the noise actually was. Peter called across to me, "What's that?"

"VAC machine," I replied. There's a red light flashing and this noise. Has it gone wrong or something?"

Peter immediately came over to inspect the device. The dressing was still taut but the alarm, on closer inspection, indicated that the vacuum had somehow become broken. There had to be a leak. Peter inspected the whole dressing really carefully and could find no evidence of a leak anywhere. He consulted the instruction sheet which the District Nurses had thoughtfully left behind. There would be no point in calling the nurses as there was no night-time service in this area. Eventually, Peter took out a sheet of the sticky film and very carefully applied it over the whole wound so that there were no gaps at all. The light went out and the alarm stopped.

Relieved, Peter put all the stuff away and we both settled down to sleep. Within fifteen minutes, the alarm began to sound again. I am absolutely sure now, with hindsight, that this must have been Psyche-Imp activity because he'd been inexplicably quiet for several days and I'd had virtually no panic attacks or any other troubles to speak of. Peter came back to inspect the device (which had only been changed the previous day) and could find no leakages at all, nor any other reason for there to be an alarm sounding. Again he tried to patch over any part of the film where there appeared to be a crease but it had no effect. The alarm was one of those electronic, particularly irritating ones which really get under your skin quickly. We were both becoming increasingly frustrated. Peter studied the instructions again and then found a telephone number, apparently manned twenty-four hours a day, which he called.

I shuffled into the kitchen with the wretched machine bleeping as I made a cup of tea for both of us. When I returned to the room, Peter was looking very annoyed and was arguing, as politely as possible with the operative on the other end of the phone.

"Look, Madam, I know this area extremely well. I am an RGN myself, I live in this area, work in this area and I am telling you there is no service here at night!" Peter insisted. He listened to the reply and sighed. I saw him scowl fiercely. He drew in a breath, "I dare say, but in this area ..." he turned toward me, an incredulous expression on his face, "You cannot possibly state ... pardon? What ..." The telephone hung limply in Peter's hand. "She hung up on me!"

He explained that the operative on the other end, rather than talk him through what may need to be done with the machine, had informed him, in an icy tone, to telephone the night-time District Nurse service and ask for a nurse to visit. She simply would not accept that there was no such service in this area and eventually, became almost offensive, before hanging up the phone.

"Right," said Peter, recovering his calm. "I am a registered nurse. I've changed this dressing and bag before and so, since that's all a District Nurse could possibly do, that's exactly what I'll do. I'll just get all the stuff ready and then we can sort that bloody alarm out."

Whilst waiting for Peter to get everything ready for the change, I switched the machine off because the alarm was really getting on my nerves and making me increasingly irritated.

It didn't take very long for Peter to change everything. He stripped the wound and stoma down, cleaned everything thoroughly and methodically re-did the whole dressing and bag. Finally, he switched the VAC machine on and we watched as the air began to be sucked out of the grey foam dressing until the wound was once again a flat, grey strip across my abdomen.

Peter had not even finished clearing away all the packages, old dressings and things when the alarm sounded again. Astonished, he turned and stared at me.

"What? I didn't move!"

And so it went for a long time during that night. Time and again, Peter patched and changed the dressings, the sticky film, then the whole thing again and time and again, the machine alarm went off. In the end we both gave up and simply switched the vacuum off. At least we could then get some sleep.

The next day, Peter called the nurses and someone came out. We demonstrated that, within a few minutes of switching the machine on, the alarm sounded, although there appeared to be nothing at all wrong with the dressing. The answer was to change the machine. Clearly, the one I'd had developed a fault sometime after fitting it. With a new machine on the same dressing, everything was just fine.

I knew I only had a week or two left of the VAC therapy and, although the wound had grown considerably narrower and shallower with the machine, there was still quite a sore and raw open slash down my middle. I asked one of the District Nurses whether the wound would ever completely close up and she shook her head.

"I'm afraid not. It will heal over, but you'll always have that deep cleft. If it really bothers you, what about asking the GP if she could refer you to a plastic surgeon? They'd be able to fix it soon enough."

This was not the news I'd wanted. Oh no, not at all the news I'd wanted. Psyche-Imp immediately appeared from nowhere and crawled up my back to whisper in my ear. By the time the nurse had left, the little blue imp had persuaded me that I would be forever ugly, deformed and would never again be able to wear any decent clothes because everybody would be able to see that I had a 'bum' on my ever-growing tummy. Psyche-Imp also pointed out that I was rapidly getting fatter and already looked pregnant. In moments, my self-esteem dropped away to nothing.

Although I kept going through the motions of moving about, I felt so low, in myself, I seriously considered cancelling the Sport Relief Mile. In addition to my self-image problem (and nobody had answered the District Nurse's referral about body-image) I also found I had a great fear of becoming fat. I seriously considered taking up smoking again.

One morning, I sat down at the computer intending to write and found that I could not settle at all. I kept stopping what I was doing and looking around as if searching for something. Eventually, I realised it was the cigarettes which had been ever present during all other times when I wrote. I'd got through ever so many fags because I lit one, inhaled the first puff and then set it down in the ash-tray beside me whilst I wrote. By the time I picked it up to smoke it, generally it had burned away and so I would light another and repeat the process the whole time I was sitting at the computer. Once I began to really think about it, I realised that perhaps twenty or more of my forty a day habit had been burning away in the ash-tray beside me. Briefly, I thought it was a good thing I no longer smoked.

That feeling soon vanished when I found I could not settle at all to write anything. I told Emily we were going up to the shops and I wanted her to come with me. On the way, as I drove, I explained that I intended to buy some cigarettes and resume my smoking habit. Emily counselled me against it but at the same time, she seemed to understand that I felt unable to write without them.

I purchased one pack of cigarettes and a lighter and drove home again. Once I got inside, I had to search for an ash-tray. Whilst I unwrapped the cellophane packaging, I told Emily how surprised I felt at the price of cigarettes and found it hard to believe they had increased in price so much in just three months. I took a cigarette out of the packet, put it in my mouth and sucked inwards as I applied a too large flame from the lighter. Emily watched with an expression of doubt and anxiety on her face.

I didn't cough; neither did I taste the tobacco on the first two or three pulls I took. And then, when I did get a taste of it, I screwed my nose up in disgust.

"Yuk! That's horrible!" I exclaimed. I pinched the end off the cigarette and shook my head. The whole room stank of tobacco as well. "Gods, Em, it's awful!" I exclaimed. Emily nodded miserably.

About an hour later as I sat at the computer again, I tried, with the same cigarette – or the half a cigarette remaining. This time, I got the taste immediately and actually had the need to spit into the ash-tray. "Oh no!" I moaned. "It really is so horrible and I can't do it! I'll never be able to write again and I'm going to be as fat as a pig for the rest of my life!" Once again, I put the cigarette out.

This time, I emptied and cleaned the ash-tray and buried the pack of cigarettes deep inside my bag. I knew I couldn't smoke them but I so wanted to write and felt completely unable to do so without the crutch of cigarettes. I kept trying to tell myself how foolish I was being and Psyche-Imp, appearing once more as if by magic, kept insisting that, without the cigarettes, I would never write again.

On 20th February, Andrea came along and removed the VAC therapy machine for the last time. I told her I felt very vulnerable about being without the security of the film, worried that the ileostomy bag would not be so secure and so would leak into the wound again. I was not at all happy about the therapy being discontinued because I still had a wound which could become infected.

Andrea did her best to reassure me and filled the wound with Sorbisan or something similar and used a shower proof dressing to cover it. The dressing, which resembled a large plaster, partially covered the edge of the ileostomy bag. It neither looked nor felt secure to me and I remarked upon it. Andrea reassured me as best she could and told me she'd see me in four days because I had an appointment at the hospital to see Mr. Billings two days ahead and someone at the hospital would change the dressing for me. She reminded me to make sure I took dressings with me when I went.

That night, I felt so grateful that Peter was here with me because, despite Andrea's reassurances, the bag came unstuck and a great quantity of liquid shit ran into the wound before I'd even realised it had happened. Peter patiently cleaned and cleared it all out and re-applied a fresh bag and re-dressed the wound. Clearly, I had been correct and the ileostomy bag was not in the least secure.

In the morning, the bag had leaked again. This time the whole bed was covered in liquid poo, the room smelled like a sewer and I was very distressed. Peter cleaned the evil-smelling filth from the wound first so as to minimise the risk of infection, but both he and I were already worried. Peter telephone the Colorectal nurses later that morning and explained the situation. Jaime agreed to meet us the following day at the hospital appointment where I would see Mr. Billings about the loops of tension stitches now clearly visible all throughout the wound and above it.

Peter was unable to come with me as he had to work and had already taken a lot of time off, so Emily accompanied me to the Maelor. On the way there, as I drove, I kept sniffing the air and asking Emily if she could smell anything. She said mostly that she couldn't, but now and again, she replied that she did 'get a brief whiff' of something.

When we got to the hospital, we met Jaime and Claire, two Colorectal nurses. I lifted my loose top to show them the bag and completely failed to notice that it had come adrift from my abdomen. In all fairness, they didn't notice either. Jaime said she had a new type of bag she would like to try out and that she would visit me at home with the District Nurse in a day or two.

After that, I was shown into an examination room and a nurse took down the dressing ready for Mr. Billings to come along and look at it. The loops of stitches were clearly visible and a faint, sickly-sweet smell was coming off the wound as well as the ever present scent of poo coming from the edge of the bag where it had come away from my skin on the left hand side again. I pointed it out to the nurse.

"Don't worry about that, love. I'll sort it all out after Mr. Billings has had a look at these stitches. I expect you brought spare dressings and spare bags with you, didn't you?"

I agreed that I had indeed brought everything which would be required.

At that point, the door opened and Mr. Billings sauntered in. "Hello, You," he greeted me. "What's the problem with you, then?"

I pointed at the loops of stitches and, as he tugged at one or two of them, I also complained about the smell and expressed my thoughts that, due to leakages from the bag, there was probably yet another infection inside the wound.

"These kind of wounds are always full of nasty bugs," Mr. Billings replied. He turned to the nurse. "Pull on these until they won't go any further and then simply cut them off."

"Um ... won't that just leave bits of stitch floating about inside me?" I asked.

Mr. Billing grinned. "Probably, but they won't go anywhere and will do no harm. I'm told you stopped smoking on the day of your surgery?"

"Yes," I replied. "I did."

"Good. Well, stay off the fags then," he said as he left the room.

And that was that. All the things I'd been planning on saying to him, everything I'd wanted to complain about, everything I wanted to rage about ... and I'd said none of it. Instead, I gritted my teeth as the nurse tugged on the lengths of plastic 'string' which were the stitches. I saw Emily wince in sympathy as she sat on a chair opposite the couch upon which I lay.

The nurse cut away two lengths of about four inches, one of about two inches and five of an inch or less. None of those five pieces would move at all when she took hold of them and tugged. I peered down into the gory cavity and asked if she could take a swab whilst she was there. She told me she was not permitted to do so and that I should approach either the District Nurses or my GP about it if I thought I had an infection. She then set to changing the bag for me.

I noted that where the bag had come away, liquid shit had settled on the skin to the left of the stoma. This was quite difficult to clean away and beneath it, the skin was red and raw. The nurse dealt with it all, stink and all, as if it were the most normal thing in the world.

"Tell me," she asked, as she cleaned the stoma itself, "How do you manage to change to your bag when the lumen points down at your feet? Do you use a mirror?"

I admitted I did not and that I had never yet been able to change the bag myself, not just because the lumen pointed downwards instead of straight out but also because the underside of the stoma had 'dehissed' and there was a gap, probably about two millimetres wide between the edge of the stoma and the slash in my skin where the stoma poked out. The nurse inspected it.

"Haven't you asked if someone could arrange to have it stitched back down?"

I shook my head. None of the Colorectal nurses seemed to think this necessary, even though the gap often bled when the bag was being changed. It was apparently, just a minor annoyance.

When the bag and dressing had been reapplied I got up, holding the bag in place as I moved. "I knew it was me that was stinking on the way here," I joked with Emily.

Two days later, Jaime came along at the same time as Sarah, the District Nurse. She brought with her some strange looking bags with a rigid plastic dip in them.

"These are rigid, deep convex bags, Kat and I think they may be the answer to your leakage problems. I'm going to cut one and put it on for you now and then Sarah can do the dressing afterward."

I watched as Jaime cut the hole in the convex plastic just off to one side. Having done this, she held it up and snorted with laughter. "Silly me! I've cut it going the wrong way! I'm trying to cut it so that more of the bag is over to the right and less to the left near the wound. I think it will stick better that way." She immediately threw that bag away and cut another.

The bag felt surprisingly comfortable (much to Psyche-Imp's disgust; he'd sat on the rail of the bed watching the proceedings and preparing himself to pounce on me). As it was, I managed to avoid all panic whilst Jaime was with me. Sarah watched and listened as Jaime explained how the convex bag would work, namely by pushing the stoma outward so that the crooked lumen would be well inside the bag and so preventing the poo from leaking out of the sides. Jaime gave me a whole box full of the bags and told me she'd left a template for me to draw round so I could cut my own. Whenever I felt ready, I could order more bags from a company called 'Amcare', who would obtain the prescription from the GP on my behalf.

I certainly felt more secure with the new bag in place but, even though I'd asked Sarah about having a swab done, she'd said she couldn't smell anything bad in the wound and that, at any event, late afternoon was not a good time to take a swab as it would not be collected to be taken to the lab until the next morning. I had to accept what she said.

That day, Emily came with me and I managed to walk all the way to mosaic at the top of the hill at Ifton Meadows, leaning on my walking stick and without using the GTN spray at all. I felt kind of elated. Emily thought I'd be able to 'do' the Sport Relief Mile after all and promised she would stay with me all through what for me would be a walk and for everyone else, a run.

Several days passed and the new convex bag didn't leak at all. My confidence began to grow and I ventured out a few times to the shops. I needed to purchase yet more clothing because I'd outgrown the size fourteen stuff I'd been wearing and even some of the newer size sixteen things were a little snug as well. I still felt incredibly fat and ugly but had no idea what to do about it. I'd never needed to go on a diet in the whole of my life. Besides, with an ileostomy, there are a number of things one is not supposed to eat because it can cause problems and salad was one of them. I kind of missed salad, especially plum tomatoes and crispy lettuce.

Even despite eating a great deal of starch and carbs the bag contents were still completely liquid. I asked Jaime about it on the phone one day as it was worrying me. I'd also noticed that, if for any reason, I felt a bit anxious or Psyche-Imp was busy causing a panic, the bag filled very quickly indeed and it filled with total, evil-smelling water. She recommended Jelly Babies again and suggested potatoes, long grain rice and various well-cooked vegetables (all of which I was already eating). Apart from trying to control the output with Loperamide, she had no other ideas.

Purely by accident, a week or so later, when my order arrived from Amcare, there was a 'free samples' box of goodies inside the pack. I discovered one of the samples was little strips which could be placed inside the ileostomy bag and which would turn liquid into gel – much like the strips which used to sit inside the VAC therapy machine tank. I immediately rang Amcare and asked if these were available on prescription and they told me they were and that, should I order some, they would collect the prescription on my behalf from the GP. I put in an order straight away.

I bought a couple of tops from Sainsbury's in size sixteen, bemoaning my fate of being 'a fat cow' as I did so. I'd been a size ten ever since I could remember and the larger sizes looked like tents to me, even though they fitted really quite well.

I felt pleased and encouraged however, when I managed to get a total of sixty pounds in sponsorship to 'do' the Sport Relief Mile. I made sure that I walked a little almost every day. I was determined that I wouldn't use a walking stick even if I had to walk it rather than run it. I persuaded Uther, his friend, Chris and another of his friends, Gemma to come run with us. Peter had no choice. I just told the poor man that was what was happening. Gemma said she'd walk round with me and Emily said she's join us. The Mile was scheduled on my birthday, twenty fifth March.

During the first week of March, I asked the visiting District Nurses several times if they could please take a swab of the wound as, to me, it smelled very strange. Each time they told me they could not smell anything unpleasant and that a swab wasn't necessary. In the end, when the wound began to feel itchy and sore as well and none of the nurse's were prepared to take a swab, I telephoned Chirk hospital and asked the Sister there if she could do it for me. At first, she refused, saying she could not over-rule another nurse's decision. Irritated, I replied, "Very well. I'll drive over to the Maelor and ask them to look at it instead." At that point, she decided perhaps she should take a look and asked me to come along to outpatients before twelve noon that day.

When I arrived at Chirk hospital, the Sister was as friendly as she always had been whenever I'd visited but she told me she'd spoken to the Sister in charge of the District Nurses. The District Sister felt, if I was well enough to take myself to Chirk Hospital for a swab to be done, then her nurses didn't need to visit me at home any longer. From now on, I would have to attend at the clinic in Chirk twice a week to have my dressing checked and changed. I think the Outpatient Sister was surprised when I grinned widely and said that was a much better arrangement for me as it meant I didn't have to sit at home any longer waiting for the nurse to turn up. She took the swab, re-dressed the wound and I went home.

Two days later, I received a call from the GP surgery. Elaine told me that I needed to come along and collect a prescription of antibiotics. Apparently, I had, of all things, a Tonsilitis bug inside my wound! I'd been sure there was an infection, but not one like that. I went to collect the prescription later that day.

Fortunately, over the seven day course of antibiotics, the wound stopped feeling sore and itchy and even the amount of slough and exudates improved. I also found life a lot easier because I could go to the clinic at an appointed time, get the wound seen to and then come away again and do whatever I felt I wanted to.

Psyche-Imp had been completely absent for well over two weeks. My confidence had grown and I had become used to being on my own for a few hours a day. I was sitting at the computer, minding my own business, messing about on Facebook when the phone rang. I reached up and answered it.

It was a reporter. I stared at the handset for a few moments before saying, in a suspicious tone of voice, "Where did you get this number from?" There was a long pause.

"Does it really matter where I got the number from?" the man asked. "Somebody who knows you quite well gave it to me and said you would be willing to talk to me about Jimmy Savile and your time at ..."

"Leave me alone!" I screamed down the phone. My hands were shaking and my stomach had knotted. Psyche-Imp appeared out of thin air and scrambled up my back onto my shoulder. "Don't ring this number again!" I bawled and then slammed the phone back on its stand. As soon as I'd put the phone down, I felt sick in the pit of my stomach, so much so that I almost lost control and actually retched!

"Aha!" howled Psyche-Imp, capering over the computer keyboard. "You're gonna be sick and there's nobody here for you. You're all on your own and you can't do it. You'll die! You'll be sick and choke to death and they'll come home to find a corpse where you should be!" I clutched at my stomach and tried to stand up. I could feel the ileostomy bag filling rapidly and lifted my top to glance down at the bag. Brown fluid was actually jetting from the stoma; it was beyond gross and possibly the most disgusting thing I've seen. I swallowed hard and tried to control the shaking.

Eventually, completely unable to shake Psyche-Imp and also unable to control the violent shaking my body was enduring, I tottered into the downstairs toilet, feeling that, even if it did make me vomit, I had to empty the bag because it was filling so fast it would likely burst if I didn't. The prospect of being showered by the contents of an exploding bag almost caused me to retch too.

My hands shook horribly as I gathered everything ready for the emptying routine. The jug was almost completely full and yet more was flowing from the stoma still. I re-fastened the vile bag and got rid of the contents of the jug. It seemed activity, even this foul activity (which involved a lot of bleach and air fresheners) was better than nothing. The shaking had become a little less.

When I'd done the bag and washed my hands, I went to the kitchen and went through the motions of making a cup of tea. I slopped water on the counter and nearly missed the cup altogether as I poured the boiled water on the teabag. As I stirred the milk into the tea, the phone rang again.

Certain that this time it would be someone with whom I could chat, and so chase Psyche-Imp thoroughly away, I rushed into the lounge with my cup and answered the phone. "Hello?"

This time it was a woman. Also a reporter. She too would not tell me where she got my telephone number from and when I told her I had nothing to say to her, she remarked "You had plenty to say to Newsnight last year, didn't you?" My stomach clenched. I put the phone down without saying any more.

I was so relieved and pleased to see Damon when he came in. I told him I'd had a couple of reporters phone and that it had panicked me. He begged to be permitted to answer the telephone if it rang again. I agreed that he could. In the meantime, he entertained me and acted the fool until Psyche-Imp found he could no longer stress me and so slunk away. I asked Damon if he could think of anything awful for me to do to the imaginary imp and he had a whole catalogue of dreadful things – none of which I now remember, but all of which had me rolling around with laughter.

Psyche-Imp had been well and truly banished. If only I could say the same about the reporters!

Several times over the next few days, I had telephone calls from reporters, not just to my landline but also to my mobile phone. I felt so enraged and realised that the only place they could have all got my numbers from was the BBC! When I later found a few emails also from reporters I knew for certain that the BBC were to blame. I didn't dare telephone them to complain because that meant drawing attention to myself even more and I didn't want to do that. I began to have bad dreams and to wake up frequently during the night and panic for no apparent reason.

Somehow, I managed to get through to my birthday and the Sport Relief Mile. I'd bought a pair of trainers online and the Sport Relief tee shirt and socks. Peter drove us all to The Venue near Gobowen and, after the obligatory instructions, we set off. Gemma, Emily and I were the last to leave; the others were of course all running and I was walking.

I started off well enough at a reasonable pace, but, after probably five hundred yards I found I had slowed considerably. By the time Gemma, Emily and I had covered another hundred and fifty yards, the first of the runners were passing us on their way back to The Venue! First Chris, then a few others and then Peter and Uther raced past us and we hadn't even got halfway yet. I began to fear I might not make it!

I am glad to be able to report to you, dear reader, that I did complete the Sport Relief Mile and I got my medal, as did both Gemma and Emily. It took me very nearly forty minutes but I did it and all without a walking stick too. That I ached all over is a given, but I felt really pleased with myself. I saw this as a major hurdle which, although it took ages, I had achieved. If I could do this, then surely, I could get a lot better and do lots more too.

In the first week of April I attended a hospital appointment at Chirk to see someone called Yvonne. She was Mr. Billings' 'Nurse Practitioner' and it was her job to monitor my progress. I took my friend Hannah with me to that appointment.

Yvonne asked several questions about my general health, and then peered at the watery contents of my bag and told me I wasn't eating nearly enough. She instructed me sternly to eat lots more. Of course, I protested that I already ate like a pig and nothing made any difference! I exclaimed that I was fat and ugly and couldn't bear to put on any more weight, not even to please her.

Bemused somewhat by my outburst, she soothed me and told me to speak to Jaime to ask for help in thickening the output up a bit. And then she wanted to 'examine' my back-side!

Mortified, I complied. It never occurred to me to refuse in fact. The examination hurt and I listened as Yvonne told me she could feel the 'anastomosis' – or the join in my colon and that it felt, to her, as if I'd had a bit of a leakage but that it was all right now. She also said there was a lot of 'poo' there that needed to be shifted. I should ask the District Nurses for suppositories and, if they didn't work, an enema! I questioned her as to whether the constant sensation of needing to poo could be caused by this 'old poo' being 'stuck' in there and she agreed it would indeed cause just that sensation.

Yvonne asked if I'd had my X-Ray yet. Since I had no idea what X-Ray she meant, she deduced that I had not and told me she would book it directly. I didn't give it much thought, to be honest.

I asked the GP in fact for the suppositories and, although I followed the directions exactly, they completely failed to work. The GP advised me to stop stressing and leave well alone. She herself did another examination and said she couldn't feel anything untoward at all.

Days passed into weeks and I realised that now, the bag only leaked about once a week or less. It was always at the same place, on the left of the stoma, right next to the wound and was dealt with mostly by Peter but once or twice by me and Uther together. All in all, I managed to get along somehow. It certainly made a great deal of difference to my life not having to remain close to a toilet at all times. I took a chance and booked a week's holiday in Cornwall in September.

In the second week of May, Andrea decided I no longer needed to visit the clinic because, she felt, I no longer needed any kind of dressing on my wound. There was still a deep cleft in my stomach, but the wound itself was now just an inch or so long and quarter of an inch wide and no more than a slight 'sore-looking place' in the centre of the cleft.

The first few days with no dressing on the wound at all felt rather strange but I soon got used to it. I began to make sure I went out every single day, even if it was only up the hill of Ifton meadows with the dogs or to the shops. I still got the angina attacks but I'd learned to put up with them now and never even bothered to mention them to the GP any more. I'd grown used to the stiffness of Fibromyalgia and found that the pain killer for the anastomosis 'Tramadol' was also very good at controlling Fibro pain too.

I was shocked when I sat on the settee one day and went to cross my knees. I was unable to do so! I stared down at my legs and tried again. The manoeuvre was totally impossible – because my legs had grown so fat! If I could have cried, I would have done so then. I had used to sit with my legs crossed at both knee and ankle and now I was so incredibly fat, I couldn't even cross my knees. I stood up and went to the kitchen to weight myself. No surprise that I felt fat. I now weighed twelve stones and two pounds. That's three stones heavier than I'd ever been in my entire life before. I'd never even been that heavy when pregnant.

Dejected, I sat down and stared at my hands. Psyche-Imp crawled up my leg and sat beside me. "Poor, fat Kat," he began.

"Shut up, you little creep!" I snapped. "It's because I stopped smoking and kept eating like they told me to do. Now I'm a fat cow and I'll have to live with it." I swatted him out of the way and went to make a cup of tea.

Several months passed by during which time I did all manner of things I'd been unable to do before. I visited lots of stately homes and castles. I walked around them with the aid of a walking stick, but before I'd had the Tramadol painkillers I'd never have been able to do that. I went on a couple of weekends camping too. It was stressful and rather uncomfortable sleeping on an air mattress, but certainly something I had never expected to be able to do again ever. That it poured with the rain the first time is no surprise. The year 2012 was not a good summer for anybody.

All through the year I was plagued on and off by reporters. Sometimes they came knocking at the door. At other times they hounded me by mobile phone and house phone. Once, I was accosted in the Iceland store by a man who had followed me and then introduced himself as a journalist. I threatened to clout him if he didn't sod off and leave me alone.

Of course, anyone who knows me, knows that when the story broke on September 30th 2012, I then gave in and finally agreed to speak to Mark-Williams-Thomas about Savile. I wasn't exactly conned, but he led me to believe that what I said would be tacked onto the end of his documentary programme and that all the people in the documentary had waived their right to anonymity. I waived mine too. Then I discovered that I would appear on the ITV news on my own and be the first to publicly reveal the ancient truths. I need to say no more than there then followed a media storm during which time I was hounded, harangued and harassed as if I were a major celebrity. It was not fun and there was nothing pleasurable in it and, contrary to popular belief, I earned absolutely no money from simply telling the truth as I experienced it. Even so, rumours abounded locally. I digress.

Just recently I was summoned to the hospital to have this so-called X-Ray along with the 'water-soluble enema' which went with it. I'd put it off twice because the person doing the procedure was male and I felt uncomfortable about that. With a Colorectal nurse to hold my hand during the whole thing, I could hardly refuse.

Peter drove me to the hospital. We were met by Claire, the Colorectal Nurse and didn't have to wait long; I was invited to change into a gown, and given a very fetching pair of 'colonoscopy bloomers' with which to protect my modesty. I changed and trailed into the X-Ray room with Claire following me. She was wearing an enormous, lead-filled overall to protect her from the radiation. It did cross my mind that I'd already been exposed to so much radiation that this could not be a good thing for me. Too late now!

The procedure was not as bad as I'd feared. The stuff the fellow injected into my rear felt cold, that's all. I was required to turn this way and that way. Onto my back, on my left side and then my right side. After just a few minutes it was all over and the man told me had had removed as much fluid as he could do but that, should I still need the toilet, there was one adjoining the examination room.

I sat up and listened as he instructed me that the liquid used should all come out straight away but that, should I lose any clear fluid over the next few days, I should not be alarmed. He also advised that the stuff tended to be rather sticky and so advised I use wet wipes rather than toilet tissue. I snatched up my basket of clothes and disappeared into the toilet.

He had been right. There really wasn't very much left to come out. I sat there for perhaps ten minutes and when I was sure it had all gone, I got dressed and left the toilet via the other door. Claire and Peter were waiting for me. I thanked Claire for her support and together we walked out of the hospital.

We were about halfway home when I got a very unpleasant pain across my middle and felt distinctly sick quite suddenly. Of course, I told Peter. He didn't appear to be concerned. He actually said "Well, you felt sick before we came out so I expect it won't get any worse. Have another anti-sick pill. I'm sure you've probably got some with you."

I did have them with me and I took one. I searched my bag for an Extra Strong Mint but I couldn't find any. In the next moment, two things happened at once.

Psyche-Imp appeared from nowhere and head-butted me right between the eyes. "You're gonna puke!" He crowed. At the same time, the world fell out of my arse.

Fortunately, Peter had the forethought to use one of the dog toilet training pads (similar to an inco-sheet) on the passenger seat of his car. Terminally embarrassed, I told Peter what had happened and caught my breath as another wave of extreme pain gripped me across my abdomen. I had to clench my teeth so that I didn't retch.

Matters were not helped in that we were kind of stuck in a traffic jam! The vehicles crawled along and all I could think of as I tried to swat Psyche-Imp out of my line of vision, was that I needed to get home and sit on the toilet. I hadn't felt like this for many, many months.

Psyche-Imp was not going to be sent away this time. He had other ideas. He sat on the dashboard of Peter's car with his bony legs crossed at both knee and ankle (just how I used to sit when I was thin) and he mimed vomiting over and over again. I tried to look away and watch the scenery but panic began to build and very soon was beyond my control. Peter could do little to help me other than chatter – which he did.

As soon as we arrived home, I rushed into the little downstairs toilet and plonked myself down on the toilet. I was appalled that what had flooded out of me in the car was not the clear fluid I'd been led to expect but what appeared to be blood and lots of it.

My heart began to pound painfully. I had spots winking in various colours in front of my eyes and felt intensely grateful that I was already seated or I would have fallen over. I could feel more flooding out of me, not just liquid but what felt like solids as well.

Peter called out to me asking if I was all right. At that time, the pain had subsided and Psyche-Imp was nowhere to be seen. I agreed that I thought I was but that I was freaked because what I'd thought was fluid from the enema seemed to be blood ... and some very hard and ancient poo as well.

Peter called back that it probably wasn't all blood. He suggested that any old poo still stuck inside would be very dry having been there for ten months and that perhaps the enema had shifted it. The blood was probably due to the inside of the colon being scratched by the hard faeces.

I agreed, that was probably it. He asked if he could get me anything and I said yes, he could make me a cup of tea. I cleaned myself up and then stood up to empty the bag into the jug at the sink just as I always did. I glanced back at the toilet I'd just vacated and saw the deep red of blood in the water and felt my heart quicken. I turned away and tried to concentrate on the task of emptying the bag which had mysteriously filled from barely anything to almost overflowing in a matter of ten minutes. The jug was full to the top. Just as I had cleaned and re-fastened the spout of the bag, I felt more coming from the rear. Leaving the jug standing in the sink, I quickly sat back down on the toilet and felt another flood leave me.

A hand appeared around the door bearing a cup of tea and I accepted it gratefully. I'd managed just one sip of the tea when a huge wave of intense stomach pain gripped me and I retched.

Of course, instantly, I panicked. I yelled to Peter to bring me a bowl as I was stuck on the toilet and was going to be sick. When Peter opened the toilet door to pass the bowl around it, unfortunately, Odin, one of the kittens, leaped in through the gap and jumped up to the sink ...

I'm not going into further detail. I'll let your imagination do the rest in that regard, dear reader. I can just tell you that I sat there miserably panicking, with Psyche-Imp chasing a shit-covered kitten all around the tiny room. I felt like I couldn't breathe at all and the pain in my stomach was dreadful. I knew I was going to vomit. It could not be avoided.

Bless his heart, Peter came round the door and squatted down in front of me, rubbing my leg, holding the bowl for me and he talked and talked. The panic would not lessen in the least. My heart raced, I felt dizzy, and I felt like I couldn't breathe.

After an hour of sitting there, Peter persuaded me to come sit in the lounge. He told me he'd covered the settee in inco-sheets and that it would be much easier to support me in the lounge, whether I shit myself or not.

In the end, I was persuaded. I sat on the settee with the bowl between my feet and Peter rubbed the small of my back and talked. Emily was there too (although I cannot recall why) and she talked too. Periodically I retched long and hard, although I did not actually vomit. I am convinced that the only reason I did not vomit was that I'd had two anti-sick pills in quick succession and there was nothing in my stomach to sick up. My ileostomy bag had almost filled up again too so my stomach must've been completely empty as I'd eaten virtually nothing that day. Every now and then another flood of fluid left me. I had no control whatever over either end of my body and it was vile and terrifying. Psyche-Imp is the reason I kept retching I am absolutely certain. He kept punching me in the throat and saying dreadful things. I became convinced, as I sat there in my puddle of blood and shit, that I would die, right there, right in front of Peter and Emily. After all I'd been through, it was going to end in the filth and vileness I'd so feared for so long.

It should not be possible for the human body to sustain a high level of anxiety or panic for very long. In fact, most psychologists or cognitive behavioural therapists will tell you the limit is usually around forty minutes. Every time the panic began to subside a little, Psyche-Imp reappeared and caused another wave of it to start.

Emily went home after a few hours. She looked very worried and told me she hope I felt better soon. I couldn't reply because I was concentrating hard on not retching at the time and my whole body was shaking in an uncontrollable manner.

This miserable state of affairs lasted, in total, just a little over eight hours. By the time I'd had a third anti-sick pill and a couple of valium, not to mention eight hours of being talked to and having my back rubbed, the panic suddenly vanished and I felt exhausted. I still felt decidedly strange but at least the worst was over. It was around midnight.

I managed to take myself back to the toilet and clean up the shitty mess the cat had made. I also emptied the bag again and cleaned the toilet. Peter disposed of the blood-soaked inco-sheet and spread out another one for me to sit on. He also brought me clean underwear and pyjamas. I did end up getting a little sleep that night but only because I knew Peter was here with me in case I panicked again.

It took three days to get back into eating normally again. I telephoned the Colorectal Nurses and spoke to Jaime. She thought what had happened was extreme and that I should visit my GP about it. She'd never heard of anyone reacting to the water-soluble enema in that way before. I told her I would see the doctor, but, at the time of writing, I haven't yet done so. Mainly, I am mightily scared that there is something pretty horrible wrong in there.

This time, having survived cancer once, I don't actually want to know what is wrong with me. I just want to keep it firmly under control. If it's anything serious, I'm afraid I just don't want to know. I've got an appointment to see that Yvonne woman again at the end of November. She's told me that I'll be having my ileostomy reversed at some point. I've also told her, and my GP and Jaime (and in fact, anyone else who will listen) that I don't want the stoma reversed. I now have a life. I no longer have to remain within ten feet of a toilet. I can get out and about and do things now. They all seem to have forgotten that, along with the cancer, the second colonoscopy showed that I also have Diverticular Disease. If I had a reversal, I would just go back to intermittent diarrhoea and a reclusive, miserable lifestyle. No thanks!

If anyone could come up with a way to get rid of that blasted imp for once and all I'd love to hear it. Feel free to contact me via Twitter or even email with any idea you may have! I'm certain that, so long as he exists, I will continue to be fearful and continue to suffer these dreadful panics. I am equally sure that emetophobia is an almost impossible phobia to cure. (I know this as I've seen multiple cognitive behavioural therapists during my lifetime and every one of them has failed to cure or even lessen it).

Chapter Eight: Thanks

There is an old adage 'A friend in need is a friend indeed.' However, I used to say 'A friend in need is a pain in the arse!' I can only say that I have had and been a pain in the arse for about eighteen months now.

I thought Lesley was such a steadfast and stalwart friend; I've known her almost as long as I've lived here. She certainly got me through all the tests and the early part of treatment, but then, just as I managed to get a care package so that I could at least pay her a bit for her time and care, she suddenly stopped speaking to me. She didn't turn up as arranged nor visit as a friend anymore and refused to answer my calls and messages. That occurred shortly after I had my operation. I still have no idea what I said or did to have caused such a staunch friendship to turn into obvious hatred and disdain. She has not spoken to me or even glanced my way since January 2012. It makes me sad of course. I always like to know at least what wickedness I have been guilty of to make others turn their back upon me so absolutely. Thanks anyway, Lesley.

Rosemary keeps on expressing her regrets and feelings of uselessness that, apparently when I needed her most, she wasn't here. Well no, but that would be because her husband had a stroke and she herself was dreadfully ill! She went on to suffer from Bell's Palsy caused by Shingles (or perhaps it turned out to be some other type of palsy). Anyway, twelve months later she is still suffering the effects of her Shingles and palsy although Tom, her husband, has recovered pretty well. She's been my best friend for thirty five years; I am still trying to get it through her head that I do understand

and am grateful that whenever she could be here, she was. Thanks, Mrs. Woman! (Rosemary)

Emily ran around me like a blue-arsed fly. She'd never had any experience of 'Personal Care' before and yet she pitched in with gusto. She sometimes helped with the changing of the bag, or the cleaning of the wound. She came with me to support me through appointments and, once I could get about, she accompanied me to make sure I didn't keel over or pass out or panic. She has never refused to do any job, however grotty. When I was getting up and about a bit but still not back to speed, she did everything from cleaning a shitty dog yard to changing kitty litter trays. She runs errands and waits on my boys like a slave. She appears to be incredibly patient and has never said anything nasty (although, in her shoes, I'd have plenty of nasty stuff to say or shout). She has been and still is being an absolute star. Thanks, Em!

Peter has tried especially hard. That man is either completely, utterly stupid or still has very deep feelings for me. He swears it is the former. I think it is the latter. I've decided not to argue with him about this as arguments are futile (and we still manage a fair old few even now). Life is too short and it really doesn't matter. The fact remains, when needed, he is always here for me, no matter what his other commitments are. He has crawled out of a warm bed and come to my house in the middle of the night to cope with everything from a large spider running about to a totally split stoma bag and liquid shit everywhere. He has sat and endlessly rubbed my back, feet, shoulders to try to rid me of Psyche-Imp induced panics and cramps. He's cleaned up more shit than any human being should ever have to clean and he's mopped up blood and gore too. He often changed the wound dressing, both when I had the wadding and the VAC therapy. Many times he's staggered through the door after a twelve hour nursing shift, looking like a zombie and yet has set to with a will to get me and my bloody and shitty problems straightened out. He quite often falls asleep whilst sitting on the settee, in mid sentence. He's done his utmost to protect me from the vultures that are The Press and has chaperoned me to so many appointments and then dealt with the Psyche-Imp induced panics during and afterwards. It doesn't seem enough, but: Thank you, Peter.

As for my boys, there is so very much I need to say to them and so much I have to be proud of (despite the fact that Peter often thinks they don't do enough for me). They are each of them, so different and yet they do what they can. It may not involve large amounts of housework, dog-walking or other things I ask them to do and they forget, but companionship goes a long way. I'm their mother, so of course I think they're fabulous (even sometimes in the face of the evidence that they most certainly are not). They have been absolutely brilliant almost all the time and still are. I can't believe I thought I wanted to die and leave them behind! I told you I was selfish!

I've said sometimes how Uther very often upset me by being apparently angry or scornful; I now recognise that it was his own fear which caused him to react the way he did. That and he himself had troubles. After all, during 2011 his whole life fell apart and then I had cancer too. That he loves me I am certain, it's just that my timing in this particular instance absolutely stank. The times that young man has sat up until or past four in the morning, just watching films and chatting mean a very great deal to me. He has also been there to help when the stoma bag has leaked or split or needs changing and Peter was working elsewhere or otherwise unavailable. He has kept me calm when there's been blood or other scary things to cope with. I'm not sure I've ever thanked him; I should have done, but as I've said before, I am an inherently selfish woman and may have forgotten. Thank you, Boy.

Of course, Zakh has largely been absent, being away at University in Leeds. He often sent and sends me texts and rings me too (frequently to beg for funds). He even encouraged me to load Skype onto my laptop so that I could see his room at uni and chat with him face to face. That he fell over playing football and shattered his leg was just another really horrible thing to add to the year 2011. Once home, after his operations and with his leg in a cast, he was very good company indeed and spent many nights sleeping in the lounge alongside me. Just knowing he was there helped a lot. Thank you, Boy.

Damon needs lots of credit as well. He has probably been the calmest of all my sons. He has been great company, talked and talks to me for hour upon hour (especially when I'm at the mercy of Psyche-Imp) about such interesting subjects and has some very new and novel ideas and concepts which certainly take my mind off my problems and my condition. He may be only fifteen in physical years, but I reckon he's about fifty in wisdom and calmness. I can always count on him to talk me away from Psyche-Imp. He can also make me laugh, both when panicking and when furiously angry or upset; that is a special talent. He tries to come across as totally unemotional, but nevertheless, he clearly loves his mother! Thank you, Boy.

There are actually loads of people to thank now I come to write it down. That's why they have a short chapter all to themselves.

There are the doctors at Chirk Surgery. OK, so I have moaned about them. A lot of the time they utterly pissed me off, frequently didn't listen and often got it totally wrong but, once we had a diagnosis, they've been very supportive, as have the reception staff. Elaine and Lynne need a special mention as they've always managed to squeeze me in for an appointment or get the doctor to visit me often at very short notice. Dr. Nicola Fox has been incredibly supportive and also, to my surprise, Dr. Brian Johnson too (I always felt he was patronising me in the past). Dr. Prigg visited a few times at short notice and wrote urgent prescriptions for the numerous wound infections I got. Thank you.

I need to thank the The Colorectal Nurses at the Wrexham Maelor Hospital, one of whom, Jaime Windsor, frequently visited my home and endlessly mopped up liquid shit and messed about with a stoma which was surrounded by raw and bleeding skin, until she had it all under control and comfortable. Claire came and held my hand during the vile enema-thing. Alison annoyed me intensely but coped admirably well with a woman who was intensely rude to her at all times and Linda always did her best for me and supported me whenever she had to, even though, again, I was incredibly rude to her. Thank you, Colorectal Nurses!

There are many other staff at The Wrexham Maelor Hospital who need to be thanked. I don't know their names of course. There are the Ward Staff who cared for me after my operation. They all did a wonderful job. There are Phlebotomists, Pharmacists, Nurses,

Doctors, Clerical Workers, far too many to even remember, never mind mention. Thanks; all of you.

Of course, I must not forget the staff at Glan Clwyd Hospital at Boddelwyddan, St. Asaph. They were all fantastic. I can recall only one radiologists' name: Claire. I saw Dr. Raavi whilst I was there, the Oncologist who advised me, even though I was Dr. Simon Gollins' patient. Jill, the Nursing Sister from the Cape Clinic; the Hospital Social Worker; Eileen on Reception. Thank you all so much.

And of course, then there are the Chirk District Nurses. Andrea Perrett was my prime nurse, but many others came along to help on different days. There was Sarah and Hazel, Tina and Julie to name but a few. They always maintained such a cheerful, optimistic calmness, even when I was so depressed I was almost impossible to reach. There were a few laughs as well, I must not forget those. Thank you all so very much.

What's that I heard you mutter, dear reader? Did I hear you say "What about Psyche-Imp?" Yes, what about that little blue sod. I'm *not* thanking him, that's for sure.

He's still around. Between creeping up on me unawares, he follows other people down the road and frightens them out of their wits before running away, leaving them to think they panicked over nothing at all.

I'm almost sure that, even though I 'invented' or 'imagined' him, the cats can see him. Either that or they stare at and sometimes chase something which really isn't there at all!

I expect, somewhere, Psyche-Imp's got lots of brightly coloured little imp friends. I dread to think what they may be the anthropomorphic personifications of though. I sincerely hope I never find out.

Oh. I just thought. There is someone else to thank. YOU, dear reader, for wading through this miserable, moaning, pathetic epistle all the way to ...

THE END

Printed in Dunstable, United Kingdom